RETHINKING PREJUDICE

"This book fills a gap in current literature: the systematic study Dorschel presents, unifying an historical treatment with proposals for acceptance today, offers a significant new contribution."
J. E. J. Altham, Gonville and Caius College, Cambridge.

Much has been written on the subject of prejudice, but *Rethinking Prejudice* offers the first philosophical monograph on the concept of prejudice. It takes its start from a study of Enlightenment thought, and pursues the topic to the reassessment of prejudice in contemporary hermeneutics. Yet history of ideas is a means rather than an end in this book. Dorschel analyzes the debates about prejudice from the 17th century onwards in order to shed light upon present concerns.

Prejudice is not something peculiar to racists and similarly sinister figures, Dorschel argues; rather, it is an indispensable part of everyone's intellectual repertoire. Racial prejudice, for example, has to be rejected not because it is a prejudice, but because it is racist. So why is it popular to reject racism on the grounds that it is a prejudice? The economy of transforming a whole complex of ethical problems into one apparently simple problem of epistemology is certainly understandable. But such transformation plays down phenomena like racism. If they are prejudices, then this is a common feature they share with a host of innocuous and even reasonable attitudes. The critical standard, Dorschel concludes, must be taken from elsewhere: if relevant phenomena are to be criticized, a genuine moral stance cannot be avoided.

Rethinking Prejudice introduces and explores a topic of wide interest, particularly to those researching within the fields of philosophy, history of ideas, cultural studies, and social and political theory.

Andreas Dorschel is a lecturer in philosophy at the University of East Anglia, UK.

ASHGATE NEW CRITICAL THINKING
IN PHILOSOPHY

The *Ashgate New Critical Thinking in Philosophy* series aims to bring high quality research monograph publishing back into focus for authors, the international library market, and student, academic and research readers. Headed by an international editorial advisory board of acclaimed scholars from across the philosophical spectrum, this new monograph series presents cutting-edge research from established as well as exciting new authors in the field; spans the breadth of philosophy and related disciplinary and interdisciplinary perspectives; and takes contemporary philosophical research into new directions and debate.

Series Editorial Board:

Rethinking Prejudice

ANDREAS DORSCHEL

Ashgate

Aldershot • Burlington USA • Singapore • Sydney

Published by
Ashgate Publishing Ltd
Gower House
Croft Road
Aldershot
Hants GU11 3HR
England

Ashgate Publishing Company
131 Main Street
Burlington, VT 05401-5600 USA

Ashgate website: http://www.ashgate.com

British Library Cataloguing in Publication Data
Dorschel, Andreas
    Rethinking prejudice. - (Ashgate new critical thinking in
    philosophy)
    1.Prejudices - Philosophy 2.Reason 3.Enlightenment
    I.Title
    128.3'3

Library of Congress Cataloging-in-Publication Data
Dorschel, Andreas.
    Rethinking prejudice / Andreas Dorschel.
        p. cm. -- (Ashgate new critical thinking in philosophy series)
    Includes bibliographical references (p.) and indexes.
    ISBN 0-7546-1387-9
    1.Prejudices--Philosophy. 2. Social perception--Philosophy. I. Title. II. Series

    BF575.P9 D67 2000
    303.3'85'01--dc21
                                                                        00-58637
    ISBN 0 7546 1387 9

Printed in Great Britain by
Antony Rowe Ltd, Chippenham, Wiltshire.

Contents

Analytical Table of Contents

69. Coleridge's Garden or the external recommendation of prejudice in education: It is undesirable, nay, impossible to bring up children on the principle that all prejudices must be abandoned.

70. This external recommendation of prejudice (§ 69) seems to extend to the domain of learning complex activities generally.

71. There are even cases of internal recommendations of prejudice where the paradox (§ 65) can be avoided.

72. To avoid the paradox for an internal recommendation of prejudice (§ 71) apparently presupposes that we keep apart their truth from their benefit. But sometimes we cannot even do this.

73. External justifications of prejudice seem to be elitist and cynical. But they do not need to be elitist.

74. Nor do they need to be cynical.

75. Again, what's wrong with prejudice? Locke's criterion: resistance to contrary evidence.

76. Locke's criterion turned against his terminology: presumption *vs.* prejudice.

77. Prejudice as a way of looking at things: this account explains how prejudice can be so persistent.

78. But (a) it is sometimes rational to resist contrary evidence, (b) the criterion (§ 75) is circular.

79. Not to be resistant to correction would mean that in principle everything is on the agenda, and there is doubt whether that is desirable. An example.

80. The attraction of hunting prejudices has been to treat moral problems without much moral ado, as if they were basically intellectual shortcomings.

81. A problem with the example (§ 79). Another example.

82. The idea of setting limits to what we should examine is not a relic of premodern obscurantism.

83. Objections: The idea of limits to examining is either (a) inconsistent because any such proposal has to be examined too, or (b), if consistent, misdirected, because it overlooks a distinction between two senses of open-mindedness.

84. But the idea of limits to examining appears inconsistent (§ 83 (a)) only if 'examining' is used ambiguously for 'thinking about a matter' and 'submitting other people to experimental testing'.

85. It is possible to distinguish two conceptions of open-mindedness (§ 83 (b)); but both are inappropriate to our fundamental moral beliefs.

86. Swift's 'Modest proposal'.

Preface

There are some enterprises in which a careful disorderliness is the true method
(Melville, *Moby-Dick*)

The expulsion of prejudice is the centrepiece of intellectual progress, as it has been understood since the Enlightenment. 'Prejugès detruits, les progres de l'esprit humain', Friedrich Schlegel[1] summarized in 1797 what the 18th century had begun to fight for. That this fight has not been successful since is obvious; but this does not invalidate it. There is no reason to believe that people in the 20th century had *fewer* (rather than merely different) prejudices than people had in the 18th century; yet we might simply conclude that the fight has not been conducted resolutely enough. The question whether or not this might be the right conclusion, however, depends on an answer to a more fundamental question: whether prejudices, as such, are a proper object to fight against in the first place. The argument of this book is an attempt to show that they are not.

The charge that the Enlightenment battle against prejudice is misdirected is of course as old as the battle itself. It has been claimed that prejudices embody the wisdom of tradition and should therefore be revered rather than attacked. The most obvious alternative to an untenable thesis is its opposite; but it need not be the right one. If the following argument is sound the celebration of prejudice is no more justified than the Enlightenment attempt to destroy it. Prejudices can be true *or* false, intelligent *or* stupid, wise *or* foolish, positive *or* negative, good *or* bad, racist *or* humanist, and so on – and they possess none of these features simply *qua* prejudices.

The concept of prejudice has been thought to play a decisive part in the Enlightenment's programme of separating reason from unreason. I shall argue that it is unfit to serve this function. Prejudices are neither necessarily worse nor better than, say, judgements, thoughts, beliefs or opinions, all of which can be reasonable or unreasonable. Prejudices have their place among the ways in which human beings relate to the world, and can thus be in place or out of place just like any other ways. They too are part of our intellectual resources. Prejudices are out of place in some contexts, but so is any other way in which we make up our minds. Arguments are out of place in, for instance, a declaration of love; but this also does not prove that anything is wrong with arguments *qua* arguments. Particular prejudices of course can and should be criticized (or praised) according to the apposite standards; but criticism or appraisal of prejudice *qua* prejudice is arbitrary: those who dislike prejudice call it bias, those who like it dub it intuition.

At first glance, it seems particularly easy to make the case sketched above. For we could simply stipulate a *definition* of prejudice free of any negative or positive valuation. But this degree of abstraction would render the account pointless. It would be pointless because critics as well as apologists of prejudice could plausibly object that they did not mean *that* by prejudice. This reply would be apt in so far as the stipulated definition remained unrelated to their claims, and any appeal to the fact that the words they used are still used today would be naïve. Words do not have fixed meanings. Like colours, their meanings can be changed by the background in which they are set.

Only like-minded people would be convinced by a stipulated definition. Hence we cannot avoid grappling with the characterizations of prejudice passed on to us by the philosophical tradition. The history of the debate about prejudice since the later 17th century has been a history of attempts to inscribe value into the meaning of this term – a term which before that time had been generally neutral, and only carried a positive or negative charge in particular contexts. (The term 'prejudice' originated in the language of jurisprudence; there it meant a judgement pronounced before the final sentence.[2]) As a matter of politics, the attribution of negative value to prejudice has been successful; but as a matter of logic, it has not. Our method will therefore be to examine the relevant arguments, both actual and possible, in their proper contexts.

No analysis of 'ordinary language', that once fashionable method of Anglo-Saxon philosophy, can in our case furnish a viable alternative to the study of intellectual history. Everyday talk of prejudice is a pale reflection of the Enlightenment account, without, for the most part, knowing that it is. Watered down as it is, it is in general far less instructive than the philosophical originals from which it is derived; hence it is the latter we ought to face.

Historical study of concepts and ideas therefore plays an important rôle in this monograph; but it does so as a means, not as an end. Its object is systematic. References to past masters are designed to bring an absent speaker into the discussion, not to give a chronological account of everything that has been said on the subject. Therefore the order in which the arguments are presented follows the logic of the problem; it does not necessarily coincide with the historical order in which they appeared.

The progress of the argument is as follows. *Chapter One* (§§ 1–17) reconstructs the Enlightenment's main objection to prejudice. Its conclusion that all prejudices must be destroyed is challenged. Focusing on the context of decision and action, a *prima facie* case in favour of prejudice is built.

A number of Enlightenment authors have fastened on lack of experience as the defining defect of prejudice. This is explored in *Chapter Two* (§§ 18–43). The objection is not altogether pointless; but the relationship between prejudice and experience turns out to be more complex than it is represented in that objection.

Chapter Three (§§ 44–54) considers a particular defence of prejudice, developed in hermeneutics. According to its hermeneutic defenders, prejudice is a condition of the possibility of understanding. This vindication, however, inflates the notion of prejudice and confuses it with a number of notions that are adjacent, but should be kept distinct; in particular, it distorts 'prejudice' by confusing it with concepts such as expectation, anticipation, perspective, or point of view.

The problem of prejudice is investigated at a more basic methodical level in *Chapter Four* (§§ 55–74). Recommendations of prejudices are subject to a paradox: a prejudice, in order to be recommended, *i.e.*, distinguished as something good, must have been examined. But then, apparently, it has ceased to be a prejudice and has become a genuine judgement. The paradox can be circumvented by distinguishing between, first, recommendations of prejudice in general, secondly, external and, thirdly, internal recommendations of prejudices.

Chapter Five (§§ 75–100) drives home the general conclusion of the book. To make the case for a reinterpretation of the concept of prejudice, it addresses particularly contentious issues. It takes up what may appear to be the severest charge against prejudice, that of dogmatism and fundamentalism. If and in so far as that charge is true of, *e.g.*, racist prejudices, I shall argue, it is also true of a humanism that is strong enough to oppose racism. The point of this is of course not to show that the one is as good as the other. The point is, rather, that critical standards cannot be simply derived from a demonstration of prejudice. While the latter suggests a cognitive problem, the final chapter of the book concludes that there is no substitute for taking a genuine moral stance. Along this line of thought the elimination of prejudice is not desirable; what is more, towards the end a sense is indicated in which prejudice is indeed indispensable.

(A much more detailed breakdown of the argument is to be found in the *Analytical table of contents* which forms the previous section of this book.)

It should be clear, then, that this study aims neither to extirpate prejudice, nor to celebrate it – in the spirit, for instance, of that brilliant reactionary, Joseph de Maistre.[3] But nor does a 'neither – nor' approach provide a middle ground on which a moderate account of prejudice might easily settle. On the contrary, the following pages try to explore the difficulties in thinking about prejudice. Prejudice is a pervasive theme of modern philosophical thought; yet at the same time it is elusive. It requires thinking in more than one register; so literary fiction has proved to be as relevant to it as logic, Swift and de Sade have turned out to be as instructive for its study as Descartes and Kant.

At the same time, the iridescent and elusive character of the subject is no excuse for being elusive in the way it is presented; on the contrary, I shall suggest conclusions wherever the topic allows it. The whole endeavour of this book rests on the supposition that prejudice is a concept that can meaningfully be discussed, though that discussion does not terminate in a list of 'necessary and sufficient conditions' for that concept. But that is true of most concepts that are not either trivial or linked with strictly technical terms. It is also true that sometimes, depending on the context in which prejudice is explored, the best one can do is to approach this perplexing subject from different sectors of its logical periphery, balancing error against error. Yet even that, admittedly toilsome, procedure promises a gain in clarity. Those passages which seem to reveal complexity rather than conclusions remain tied to the general drift of the argument, *viz.*, to regain the older understanding of prejudice, according to which prejudices can be true or false, intelligent or stupid, good or bad. The argument attempts to achieve this by way of scrutinizing the flaws of a still dominant tradition according to which prejudices *qua* prejudices must possess the negative quality of each of those pairs of features. (The opposing tradition, attributing positive quality to prejudice in the same fashion, has never been dominant.)

'Prejudice', in the Enlightenment usage of the term, was as much a weapon as a concept. Thus the influential modern definitions of prejudice imply a negative assessment of it. They represent prejudice as *constituted* by a mistake; by implication, we could not say what prejudice *is* without pointing out what *is wrong* with it. Such definitions involve, for instance, the idea that prejudices are hasty or even false; though that is not all they say. There is no other way to engage with the authors of these definitions than to venture on their troublesome link of the two questions: What is prejudice? and: What's wrong with prejudice? For anything else would do no more than decree from the outside, and it is hard to see why anyone should accept a definition not shared by himself, if no argument has shown up weaknesses or even inconsistencies of his own position. Thus the systematic and the historical problems of prejudice are inextricably linked: the systematic point can only be established by an examination of the history of the problem from the inside, and this in turn forces us to address the two questions of what prejudice is and whether anything is wrong with it jointly.

To proceed in this manner runs counter to a strict ideal of method. But a method is good, as opposed to merely strict, if it yields insights; and precisely the inquiry into whether prejudice must be repudiated or may be defended, *i.e.*, the second question, will prove most instructive as regards the first question, about what it is. There is only a superficial paradox in the claim that the way to overcome the modern blend of description and evaluation in explaining prejudice is to meddle with it. Errors that have been epoch-making elude schoolmasterly censure. Understanding the philosophical problem of prejudice is, in a crucial respect, a matter of seeing the plausibility of the traditional formulations of the problem. Seeing the plausibility of an account, on the other hand, is by no means the same as accepting it. What is plausible is what is able to make us applaud immediately after it has been presented; our applause is far from being reserved for things which are true. But the immediate impact could even pass away, yet plausibility may remain. This is how disagreement with a position that has been important in the history of thought often, perhaps typically, comes about; a position which we found adequate in many ways – comprehensive, clear, relevant, interesting, reasoned – and, on this ground, worthy of closer study turns out not to be true in the process of such study. In a number of cases, therefore, the argument of the book attempts to show the plausibility of views that in due course of the reasoning turn out to be in important respects mistaken. Only when we face the strengths of a tradition that has managed to present errors as insights, have we a chance of overcoming it.

Notes

1   *Philosophische Lehrjahre* I, p. 57. Accent marks *sic.*
2   Meiszner, Art. 'Vorurteil', col. 1856.
3   *Etude sur la souveraineté*, I, 10, p. 375.

Chapter One

On Enlightenment, Especially on its Conclusion that all Prejudices Should be Abandoned

1. What is prejudice? Many European languages represent the phenomenon in question in the same way. Πρόϰριμα, praeiudicium, pregiudizio, prejuicio, préjugé, prejudice, Vorurteil: The first part of these words tells us that it is something which comes 'before': to hold a prejudice is to judge ahead of time.[1] A prejudice seems simply to be a premature judgement.

Etymologically, this idea of prejudice as precipitate judgement is correct; but conceptually, it is too wide an idea. For it would make even the most banal errors of judgement into prejudices. If I judge that all doorknobs are coloured gold, because I have seen a single brass doorknob, my judgement is certainly precipitate; but it would seem strange to call it a 'prejudice'.[2] Prejudices may share an important feature with such trivial mistakes, but at the same time the word clearly suggests something more special. In fact it would not be unreasonable to regard *all* errors of judgement as in some sense the result of precipitation. Whoever errs, judges about things he does not yet fully understand. He could, we suppose in any case of error, by way of ongoing scrutiny arrive at a correct view. 'Prejudice', however, is not a synonym for mistake. If prejudices are errors, they are errors of a very particular sort.

2. This does not mean that we have begun in the wrong place. The formation of the word is significant. Even if we assume that the meaning of 'prejudice' has changed – as it seems to have done in the age of Enlightenment – that change must have made sense in terms of the word's original meaning. There must have been a reason why that particular word was chosen for that particular new task. So we have been right to start as we have done; but we have to be more precise.

The first part of the English word 'prejudice' and its European equivalents, we have said, tells us that it is something which comes before something else. But before what? Perhaps before we get to know what the prejudice is a judgement about. In prejudice we pass judgement on something before we have actually encountered it. Prejudice, it appears, precedes actual experience; hence it is not based on it. Since it is formed *before* evidence, it is therefore formed *without* evidence. Someone who is the victim of his prejudices ('la victime de ses préjugés'), says the author of a radical Enlightenment pamphlet on this subject, du Marsais, has neither experience nor reason ('n'a ni expérience ni raison'). According to this work, the *Essai sur les préjugés* edited by d'Holbach in 1770, a prejudiced person is the hapless plaything of his own inexperience ('le jouet infortuné de son inexpérience propre').[3]

The claim that prejudices lack experience raises two questions: Why should experience be so important? And: What follows if prejudices lack experience?

First, why should experience be so important? Experience, in a significant way, always has to be *my* experience. If someone else reports a certain experience to me, then, strictly speaking, I do not *have* that experience. It follows that as long as experience forms the basis of my beliefs, I am the author of my beliefs. On the other hand, if I labour under prejudice, it seems that I am not the author of my beliefs. My beliefs are guided by others. Freedom from prejudice, then, is intellectual autonomy, and I have acquired it as soon as I can substantiate every judgement I make by appeal to my own experience. This seems to be the reason for the importance of experience, stressed permanently by du Marsais.[4]

Secondly, what follows if prejudices lack experience? As du Marsais's choice of words (*e.g.*, 'infortuné') indicates, his remarks are not meant as a mere description of prejudice. They are at once an assessment of it. Prejudices, du Marsais suggests, are something we have to dispose of altogether. Being void of first-hand experience, prejudices separate us from reality. ('First hand', in this context, does not state an additional condition. It only makes explicit an implication. For what is merely second hand is, strictly speaking, not an experience at all.) To approach reality would mean, as du Marsais puts it, to cut through the veil of prejudices.[5]

The Enlightenment which invented – or discovered? – prejudice as a *philosophical* topic, brought it up mostly to reject it. The elevation of prejudice from an inconspicuous legal term to an epistemological, moral and political *cause célèbre* was intended to do away with it; this motif lasts from the early to the late stage of this intellectual movement. Bacon's preface to his *Instauratio Magna* from 1620,[6] for instance, as well as Poullain de la Barre's treatise on the equality of sexes from 1673 (which, as its subtitle – 'Où l'on voit l'importance de se défaire des Préjugez' – insinuates and its preface points out, was intended as a case study in a Cartesian treatment of prejudice),[7] d'Alembert's preliminary discourse to the *Encyclopédie* from 1751,[8] du

Marsais's essay on prejudice from 1770,[9] Kant's article on enlightenment from 1783[10] or Condorcet's outline of the human spirit's progress from 1793/94[11] mention prejudice merely as something from which men, by the use of reason, have to rid themselves. They have to do so completely, these authors urge, for if only some prejudices were eliminated, while others were kept, the result would be inconsistency.[12]

3. Our analysis has revealed three distinct elements of a critical theory of prejudice: Firstly, prejudices lack experience; secondly, the self should be in control of its beliefs, which is the case if these are founded in its own experience; thirdly, therefore prejudices should be abandoned.

The argument may at first appear cogent. But actually the logical nexus is less tight than it seems to be. This is not hard to discern for the second element which is supposed to hold the inference together. The link between experience and cognitive autonomy is not as compelling as has been suggested. Certainly, experience must be *my own*, in the sense in which this has been asserted. But it does not follow that, conversely, every insight that can properly be called my own has to be derived from experience. Looking for empirical evidence is just one way of checking or examining a question for myself; thinking things through is another way to do this, especially where the matter is not one of observation at all. What I myself have thought can be attributed to me as basis of *my* insight with no less right than what I have experienced.

The inference is thus rendered invalid by its second element. We are left with three claims whose logical relations need to be re-examined: Firstly, prejudices lack experience; secondly, prejudices signal the absence of intellectual autonomy; thirdly, prejudices must be abandoned. We shall now continue our scrutiny of the second claim (§§ 4–7). The first claim, concerning experience, will be taken up later (§§ 9, 18–34), while the third question, whether prejudices can and should be abandoned altogether, will be with us throughout these investigations (in the present chapter §§ 8, 10–17).

4. The maxim of enlightenment, or of unprejudiced thinking, says Kant, is always to think for yourself.[13] Prejudice, then, is simply failure to think for oneself, or intellectual heteronomy.[14] A person fails to think for herself, Kant says, when her understanding is guided by someone else.[15] Consequently, if we want to know what is wrong with prejudice, we merely have to consider what it is *not* to think for ourselves, or, to have our understanding guided *not* by ourselves, but by someone else.

We might first suggest that a person does not think for himself, when he takes into account what others think. This cannot be right, however. Understood in this way, thinking for oneself would be neither desirable nor even possible. A self-thinker of this sort would be an incommunicado; but then it is doubtful whether a person could think at all if deprived of communication. We do not wish, nor, it seems, are we capable of doing our thinking alone to the point of not even considering others' views.[16]

We ought, at any rate, have some way of distinguishing autonomy from autism. Diderot insists that the eclectic, who is by definition someone who takes the thoughts of others into account, thinks for himself ('penser de lui-même'):[17] he thinks for himself what others have thought already, and he is in no way inconsistent in doing so.

5. How else might we interpret the idea that someone fails to think for himself? We might find it more appropriate to say that a person's understanding is guided by another, if he acts on the basis of somebody else's judgement without checking its accuracy himself. The demand that men should purge their minds from any opinion merely adopted rather than examined independently was indeed frequently voiced in Enlightenment quarters. Kant himself suggests this reading. In his essay on enlightenment, he has the unenlightened person explain herself thus: I do not need to think, if only I can pay; others will undertake the annoying business for me.[18] As Rüdiger Bittner points out, the analogy here is with a person who, for instance, pays someone to clean her windows because she doesn't want to do it herself. Just as in this case the person eventually enjoys a clear view without doing a hand's turn herself, so the unenlightened person, according to Kant, avails herself of the results of another's reflections without herself following the train of thoughts that leads there.

Yet here again thinking for oneself seems to be unattractive, if not impossible. 'I hate to prepare my tax return and get an accountant to do it', Bittner says. 'Here indeed I do not need to think if only I can pay. I accept the accountant's judgment without checking its accuracy, and yet I act on this basis, since it is still me, not the accountant, who is declaring my income to the tax authority and who is legally responsible for the declaration. However, saving myself some thought by paying does not seem such a terrible thing in this case'. So one wonders what should be wrong in principle with not thinking for oneself, understood in this way.[19]

6. Bittner sketches a third interpretation, formed in response to the failure of

the previous one: 'Sure, there is nothing wrong in general with relying on another's judgment. There is something wrong with it in particular instances. Sometimes people give more weight to another's judgment than is warranted in the case at hand. It is all very well to pay somebody for preparing your tax return. It is a mistake to pay somebody for telling you what to do in every situation of life and always to feel bound to that person's orders. This is the sort of mistake that Kant has in mind when he speaks of somebody being guided by another, and it is the sort of mistake that enlightenment is intended to overcome'.[20]

As Bittner makes clear, however, 'the injunction not to let oneself be guided by another becomes useless on this reading. The injunction now means: Do not put too much weight on others' judgments. This, however, while difficult to do, is trivial to say. We would need to know what the right weight is in any particular case in order to use that rule, and this is just what we do not know'.[21]

As a number of Enlightenment authors have plausibly pointed out, authority is a major source of prejudice.[22] Evidently, the third interpretation refers to cases where people rely too heavily on the pronouncements of authorities. One of Kant's contemporaries who made the point in this way was Thomas Reid. In a chapter entitled 'Of Prejudices, the Causes of Error', Reid set out to illustrate the most influential classification of prejudices, that of Francis Bacon, 'that wonderful genius';[23] referring to what Bacon called the *idola tribus*, Reid claims it is a defect common to the whole human species that 'Men are prone to be led too much by authority in their opinions'.[24] But it is a tautology to call this a defect; there is nothing in the world that one should do '*too* heavily' or '*too* much'. Μηδὲν ἄγαν teaches us nothing; for how could 'too much' be understood if not as that which goes beyond the proper measure of something.

But by this third interpretation Kant's imperative to think for oneself rather than to have one's understanding guided by another is not only rendered useless. The interpretation actually misrepresents what is going on. The salient point is that there is no way to rely on the pronouncements of an authority except by accepting him as authoritative, *i.e.*, *thinking for oneself* that he is endowed with the pertinent qualities. (Toland crudely insinuates that a prejudiced person is 'led like a Beast by Authority',[25] as if such an idea had ever been heard of among animals.) Of course people make mistakes here as they do in any other sort of reasoning. They rely on authorities who do them harm. They attribute qualities to others that these do not possess. But then their errors are mistakes *of* reasoning for themselves, not something opposed to it. Relying on authority does not preclude the use of one's own understanding, but is a particular form of it (and, like all other forms, liable to error).

It is sensible to trust many, though not all, tax accountants in matters of tax returns because they have learned their business and have no interest in their clients' returns being low; it may be unwise to trust them in many other matters, and it was definitely a bad idea for a German worker to trust Hitler in 1933 on the ground that his party had dubbed itself a workers' party: for the objectives of a politician cannot be read off the labels he uses to sell his policies. Whoever did try to read them off in this way, was mistaken; but his mistake arose while thinking for himself. The difference between him and Bittner is not that one of them did not think for himself while the other did. Nor can we say that one relied on authority while the other did not, or that one was guided by another while the other was not. Both saved themselves a few steps in the reasoning process by trusting another person. The difference is that the one, who trusted Hitler, made an error of judgement, while the other, who trusted his tax consultant, was more likely to have made a good decision. This is not tantamount to the cheap scepticism which infers from the premise that I need evidence not only to judge a state of affairs, but also to trust an authority, that therefore authority can, as it were, never get off the ground. The premise is sound, but the conclusion does not follow. I need evidence for both acts, but this does not prove that there is no such thing as authority. For what counts as evidence will be different in each case.[26] But my counting something as evidence is not something that anyone else could do for me.

Thinking for oneself is not an achievement, but a triviality. To be thinking at all, however excessively relying on others' judgements, is to be thinking for oneself.[27] 'Have the courage to use your *own* understanding!', Kant urges.[28] But the imperative admonishes us to do something we simply cannot avoid. To use another's understanding and to use one's own understanding are not alternatives; rather, the former presupposes the latter. The worker who trusted that he would prosper in Hitler's Germany, because Hitler had declared himself a national socialist and socialism implied care for workers, used his own understanding, only he used it not well. Imposing one's thoughts on someone else is impossible, even though such imposition is frequently deplored. If one person rejects another's views, because *he* doesn't think they hold water, force is capable merely of making him *pretend* that he shares them. Even the zealot who burns heretics on the authority of the church has to think for himself that he knows the church which is in possession of the authority. Thinking for oneself does not preclude the most unenlightened content.

7. All thinking, however many errors it involves, however much it uses others' thoughts, and whatever its content may be, is thinking for oneself (§ 6).

There is, however, an objection to this analysis. It seems to rely on an equivocation. The zealot (§ 6) thinks *that* he knows the church which is in possession of the authority, but he fails to think *about* the church. In general we can think that something is the case without thinking much about it at all.[29]

Now it is clearly sensible to distinguish between thinking and reflecting. Reflection is a form of thought, but it requires more than simply thinking that something is the case. Thought is about things, reflection is about thoughts about things.

Yet the difficulty is to see how this might constitute an objection to the analysis that has been presented. If Kant really wanted to urge that we should be reflective rather than merely think, it would be hard to understand why he did not simply say this. For in German the contrast between 'Nachdenken' ('reflection') and 'Denken' ('thinking') is readily available, and there would have been no reason to invent a term like 'Selbstdenken' ('thinking for oneself') which must be understood as opposed to an not only artificial, but truly odd 'Fremddenken' ('another one doing the thinking'). These are different distinctions. When Kant introduced the latter, unusual one, he must have meant it. The argument that the second distinction fails (§ 6) applies both to thought and reflection. Just as all thinking is thinking for oneself, so all reflection is reflection for oneself. But a distinction where one of the concepts distinguished covers the whole domain, so that it contrasts with nothing, does not distinguish anything at all; it merely appears to do so.

However even if, for the sake of argument, we assume that Kant really wanted to urge us to be reflective rather than merely think, we do not appear to be in a better position. Unlike the distinction between thinking for oneself and something for which it is even difficult to find a name in English, the distinction between thinking and reflection is of course a valid distinction. But first, although both modes of the mind can be distinguished, they do not seem to form a pair of alternatives in the sense that one could be reflecting *instead of* thinking. Whatever reflection we consider, we find that its very possibility depends on a host of thoughts that are taken for granted, *i.e.*, precisely not reflected upon. Secondly it remains unconvincing that, would the injunction to reflect be followed, we would necessarily reach conclusions that ruled out prejudices. It is possible that the zealot (§ 6) not only thinks that he knows the church which has got the authority; he might also reflect on the source of this thought. He can tell the mark of the true church; he has found the signs of divine blessing everywhere in its past and present. To dislike this particular reflection is no reason to believe that it is not reflection; the person has effectively moved from asserting a belief to the different level of justifying it. Justifying an idea is a thought about thinking: a case of reflection. If we still hold the zealot's attitude to be unenlightened, this merely shows that reflection as such does not preclude unenlightened attitudes. With the demand to be reflective we get stuck in the same kind of formalism as with the admonition to use our own understanding (§ 6). Poor reflections are also reflections, they just do not help us on.

8. So what does help us on, if thinking for oneself (§§ 4–6) and reflection (§ 7) as such do not? The particular sort of reflection we call 'examining' might seem a promising candidate. Admittedly, it may not obviously rule out the religious zealots (§§ 6–7) who were paradigm cases of prejudice for the Enlightenment. After all, those zealots formed what is known as the Inquisition, and inquisition is just a synonym for examination. But it may properly be asked whether we are entitled to take the self-description of those people at its face value.

In order to rid oneself of all prejudices, Descartes says, the only thing needed is resolution not to affirm or deny any of the things we have previously affirmed or denied until we have examined it afresh.[30] Du Marsais, accordingly, defines prejudice as a judgement passed before examination: 'le *préjugé est un jugement porté avant d'examiner*'.[31] Emphatically, he adds: 'L'homme est grand dans toutes les choses qu'il s'est permis d'examiner; il n'est resté petit que dans celles qu'il n'a point osé voir de ses propres yeux'.[32] These remarks suggest that by examining our beliefs we free ourselves from prejudices. And examining, according to Descartes, starts when we begin to doubt what we have previously believed.

Yet this formalism will hardly do. The Inquisition also doubted many things concerning those it examined, *e.g.*, the sincerity of the heretics. (Note that this doubt was genuine; it was not clear before the inquisition took place whether the heretics had to be classified as insincere or whether it had to be concluded that they actually believed their errors.) Conversely it seems impossible or senseless for me to doubt without at the same time believing something else. When I doubt any proposition, *i.e.*, when I question whether it is true, this presupposes not only that I believe I know its meaning, but also that I believe I know the conditions under which the doubt would be removed (though I may not believe I know the *procedure* by which I could remove the doubt).

The meaning of a belief – which makes the belief what it is – depends on its position within a web of indefinitely (though not infinitely) many other beliefs. Of course we can try and start to spell out these connected beliefs. But each belief we remove from its context for examination will require yet more beliefs for its comprehension. Of course we can and do isolate especially problematic items from this web and make them the subject of our examinations while abstracting from the relations they stand in. But then our predicament recurs on a different level. We discover that the web is not just a web, and that addressing it in this way discloses merely one dimension of it: it extends not only in breadth, but also in depth.

Whenever we become occupied with examining something, we find that it could be examined in even greater detail. We could always be more thorough and more specific. Someone who gave free play to his intellect would always be able to find in our results a matter that has not been settled. But every examination, as a definite project, needs limits to its thoroughness and specificity. These limits are not themselves a result of examination. We cannot know that there is nothing else which could be discovered if we were more thorough and more specific. But at the same time limits have to be set if any steps we take are to count as 'an examination' at all. The limits are set by our trust that 'so much is enough'. It makes sense to call certain procedures 'examinations' only if we allow for such trust; and this trust is not something that is in any obvious way opposed to prejudice. Rather, it seems to be a legitimate and necessary instantiation of it.

We showed above that prejudiced thinking cannot be set against self-thinking (§§ 4–6) or reflection (§ 7). It should now also be clear that the 'checking' and 'examining' of beliefs that we do ourselves is not opposed to prejudice in the way Descartes and du Marsais insinuate.

9. A number of oppositions handed down by philosophy or common sense – prejudice *vs.* thinking for oneself (§§ 4–6), prejudice *vs.* reflection (§ 7), prejudice *vs.* examining things (§ 8) – have turned out to be invalid. But from this it does not follow that there is no distinction between knowing things first hand and knowing them second hand. We acquire beliefs either by ourselves or from others. We hold them either because we have observed things or because we have been told things.

Perhaps this distinction will save the critical characterization of prejudice by the Enlightenment and its correlated plea for first-hand experience (§ 2). For in its passage from a first to a second, a third and perhaps still further hands, knowledge usually seems to deteriorate.

When people have got to know something first hand and then go on to spread it in the form of a story, they often encounter some resistance. Is what they have to say sufficiently exciting? The question is, whether *the story* is interesting enough, but what really bothers the tellers is that *they* are questioned: The suspicion is in the air that they might be rather dull fellows. For such an emergency – and most of us consider a challenge to our reputation an emergency – there is a well-tried remedy. To paraphrase Montaigne, people cover the gap with a false patch.[33] Nor are such additions and changes induced merely by lack of interest. Paradoxically, men will often deviate from the truth precisely to defend their credibility. As the story is in due course presented to new audiences, new opposition may be encountered; consequently new additions and changes are deemed necessary. Apart from such apparent or real requirements of successful communication, there is also the luxury of vanity which, after all, does not want to be stingy. '[N]ous faisons naturellement conscience de rendre ce qu'on nous a presté sans quelque usure et accession de nostre creu', says Montaigne:[34] we naturally scruple to pass on what was lent to us without some interest and addition from our own. Sardonically Montaigne adds that 'le plus esloigné tesmoin en est mieux instruict que le plus voisin, et le dernier informé mieux persuadé que le premier. C'est un progrez naturel. Car quiconque croit quelque chose, estime que c'est ouvrage de charité de la persuader à un autre; et pour ce faire, ne craient poinct d'adjouster de son invention, autant qu'il voit estre necessaire en son compte, pour suppleer à la resistance et au deffaut qu'il pense estre en la conception d'autruy':[35] The remotest listener to the story is better instructed than the witness, and the last to be told of it is more convinced than the first. This is a natural progression. For whoever believes anything esteems it a work of charity to persuade someone else of it, and in order to do so does not hesitate to add out of his own invention as much as he sees to be necessary in his story to overcome the resistance and the incomprehension he attributes to the other person.

Is it not in just this way that prejudices come about?

Montaigne here, as ever, is a keen observer of human affairs. He has acutely captured the deployment of gossip. But is what he says the whole truth on the subject of first- and second-hand knowledge? Montaigne would have been the last to claim that. According to his own testimony, what mattered for him was dispute, not the truth; after all, he thought, anyone can tell the truth, but only few people can present a persuasive argument.[36]

So the question whether first-hand knowledge is necessarily superior to second-hand knowledge is still with us. To approach an answer, let us suppose that someone becomes an eye- and ear-witness to a certain incident. On the one hand he is now able to describe what he has seen and heard, and he reports this to another person. On the other hand, let us further assume, he has misunderstood what the occurrence he saw and heard meant, because he did not know its context. The person who hears about the event, however, may have such knowledge, and may therefore be able to understand the event. He may know, again merely second hand, that a certain gesture whose appearance was described to him signifies something peculiar among the people who have been observed. Although everything he knows he knows only second hand, he knows more and better than the witness.

What we have merely been told may in important ways go beyond the limitations of what someone 'has seen with his own eyes'. If such cases can occur – as they do in fact – the Enlightenment idea that a hierarchy of value for beliefs is provided by knowing their sources – first-hand beliefs ranking *eo ipso* higher than second-hand beliefs – goes by the board.

10. Furthermore, irrespective of the question whether second-hand knowledge is ever better than first-hand knowledge (§ 9), the former seems to be plainly indispensable. If first-hand acquaintance – 'voir de ses propres yeux', in the words of du Marsais quoted earlier (§ 8) – was the condition of a genuine judgement, then it is clear that all of us will have many more prejudices than actual judgements. It is evidently not in our power, nor do we have the time, to check everything ourselves.[37] Quantitatively and qualitatively by far the most substantial source of our beliefs are other people who in turn have got most of their beliefs from yet others. Private or personal knowledge, *i.e.*, what individuals discover by observation and remember, or infer from those actual or remembered observations, constitutes a minute fragment of the whole range of what we claim to know.

On an Enlightenment view, one might go so far as to acknowledge that those remarks state a fact about most of our mundane beliefs, though a deplorable one. By way of contrast, on the Enlightenment view, science provides the paradigm of what human knowledge should be like.

But the contrast between the everyday realm of received opinions and science as the domain of direct experience will not do either. A physicist would have done for himself only a tiny fraction of the experiments he makes use of in his work. Researchers have to rely for their facts on the authority of fellow researchers, very much as all human beings must do in relation to their fellow human beings. Even the boldest innovations in science spring from an extensive range of information which researchers accept unchallenged as a background to their own particular problems.

What an individual can achieve, even if he spends his whole life on some matter, on the one hand, and what societies have already achieved, on the other, seem incommensurate. This is why Charles Pinot-Duclos, Edmund Burke and William Hazlitt claimed that to step out of prejudice would be to step out of society. '[L]e préjugé est la loi du commun des hommes', Duclos remarked;[38] for the fabric of common sense, he had discovered, is not so much judgement, but prejudice. Prejudice, according to Burke, is the impingement of others' thoughts on our own; not only old (§ 55), but common opinion. Mediated through authority, others' thoughts are no longer alien and foreign to us, but habitual and natural. Without prejudice each individual would have to trade 'on his own private stock of reason';[39] but then the individual will not get far. For deprived of social resources of belief, Burke says, '[t]he individual is foolish',[40] *viz.*, to put it more politely, severely limited in his or her outlook.

The point, however, is not just that the individual would function less efficiently when deprived of prejudice; rather, Burke argues, such a human being could not subsist at all. The elimination of prejudice that pure reason demands thrusts out communality and thereby also destroys the society based on it. Where '[p]ersonal self-sufficiency and arrogance (the certain attendants upon all those who have never experienced a wisdom greater than their own) would usurp the tribunal', Burke says, 'the commonwealth itself would, in a few generations, crumble away, be disconnected into the dust and powder of individuality, and at length dispersed to all the winds of heaven'.[41] In William Hazlitt's words, to eliminate prejudice 'would be to unravel the whole web and texture of human understanding and society'.[42] But there is no human life except in society. Therefore human beings must share in a common stock of belief. Of course, we may want to add, they do not have to adopt each and every element of it uncritically. Yet precisely in order to examine part of that common stock of belief, they have to take over a much greater part of it upon trust, *i.e.*, in the form of prejudice (characterized, in the present argument, by being second hand rather than first hand).

11. The defence of prejudice roughly represented here (§ 10) was contemporary with the late Enlightenment's attack on it. Its conservative appreciation of tradition rather than innovation (cf. § 55) and its anti-individualistic preference for trust in the community over dependence merely on one's 'own private stock of reason'[43] are intertwined. The two rejected attitudes were originally seen as one: originality. What aspires to originality must be both new and individual. This aspiration was then the fashion of the day; 'original' and

'original genius' appear in titles of books after 1750: Edward Young, *Conjectures on Original Composition* (1759); William Duff, *An Essay on Original Genius* (1767); Robert Wood, *An Essay on the Original Genius and Writings of Homer* (1769, 1775). Young denounced the acquirements derived from society – precisely those that Duclos had praised at the beginning of the same decade – as mere 'borrowed knowledge', much inferior to genius, which 'is knowledge innate, and quite our own'.[44]

Admittedly, not all of the apostles of originality regarded solipsistic reliance on untutored spontaneity as the hallmark of genius; but some did. If the wealth of human culture is communal, however, not much is to be expected from what is new simply because it originates in the individual.[45] The conclusion, explicitly drawn by Goethe,[46] is that a thought is rarely good *and* original; as a rule, original thoughts will be folly. The very fact that the original genius is a visionary, *i.e.*, that – as the praise of his admirers goes – 'he has seen things which others do not see' should render us cautious towards him. And, to put it even more pointedly, an absolutely original work would be absolutely unintelligible. In so far as a man uses language, he employs something that does not originate from himself but from the totality of his predecessors, and the novelties he might achieve are, by combined social and linguistic necessity, variations and extensions of conventions that exist by virtue of past usage (cf. §§ 31–32).

As the title of Robert Wood's book indicates, the 18th century concept of originality was projected back into history. For this purpose, of course, history had to be handled somewhat roughly. Homer, after all, had his predecessors; he may have *been* his predecessors, if the theory is correct that he was a tradition, not an individual.

Of course all this does not mean that those artists who around 1800 considered themselves original geniuses could not have produced great art. What it means is that in their theorizing about what they produced and how they produced it, as distinguished from their artistic production itself, they deluded themselves. No mind is a clean slate, still less one which mysteriously creates the signs which occur on it out of nothing but itself.

12. Prejudice, Duclos, Burke and Hazlitt maintained, forms an indispensable part of knowledge (§ 10). The ideal of the *siècle des lumières*, elimination of prejudice, then, would be self-defeating: it would result, in effect, in the destruction of knowledge. What Duclos, Burke and Hazlitt took to be the demand of the rationalistic Enlightenment: to empty one's head of everything that had colonized it and to commence thinking all over again as if there had

never been anything there, they considered insanity. In the spirit of these authors, it could be said that to require people to doubt everything and to take a fresh start, each accepting only the results of his own experience and reflection, would be just as fantastic as to require each of them to build by himself the city he alone will live in. For knowledge, Duclos, Burke and Hazlitt suggested, is as much a collective enterprise as cities are: a product of the cooperation of many people of many successive generations. Intellectually, there is no self-made man.

Indeed, reasoning which in one respect everyone inevitably does by and for himself (§ 6) is in another respect inevitably social. A proof, for instance, is valid for everybody, or otherwise it is not even valid for myself. This, however, also shows the limit of the argument from society. For we cannot invert it. Because something is true, it holds for everyone; but that everyone holds something – that it is common prejudice – does not establish its truth. This reflection on the nature of theoretical reasoning seems to weaken the case for prejudice. A reflection on the nature of practical reasoning, on the other hand, strengthens it. For the latter has a different economy from that of the former.

We are acting rather than thinking beings; it thus follows that we have to have prejudices, says Friedrich Schlegel.[47] Of course, acting and thinking are not exclusive alternatives. Always or sometimes we employ our intelligence when we act. But wherever thought is applied to practice, prejudices imply a systematic and necessary refusal to consider whole sets of data. In any decision-making context it is hard to believe that prejudices are something from which men ought to, or even could free themselves. For the point is not merely that prejudices save us a lot of trouble and make life easier.[48] In this respect, one could argue that sometimes trouble is necessary and life need not be easy. But in fact, at the moment of decision, it does not merely take longer, but is simply impossible to consider every possibility and every option. Indeed, we cannot even consider every reality. Decision-making forces us to ignore the greater part of what we perceive and all we do not perceive. Without a selection that is not itself a result of examination, *i.e.*, without a prejudiced selection, we would 'get on with it' not merely later, but not at all. In this vein, more pragmatic than Burke's, prejudices can apparently be justified on grounds of economy of thought. It seems to follow that the demand to abolish prejudice, advanced by many Enlightenment authors, expresses an idle hope.

13. To examine everything ourselves is logically impossible, because examinations involve an unexamined element (§ 8). In an examined life,[49] for it to

be examined, much will have to remain beyond examination. Examining everything ourselves is also an empirical impossibility. Most of what each individual believes has to be imported, not home-made (§§ 10–12). Both conceptually and as a matter of experience, knowledge rests on trust. The foundation of knowledge is not itself knowledge. For wherever we trust, we do not, in the strict sense of that word, know.

It might, however, be argued that knowledge, as such, is good.[50] If that were true, it might seem to follow that there could not be too much knowledge. And from this, again, it might be inferred that any piece of prejudice or trust, not being knowledge, but rather ignorance, must be rejected.

But the inference is fallacious. You can have too much of a good thing. Gold may be a good thing; but as king Midas had to learn this does not mean that the more of it there is the better.

In truth the objection under discussion is not an argument against the economic justification of prejudice. Rather, it is just a restatement of the position against which the economic justification of prejudice has been advanced. Therefore the economic argument applies to this reformulation, too. The abstract claim that 'knowledge is good' simply ignores the salient difficulty. With regard to knowledge we cannot avoid compromising on its quantity. Any way we do this, however prudent it may be, has its costs. We must sacrifice breadth for depth, or, as far as that goes, depth for breadth. We limit ourselves either by specialization or by superficiality. Given that we are finite beings, there is no way of knowing everything about everything. Even if we tried to know at least something about everything, sacrificing depth for breadth, we would end up in a state of mind that would not deserve the attribute of knowledge in respect of anything. Thus we are forced to be specialists. The difference between us, in this respect, is only a matter of degree. And, to conclude, knowing much about a few things, or at least so much as suffices for our purposes, we have to make do with trust and prejudice regarding many other things. The Enlighteners believed that all good and desirable things are necessarily compatible; this is one example to the contrary.

Hence something must be wrong with the principle that people should be open to all ideas presented to them. Certainly it is desirable to be exposed to potentially good ideas. On the other hand, it is also desirable not to waste time. If someone was open to all ideas presented, time would be wasted to such a degree that no good idea could be properly thought over. To be sure, that person's mind would be open; but it would be so open that nothing was retained. Ideas would simply pass through a mind of such constitution. In this way, the liberal ideal of open-mindedness can be self-defeating.

Exposure to potentially good ideas and avoidance of waste of time: these two requirements pull in opposite directions. The best we achieve is a balance between them. And a balance is not a stable position. Here it will be, as it were, composed of mistakes: of steps leading one time too far in one direction, another time too far in the other direction. Sometimes we must, for instance, waste time reading a book in order to determine that it was not worth reading. More often we avoid reading books we are supposed to read. The pre-screening techniques we employ, referring, for example, to book covers or the reputation of publishing houses, are anything but reliable. They amount to prejudices. Their justification is economic: they restrict the waste of time and energy so that we have enough left to study what we know to be worthwhile. We concluded above that more envisaged possibilities of what could be the case and more options do not necessarily improve our situation (§ 12): the same holds regarding ideas in general.

14. The economic justification of prejudice is, however, both limited and problematic.

It is limited in that by criticizing the Enlightenment in one respect, it has by implication to acknowledge it in another respect of equal weight. The aim of the Enlightenment's mainstream has been, it is true, a world that is transparent without remainder, 'aufgeklärt' ('cleared up'), as the German expression for that historical movement says. As against this aim, the objection has been that no one can answer each and every question for himself anew.[51] But obviously, this objection is only a partial one. For when we say that we cannot answer *each and every* question anew, we imply that we can answer *some* questions anew. So it concedes that the Enlightenment is to some degree in the right.

In so far as it implies that concession, the objection we are considering calls for a distinction. If it is sensible and indeed necessary to leave some things to custom, tradition and prejudice,[52] while some other things need not be left to them, we want to know which things fall into which category. To decide about the essentials oneself, we have to accept what is less essential as given and predetermined. To understand what matters to us, we protect ourselves from an overload of trivia by never thinking about them. Certainly any thinking, knowing and understanding that deserves the name does more than and indeed something different from putting its subject into a box and labelling it. But any mind that attains the level which deserves to be called thinking, knowing and understanding with regard to certain subjects, will contain compartments for other subjects with labels on them such as 'None of my business' or 'Never to be thought of'.[53] This is a reasonable and quite inevitable economy of power. But it is not a solution. For it immediately raises the further question: What is essential and what is not? How to choose what we are going to decide for ourselves? In this regard, the economic justification of prejudice is problematic in the following sense. It poses a problem that it cannot cope with from its own resources. For economic considerations are restricted to means. But the question about the essentials of human life is one of ends.

15. In spite of these qualifications (§ 14), the economic justification of prejudice contains a decisive critical point. To disprove a universal thesis – such as the claim that all prejudices should be eliminated – it is enough to establish a limited claim, as in this case: *sometimes* prejudice is in place. This has been claimed to be the case in particular with regard to a type of situation that Edmund Burke has characterized: 'Prejudice is of ready application in the emergency; it previously engages the mind in a steady course of wisdom and virtue, and does not leave the man hesitating in the moment of decision, sceptical, puzzled, and unresolved'.[54]

When Burke describes prejudice as previously engaging us, as acting beings, in a steady course and saving us from hesitation, it assumes a striking likeness to instinct; before Burke, this parallel had been drawn explicitly by Hume[55] and Chesterfield.[56] To put it paradoxically, prejudice is, for Burke, *social instinct*. It precisely matches the function that had been assigned to instinct – conceived of as a natural endowment, not a social achievement – earlier in the 18th century; in the words of Pope: 'Reason, however able, cool at best, / Cares not for service, or but serves when prest, / Stays till we call, and then not often near; / But honest Instinct comes a Volunteer. / This too serves always, Reason never long; / One *must* go right, the other *may* go wrong. / See then the *acting* and *comparing* pow'rs / One in their nature, which are two in ours'.[57]

Two aspects have to be distinguished in the suggestion that we should understand prejudice as a kind of social instinct that 'is of ready application in the emergency'. The first aspect is that prejudice as a social analogon to natural instinct never misleads us. But on any sober account this would not even be true of instinct in the biological sense. It is precisely instinct which guides the mouse into the mousetrap. We therefore here drop this aspect. The second aspect is that in situations of emergency there are ways of reacting to them in which prejudice plays a crucial rôle. In this regard, Burke's remark must be considered a reserved and measured way of making the point, nay, almost an understatement.

If I were walking about at night on the outskirts of Berlin and saw a group of young men with bald heads, it would be an act of prejudice to hide myself. It would precede and not be founded in actual experience. For I have never observed or even felt such people do any harm. (In the present instance, we are employing du Marsais's criterion of prejudice (§ 2), and it seems that we are right in doing so, since the harmfulness of certain people *is* a matter of experience, not of reasoning.) Furthermore, the interpretation implicit in my reaction of hiding myself is clearly not the only possible one. For these people might be a self-help group of pitiable adolescents suffering from cancer who have just undergone chemotherapy. Comparing the possible harm of doing injustice to these youngsters with the possible harm of being knocked down, the prejudice which considers them as violent is more rational than an unprejudiced attitude towards them.

Clearly, it makes sense to characterize certain situations as cases of emergency only if we consider certain other situations as normal. But a situation like the one just described is normal in a modern big city, not a case of particular emergency (though it could of course turn abruptly into one). In fact, it would hardly be an exaggeration to claim that one could not walk across the street without prejudice.[58] As a matter of social fact, the philosophical point made by Burke seems to have become empirically even more significant in the present.

16. At first glance, the example given (§ 15) seems to offer a credible instance of the rationality of prejudice. On a closer look, however, it appears sensible to distinguish between a preliminary suspicion that is reasonable and a prejudice that is not.[59] If I were walking about at night on the outskirts of Berlin and saw a group of young men with bald heads, it would indeed be rational to hide myself. But for that to be rational, I do not have to believe that all bald-headed young men are dangerous. A conviction that all bald-headed youngsters are dangerous – the relevant prejudice – is one thing, and no reason has been stated why *that* should be rational; another, clearly distinguishable thing, and the rational attitude in this case, is a mere surmise that is in practice revealed as distrust. As we saw (§ 15), the rationality behind the latter is an extremely simple weighing of possibilities: If I am wrong, I have done an injustice to those youngsters which they will never know and thus won't hurt them, but if I am right I might have saved my life by my cautious behaviour. So I am precisely not sure that I am right, as prejudiced people are,[60] but I do admit that I may well be wrong. All I have to believe is simply that acting on a mistaken assumption in this case, given the relative unimportance of my judgement of the boys, is by far the lesser evil. In other words: I do not accept

that assumption as *true*; I merely regard acting on my suspicion as more *prudent* than not doing so.

This is of course not to claim that the alternative between a preliminary suspicion and a prejudice is always at our disposal. There is a dogmatic, assertive element in our passions. When we experience terror, this tends to come along with a firm conviction that the object of our emotion *is* terrible. Running away reinforces the feeling that someone is after me. Panic has the power to arouse strong beliefs; it can prevent us from weighing any alternatives, however simple. But all this is no objection. To distinguish two attitudes is clearly not the same thing as to contend that we can choose between them at will.

17. The reinterpretation of the example (§ 16), however, overstates the difference, particularly in contrasting it, as a case of preliminary judgement, to prejudice. A thought can only be called preliminary if some definite settlement is aimed at. But rationality does not require that someone who hides himself at night from bald-headed youngsters does not rest until he has found them in the daytime at a safe place, and can ascertain what kind of characters they are. Rather, it seems perfectly rational to consider the matter as closed as soon as one has got over the night's episode without harm. Hence the thought that has been called rational is not rational because it is preliminary; for it is not preliminary. The corresponding distinction between truth and prudence, however, is too weak to save the point. For what is prudent here must also have some foothold in reality. There would be no prudence in hiding myself if what I saw was two little girls, not ten bald-headed young men in the street. In so far as I think it probable that the young men whom I do not know will behave in a certain way, the example is a case of prejudice.

Where there may be a difference from a conviction about the young men – the contrast foil of the reinterpretation of the example (§ 16) – is in my *attitude* towards my prejudice(s). It is indeed tempting at this point to go further on and take the following line of reasoning: The crucial alternative is not, as Enlightenment authors have suggested, to have or not to have prejudices. Rather, the salient point is what attitude a person takes towards his prejudices. As Karl Kraus put it, what matters is always to remain master of one's prejudices and never to become their slave.[61] The attraction of this strategy cannot be denied; however, it is exposed to a difficulty that seems hard to overcome. According to the strategy what separates the rational from the irrational is not the absence of prejudices, but the attitude taken towards them. The attraction, then, is this: Prejudices set limits, and limits need not be at all harmful, indeed, they can be helpful (§§ 12–13). But the difficulty follows in the wake of this attraction. They *can* be helpful – provided we discern what the limits are. We can only take up a certain stance towards our prejudices when we *know* our prejudices. But when a prejudice is recognized *as* a prejudice, it ceases to *be* a prejudice. Concern about prejudices arises from the fact that those who have certain prejudices never suspect that they are prejudices.[62] They believe that their own beliefs are, quite simply, the most natural thing in the world. Nature is commonly opposed to custom. But in social contexts the word 'natural' is used for customs one is so accustomed to that one does not even see them as customs. In Montesquieu's *Lettres persanes*, the Parisians are reported to have asked Rica: 'Comment peut-on être Persan?'.[63] 'How can one be Persian?': obviously, those who asked the question thought that there was something unnatural about not being a European. In so far as we are not conscious of our prejudices as prejudices, they possess the notorious tenacity of the obvious which seems to preclude mastery over them (cf. §§ 53, 65).

Notes

1   Cf. Sailer, *Vernunftlehre*, p. 77: 'Vorurtheil ist, wie das Wort sagt, Urtheil *vor* der Zeit'. – Kant, *Reflexionen zur Logik*, Nr. 2532, p. 407: 'Vorurtheile sind Urtheile, die dem Verstand zuvor kommen und da dieser nachher zu spät kommt'. Kant follows Georg Friedrich Meier whose *Auszug aus der Vernunftlehre* he used as a textbook for his courses in logic: 'In dem letzten Falle übereilen wir uns (praecipitantia), und die ungewisse Erkenntniss, die wir aus Übereilung annehmen oder verwerfen, ist eine erbettelte Erkenntniss, ein Vorurtheil, eine vorgefasste Meinung (praecaria cognitio, praeiudicium, praeconcepta opinio)' (§ 168, pp. 399–400).

2   In spite of his already cited explanation of prejudice as precipitate judgement, Kant acknowledges this point: 'Das Vorwahrhalten aus unzureichenden Gründen ist nicht Vorurtheil, sondern Muthmaßung' (*Reflexionen zur Logik*, Nr. 2517, p. 401).

3   du Marsais, *Essai sur les Préjugés*, vol. I, pp. 6–7. For d'Holbach's own account of prejudice, see his *Lettres à Eugénie*, *passim*, and his *Système de la Nature*, e.g., p. XXIX.

4   e.g., *Essai sur les Préjugés*, vol. I, pp. 3, 32; vol. II, pp. 79, 92.

5   Ibid., vol. I, p. 152: 'déchirer le voile du préjugé'. Cf. p. 11.

6   'Præfatio', p. 132: 'exutis opinionum zelis et præjudiciis'.

7   *De L'Égalité des Deux Sexes*, p. ii: 'Dans le progrez de leur recherche, il leur arrive necessairement de remarquer que nous sommes remplis de préjugez [C'est à dire de iugemens portez sur les choses, sans les avoir examinées.] & qu'il faut y renoncer absolument, pour avoir des connoisances claires & distinctes' (the explanation in square brackets is printed in the margin). For the character of the book as a case study in the Cartesian treatment of prejudice, see pp. ii–iv. Cf. Descartes, *Meditationes*, Synopsis sex sequentium meditationum, p. 12: 'dubitatio [...] ab omnibus præjudiciis nos liberet'; *Principia Philosophiae*, pars I, § 75, p. 38: 'omnia præjudicia sunt deponenda'.

8 *Discours préliminaire*, p. 132: 'détruisant autant qu'il est en nous les erreurs et les préjugés'. Cf. Jeaucourt, Art. 'préjugé', p. 239: 'Que l'homme donc dépose ses *préjugés*, & qu'il approche de la nature avec des yeux & et des sentimens purs, tels qu'une vierge modeste a le don d'en inspirer, il la contemplera dans toute sa beauté, & il méritera de jouir du détail de ses charmes'.

9 *Essai sur les Préjugés*, vol. II, p. 187: 'Réformer le genre humain et le détromper de ses préjugés'.

10 'Was ist Aufklärung?', pp. 54–5.

11 *Esquisse*, pp. 242–3 (of the benefits derived from the sciences): 'Le plus important peut-être est d'avoir détruit les préjugés'.

12 Not uncharacteristic of the German Enlightenment, however, in Friedrich Nicolai's *Das Leben und die Meinungen des Herrn Magister Sebaldus Nothanker* (p. 151) it is the enemy of the Enlightenment, an orthodox preacher, who draws attention to the inconsistency of a half-hearted elimination of prejudice, while the defender of the Enlightenment, the hero of the novel, is prepared to pay the price of inconsistency: 'Dieser [the preacher] fuhr fort: "Und unsere neumodischen Theologen, die die Welt haben erleuchten wollen, die so viel untersucht, vernünftelt, philosophiert haben, wie wenig haben sie ausgerichtet! wie müssen sie sich krümmen und winden! Sie philosophieren Sätze aus der Dogmatik weg und lassen doch die Folgen dieser Sätze stehen; […] sie sind aufs äußerste inkonsequent. –" Sebaldus fiel ihm schnell in die Rede: "Und wenn sie denn nun inkonsequent wären? Wer einzelne Vorurteile bestreitet, aber viele andere damit verbundene nicht bestreiten kann oder darf, kann, seiner Ehrlichkeit und seiner Einsicht unbeschadet, inkonsequent sein oder scheinen […]"'.

13 '[D]ie Maxime, jederzeit selbst zu denken, ist die *Aufklärung*' ('Was heisst: Sich im Denken orientieren?', p. 283). 'Selbstdenken […] ist die Maxime der *vorurteilfreien* […] Denkungsart' (*Kritik der Urteilskraft*, § 40, p. 390). Also *Reflexionen zur Metaphysik*, Nr. 6204, p. 488: '*Aufgeklärt* seyn heißt: selbst denken'. Cf. Kiesewetter, 'Ueber Vorurtheil', p. 356.

14 'Heteronomie der Vernunft' (*Kritik der Urteilskraft*, § 40, p. 390).

15 'Was ist Aufklärung?', p. 53.

16 Bittner, 'What is Enlightenment?', p. 346.

17 Art. 'éclectisme', p. 36. Diderot claims, however, that thinking for oneself and relying on an *authority* ('autorité', ibid.) form an opposition. This will be discussed as the *third* interpretation of thinking for oneself, cf. § 6.

18 'Was ist Aufklärung?', p. 53: 'Ich habe nicht nötig zu denken, wenn ich nur bezahlen kann; andere werden das verdrießliche Geschäft schon für mich übernehmen'.

19 Bittner, 'What is Enlightenment?', pp. 346–7.

20 Ibid., p. 347.

21 Ibid.

22 Cf., *e.g.*, Thomasius, 'De Praejudiciis oder von den Vorurteilen', pp. 32–4, 38, 40; du Marsais, *Essai sur les Préjugés*, vol. I, pp. 8, 27; Meier, *Auszug aus der Vernunftlehre*, § 170, p. 413.

23 *Essays on the Intellectual Powers*, p. 368.

24 Ibid., p. 369.

25 'The Origin and Force of Prejudices', p. 16.

26 Cf. Hobbes, *Leviathan*, I,7, pp. 54–5.

27 Hegel, *Enzyklopädie*, § 23 Anm., p. 80: 'Man kann den Ausdruck *Selbstdenken* häufig hören, als ob damit etwas Bedeutendes gesagt wäre. In der Tat kann keiner für den anderen denken, so wenig als essen und trinken; jener Ausdruck ist daher ein Pleonasmus'.

28 'Was ist Aufklärung?', p. 53: 'Habe Mut, dich deines *eigenen* Verstandes zu bedienen!'
29 Cf. Henry James, 'Letter to Thomas Sergeant Perry', pp. 45–6.
30 'Lettre à M. Clerselier', p. 204: 'pour se defaire de toute sorte de préjugez, il ne faut autre chose que se resoudre à ne rien assurer ou nier de tout ce qu'on auoit assuré ou nié auparauant, sinon aprés l'auoir derechef examiné'.
31 *Essai sur les Préjugés*, vol. I, p. 7. Cf. Sailer, *Vernunftlehre*, p. 77: '*vor* der Prüfung'.
32 du Marsais, *Essai sur les Préjugés*, vol. I, p. 69.
33 'Des boyteux' [= *Essais* III,11], p. 1027.
34 Ibid.
35 Ibid., p. 1028.
36 'De l'art de conferer' [= *Essais* III,8], pp. 927– 8; cf. pp. 924–5.
37 On this ground, ancient Scepticism refused to doubt and examine everything, and was even willing to resort to prejudice. Cf. Sextus Empiricus, *Pyrrhoneion hypotyposeon* I, §§ 23–4, 226, 237–8, pp. 16/17, 138/9, 146/7–8/9.
38 *Considérations sur les mœurs*, p. 25.
39 Burke, *Reflections*, p. 168.
40 'On the Reform of the Representation in the House of Commons', p. 97.
41 *Reflections*, pp. 182–3.
42 'Prejudice', p. 321.
43 Burke, *Reflections*, p. 168.
44 *Conjectures on Original Composition*, p. 283.
45 Probably the first to make this point, even before originality came into fashion, was Swift in his satire 'The Battle of the Books' (1710) (see pp. 148–50). Small wonder, then, that Swift also held prejudice in esteem, cf. § 86.
46 'Den Originalen': 'Ein Quidam sagt: 'Ich bin von keiner Schule! / Kein Meister lebt, mit dem ich buhle; / Auch bin ich weit davon entfernt, / Daß ich von Toten was gelernt'. – / Das heißt, wenn ich ihn recht verstand: / Ich bin ein Narr auf eigne Hand'. This criticism of originality is pursued in a poem from *Zahme Xenien* VI, 'Gern wär' ich Überliefrung los / Und ganz original', which is central to Goethe's self-understanding; it contains the striking assertion that he is himself tradition: 'Wenn ich nicht gar zu wunderlich / Selbst Überliefrung wäre'.
47 *Philosophische Lehrjahre* I, p. 408: 'Daß wir Vorurtheile haben müssen, folgt schon daraus, daß wir eher handeln als denken'. – On the nexus between prejudice and action cf. also Amiel: 'Pour agir, il faut croire; pour croire, il faut se décider, trancher, affirmer, et au fond préjuger les questions. Est impropre à la vie pratique, celui qui ne veut agir qu'en pleine certitude scientifique. Or nous sommes faits pour agir, car nous ne pouvons décliner le devoir; donc il ne faut condamner le *préjugé*' (*Journal intime*, p. 961).
48 This is one aspect of Lichtenberg's remark: 'Die Vorurteile sind so zu reden die Kunsttriebe der Menschen, sie tun dadurch vieles, das ihnen schwer würde bis zum Entschluß durchzudenken, ohne alle Mühe' ('Sudelbücher Heft A, Aphorismus 58', p. 23). Another aspect of this remark would be to appreciate the 'art' ('Kunst') that is at work in prejudices.
49 Cf. Plato, *Apology* 38a: ὁ δὲ ἀνεξέταστος βίος οὐ βιωτὸς ἀνθρώπῳ.
50 Wieland, 'Gedanken von der Freiheit über Gegenstände des Glaubens zu philosophieren', p. 496.
51 That everyone should do so, could, even among Enlightenment authors, only in theory be called for. Enlightenment practice, of course, did not conform to this ideal. What is the *Encyclopédie* if not a monumental attempt to save individuals the effort of answering each question anew?

52 A link between these concepts has been claimed by Montaigne, 'De la coustume et de ne changer aisément une loy receüe' [= *Essais* I, 23], *passim*, and particularly p. 117: 'prejudice de la coustume'; and many authors have followed Montaigne's lead.

53 Such a division of labour between reason and prejudice has been suggested by Fontenelle: 'Les Préjugez sont le suplément de la raison. Tout ce qui manque d'un costé, on le trouve de l'autre'. As indicated, the division is not merely quantitative, but qualitative: 'Elle [*sc.* la raison] laisse à faire au Préjugé ce qui ne mérite pas qu'elle le fasse elle-mesme' (*Nouveaux Dialogues des Mortes*, pp. 344, 340). For a different elaboration of Fontenelle's idea that prejudice supplements reason cf. § 99.

54 Burke, *Reflections*, p. 168. – Henry James generalized Burke's point beyond cases of emergency: 'Cannot you imagine the state of irresolution and scepticism and utter nothingness a man would be reduced to, who set to work to re-cast his old opinions, pick them clean of prejudice and build them into a fairer structure? I'm afraid that he would find he had pulled out the chief corner stones, and that the edifice was prostrate, and he almost crushed in its ruins. In his desire to believe nothing but what his reason showed him to be true, I think he would end by believing nothing at all' ('Letter to Thomas Sergeant Perry', pp. 46–7).

55 'Of Moral Prejudices', p. 371.

56 'On Prejudices', p. 258.

57 *An Essay on Man*, III, 89–96, p. 43.

58 Horkheimer, 'Über das Vorurteil', p. 87.

59 Kant uses the terminological pair 'preliminary judgement' *vs.* 'prejudice' to draw the pertinent distinction: 'Alle Untersuchung erfodert ein Vorläufig Urtheil, auf welcher Seite wir die Wahrheit vermuthen', 'Vorläufig urtheil ist nicht das Vorurtheil, sondern ist eine Behutsamkeit, um solches zu vermeiden' (*Reflexionen zur Logik*, Nr.s 2519, 2523, pp. 403–4. Cf. *Logik*, p. 511).

60 In Kant's language: 'Die Ursache von dieser Täuschung ist darin zu suchen, daß subjektive Gründe fälschlich für objektive gehalten werden, *aus Mangel an Überlegung*' (*Logik*, pp. 505–6), 'Der subjektive Grund einer Regel zu urtheilen der vor aller Überlegung vorhergeht, *so fern er zur obiectiven Regel wird*, ist Vorurtheil' (*Reflexionen zur Logik*, Nr. 2520, p. 403 (emphasis added). Cf. Nr. 2528, ibid., p. 406; Nr. 2533, p. 408; Nr. 2547, p. 411; Nr. 2550, p. 412). Though the claim that prejudiced people hold their prejudices to be true is convincing, these definitions by Kant fail. For they do not allow us to discriminate between prejudices and errors of judgement in general (a distinction that also Kant wishes to uphold). Errors of judgement in general are subjectively held to be true, while they are objectively false, and could have been avoided by more thorough consideration of the subject matter. Cf. § 1.

61 'Das Vorurteil ist ein unentbehrlicher Hausknecht, der lästige Eindrücke von der Schwelle weist. Nur darf man sich von seinem Hausknecht nicht selber hinauswerfen lassen' (*Sprüche und Widersprüche*, p. 172). Kant recommended a somewhat similar attitude towards false judgements, though not towards prejudices: as long as we are aware that the character of the former is problematic, they can fulfil an important function for us (*Kritik der reinen Vernunft* A 75 = B 100, p. 115).

62 de Quincey, 'Philosophy of Herodotus', p. 132.

63 No. xxx, p. 129.

Chapter Two

On the Intricate Relation of Prejudice to Experience, and on its Alleged Stupidity

18. But it seems that the problems dealt with in the previous chapter do not really arise from du Marsais's thesis that prejudices lack experience (§ 2). Rather, they seem to stem from combining this (possibly true) thesis with the demand to abolish all prejudices (a link suggested by du Marsais himself (§ 2)). So whether or not the conclusion is justified that all prejudices have to be abandoned, we need to ask whether it is true that prejudice towards something and experience of it preclude each other.

Considered in its own right, however, even the latter thesis immediately seems highly dubious. It would require much sophistry to deny that generally prejudiced persons have ever encountered members of the class of whom they disapprove. Rather, we find even people whose beliefs contemporary usage takes to be the most clear-cut cases of prejudice constantly referring to experience.

For example, an infamous anti-Semite reports that in the Inner City of Vienna he encountered an apparition in a long caftan with locks of black hair. At first he wondered whether this was a Jew. For in Linz where he had lived before Jews had not looked like this. He tells us how he observed the man stealthily and cautiously. The longer he gazed at the alien face, scrutinising it feature by feature, the more his first question assumed a new form, namely: Is this a German? As a result of this experience he could no longer believe that the objects of his study were Germans of a special religious confession. He became certain that they belonged to a different nation. From the time when he began to take cognizance of (the singular form is characteristic) 'the Jew', Vienna appeared to him in a different light from before. Wherever he went, he began to see Jews, and the more he saw, the more sharply they began to stand out in his eyes from other human beings.[1]

19. What, then, is the relationship between prejudice and experience, if they are not simply mutually exclusive? Let us examine the example given. Hitler presents his change of mind as a case of learning from experience: 'Anschauungsunterricht', 'object-lesson' is the term he uses for what happened

to him.[2] He had observed certain differences, Hitler suggests, and drew his conclusion. But in fact, he had precisely not changed his conception of the world (in this instance, of what it is to be German) under the impression of contrary experience. Rather, he had measured reality by his conception of it. Since the former does not fit the latter, it cannot, Hitler concludes, be *this* kind of reality: These people *are not* Germans. The reverse case, learning from experience, might have led to a different result. Had Hitler learnt from experience, he might have concluded that the look of 'Germans' (or of Austrians – for Hitler takes it for granted that Austrians are a subspecies of Germans) was not what he had believed it to be. Perhaps he would even have had to conclude that there is no such thing as a 'German look' since 'being German' is not a visible natural characteristic, but a political and historical one: one that has to be apprehended by thought rather than by the senses.

Hitler's interpretation of his experience depends on the prior assumption that true nationality is a racial feature. Or, to put it psychologically rather than logically, only because Hitler *was* already a racist was he able to have an experience of the sort described by him at all. Far from experience producing his idea of the Jew, it is the latter which explains Hitler's experience. In this sense we could even stick to the original understanding of prejudice as something that is embraced before experience; but the point of this understanding would not be to claim that prejudiced persons have no experience of the things towards which they are prejudiced, as du Marsais seemed to suggest. Rather, it would be that they may have their experiences which, however, are shaped by their prejudices.

20. Our objection to Hitler's appeal to experience, then, is not that *our* experiences with Jews are different from his. While this is true, and significant in other respects, it would be to beg the question to use this fact as an argument.

True, Enlightenment empiricism, invoking the authority of science, presupposed that everyone's experience was essentially the same, and where it wasn't, that it ought to be the same, that is, like the experience of an enlightened man. After all, the progress of human knowledge rested on the fact that the same experiment or observation was repeatable in Paris or Peking. But however true that may be for specific spheres of the natural sciences, thanks to a massive abstraction from certain features and the isolation of others (§ 34), it is definitely not true outside those spheres. The claim that everyone's experience is essentially the same is plainly contradicted by experience; hence an empiricism which tries to uphold it is inconsistent.

21. The above account of the relationship between prejudice and experience (§ 19) rejects the doctrine that the two are simply mutually exclusive, *i.e.*, that a prejudiced person has to have *no* experience of what he or she is prejudiced about. But perhaps a prejudice is a judgement that does not take into account *enough* experience. On this account, a prejudice would be a hasty generalization. (This doctrine is a refinement of the initial idea that prejudice is premature judgement (§ 1).)

In a brief digression in Plato's *Phaedo* (89d–90b) Socrates sets out to explain how the attitude of misanthropy (μισανθρωπία) comes about and develops: A man without experience of personal relationships (ἄνευ τέχνης, literally: without skill, that is, in dealing with men), Socrates suggests, may begin by trusting somebody who, however, soon afterwards turns out to be unreliable.[3] This happens again with another person, and then with yet another one. The hero of this story, after these repeated knocks, ends up hating everyone (μισεῖ τε πάντας). He believes that there is no sincerity to be found anywhere (ἡγεῖται οὐδενὸς οὐδὲν ὑγιὲς εἶναι τὸ παράπαν).

But the hater of men has got his statistics wrong. Had he been less hasty, Socrates argues, he would have discovered the fact that extremely good and bad people are both very few in number, and that the great majority are somewhere between the two. Socrates uses an analogy to demonstrate how the misanthrope is mistaken in his generalization: It is, Socrates says, the same as with extremely large and small things; nothing is more unusual than coming across an extremely large or extremely small man, or dog, or anything else, or again, one that is extremely swift or slow, ugly or beautiful, pale or dark. As a treatment of these cases without haste would show, all extremes are rare and few in number, but intermediate cases are very common.

22. Plato, in the passage from *Phaedo* (§ 21), does not mention prejudice, whose precise equivalent would be πρόκριμα, a noun that is absent from classical Greek; it does not occur before 300 BC. If Plato intended to establish a general point in this passage, then this must rather have been the rashness of *passion*, as exemplified by hatred. Of course this does not mean that Socrates' considerations are irrelevant to the problem of prejudice; one might speculate whether it is not precisely passion which induces the precipitancy attributed to prejudice. But only in the 18th century was Plato's delineation of a specific attitude offered as a general explanation of prejudice (including, as a particular form, misanthropy (cf. § 36)). Johann Gottfried Kiesewetter, in 1790, presented a lucid exposition of the theory that prejudice is a hasty generalization.

In so far as man possesses the power of reason, Kiesewetter argues, he must strive for universal propositions that serve him as principles. For reason aims at knowing everything from foundations, or, in other words, at deriving the particular from the universal. To reach this goal, man has to obtain universal propositions. This striving for universal propositions, in order to be able to use them to found our insights and judgements, is, however, often seductive. It tempts us, Kiesewetter points out, into assuming that something is true universally when there is, as yet, no basis for holding it to be true universally. One discovers that several things of a kind possess a certain feature and generalizes over the whole kind, in order to have a universal rule. One sees that under certain circumstances something has happened several times, and then contends that under these circumstances the same thing will always happen. One has found out that some Jews, depressed by grief and misery, as it were expelled from human society, and deprived of all normal sources of income, tried to make a living by usury and fraud, and for reasons of convenience one says: All Jews are frauds.[4]

23. This theory seems to be directly applicable to our example of Hitler's anti-Semitism. When we look at the way this case is usually treated, we find some researchers who have studied Hitler's life searching for disagreeable encounters with Jews.[5] They assume that if there had been such encounters, this would explain his racial prejudice: Hitler must have generalized in an unjustified way from 'some Jews' he had met to 'all Jews'. Other biographers, however, found that Hitler was actually helped and befriended by some Jews – Jews who were themselves poor – in his critical years,[6] and were surprised that 'in spite of this' Hitler was a fierce anti-Semite. Both approaches regard the genesis of prejudices as a kind of inductive reasoning that has gone wrong. In the case of the alleged explanation the basis for the induction was 'too small'. In the case of the surprise Hitler should have generalized inductively from his positive experiences with Jews, but unfortunately failed to do so.

There is, however, reason to think that the understanding of prejudice must dig deeper. It is implausible that people become anti-Semites because they have had a couple of unpleasant encounters with Jews. And this claim is not based on empirical observation of prejudiced persons. Rather, the point is that the alleged explanation of prejudice by reference to unpleasant experience (and even the surprise if there had not been any) begs the question. For it does not account for what is crucial here, namely, how attitudes towards specific categories of people come about. 'The Jews' must already be a category of one's thinking if one is to have unpleasant experiences with Jews rather than with dentists or male persons or whatever else they may be. To account for the unpleasantness of an experience on the ground that the person was a Jew rather than a Viennese or simply this particular individual, or by appeal to the fact that the day on which the encounter took place was very hot or that one was in a bad mood because the egg one had had for breakfast had been too hard, presupposes anti-Semitism already. There are an indefinite number of circumstances that might be referred to, and the selection that an agent makes is the decisive step which the account of prejudice as a result of unpleasant experiences fails to explain. Timon of Athens is said to have had disagreeable encounters with Athenians; Socrates' theory (§ 21) could not explain why he became a hater of men rather than of Athenians or of Greeks.

Of course the empirical basis of prejudice is insufficient (for if it were sufficient it would be a warranted judgement). But this is not really what characterizes prejudices. A prejudiced person is not, as Kiesewetter insinuated, like a lazy statistician who stops collecting samples too soon because he wants to go to bed.[7] For a piling up of instances, *however much* industry is spent on it, could never establish a universal proposition. Kiesewetter's example (§ 22) covered all future Jews, and no diligence in the world would enable one to count these. But where all pains taken would be in vain, blame for laziness falls flat.

If the prejudiced person is like a statistician, then he is like one who is sure of the results of his statistics before he produces them, and who designs his statistics in such a way that his figures conform to what he had already been sure of. The characters in Plato's *Meno* (80de) discuss the paradox that we can never come to know something that is new to us, for if we did not know it already we could not recognize it even if we came right up against it. Prejudice seems to be a cognitive attitude that lives up to the severe standard set by this sophism. It seeks only what it has already found, and becomes only what it has been already. To be sure, prejudice can be substantiated by experience: but *what is experienced* is already guided by the prejudice.

24. The previous argument is, however, built on a distinction which we must fully grasp if we are not to misunderstand it altogether. To say that a certain experience had to be bad because it included contact with Jews, and, more precisely, that it had to be bad because of the Jewishness of the Jews, instantiates anti-Semitic prejudice. To believe that there are Jews does not instantiate anti-Semitic prejudice. Certainly, one has to have the latter belief to have the former; but one can of course have the latter belief *without* the former. The account of prejudice as hasty generalization presupposes that people who claim to have

had unpleasant encounters with Jews possess the concept 'Jews'; but this does not make the account circular. What makes it circular is this: The account does not make intelligible why they chose precisely this aspect to explain why the experience had to be bad. This, not the possession of the category 'Jews', manifests anti-Semitism and therefore cannot be used to explain it.

If we have fully understood the passage from *Mein Kampf* we are already familiar with such a distinction. The pretended empiricism of Hitler's argument derives its rhetorical force precisely from blurring the salient distinction, or at least a distinction close to it. What Hitler suggests is this: I have done nothing but looked at the people. Certainly, no one can deny that there were Jews in Vienna. There is nothing prejudiced about this observation, Hitler insinuates. And of course he is right. It is neither prejudiced, nor false, nor anti-Semitic, but (if we are familiar with the historical situation, as Hitler's readers were) trivial. But where Hitler's claim stops being trivial (and becomes anti-Semitic), his empiricism also turns out to be merely pretended. What Hitler really wants to say is not that there were Jews in Vienna, but that Jews can never be Austrian, and thus German, citizens. And this is something that could not possibly be determined by *looking* at them.

25. The distinction we have just drawn, however, may occasion an attempt to reinstate the account of prejudice as hasty generalization. This attempt would locate prejudice, as it were, between the two beliefs that have been distinguished (§ 24). We should all agree that, when someone says that there are Jews in Vienna, on the ground that he has seen a number of them, he expresses a genuine judgement rather than a prejudice. But prejudice, according to the new proposal, does not first come on the scene when someone claims that a certain experience had to be bad because it included contact with Jews, and, to aggravate the charge, that it had to be bad because of the Jewishness of the Jews. Prejudice can be manifest at an earlier stage. A person is, according to this proposal, already clearly prejudiced when she says '*All* Jews are such and such'. She is prejudiced, even when she says that all Jews are nice. What makes such statements expressions of prejudice is that they generalize, whether in a positive or in a negative vein.

What is it to generalize? To generalize seems to be to draw conclusions from what has been the subject of experience to what is not yet the subject of experience. On this account, there is a sense in which *all* generalizations are hasty.[8] (In the original proposal (§ 22), on the other hand, hasty generalizations were distinguished from well-considered generalizations.) We would not be hasty, if we knew all individual cases that fall under a general description; but that would be a general statement, not a general*ization*. In a generalization, we pass from what is familiar to what is unknown, and there is always the chance that what is unknown might be different from what is familiar; that it is unknown implies that we are not entitled to exclude this possibility. What, then, is the relationship between the notion of generalization and the notion of prejudice? Generalization is a transfer from the past and present to the future, from what came before to what is alleged to come later: and that 'before' is the 'pre-' of prejudice.

26. There is clearly some merit in the proposal that it is generalizing which makes something a prejudice, irrespective of whether one generalizes in a positive or in a negative vein. For it rules out a move that seems particularly unhelpful if we want to understand prejudice. The move in question is to reserve the term 'prejudice' for negative views. Of course if someone regards 'the French' as great lovers or 'the English' as polite and cultivated people we might, admitting the unwarranted generality, still want to call those views pious errors rather than prejudices. But in crucial cases, unfavourable and favourable prejudices precisely correspond to and complement each other. A nationalist does not only have abusive views of other nations, but also and primarily – for on that ground he is called a nationalist – an exalted view of his own. Since neither kind of view, the negative and the positive, is based on critical examination, the latter are no less prejudices than the former. In terms of the approach now under consideration, the positive view generalizes over the nation to which the nationalist belongs, the negative one over other nations, and these generalizations, not the negative character of one them, are 'prejudicial'.

And though this, unlike the previous point, does not constitute an argument, it is at least interesting that in the language of jurisprudence until the 17th century, 'to prejudice' could mean either to make someone's opportunities worse than they ought to be (as it still can), or to privilege, depending on its actual content. Whilst the English noun prejudice signifies today either a prejudgement or harm, the Greek verb προκρίνειν, in ancient as well as in modern Greek, is used in the sense of 'to decide beforehand', but also, more frequently, in the sense 'to prefer'; in this way, these two particular languages materialize two complementary aspects of the concept. It is also worth noting that in western Europe in the 18th century the positive use of our concept was still very much alive. Rousseau, for example, speaks of the prejudices he had in favour of Hume before he got to know him: 'J'avois donc toute sorte de préjugés en faveur de Hume'.[9] (It is harder to see how such an example could be construed as a case of generalization; for this problem cf. § 27.) In the aftermath of the Enlightenment, however, reference to prejudice as an attitude that can be positive almost died out. But actually such a manner of speaking makes perfect sense and would be worth a revival.

27. To make generalizing the salient feature of prejudice (§ 25) is again not merely to tell us what prejudice is, but also to imply there is something wrong with it. Prejudice, it is suggested, does injustice to us, whereas an unprejudiced outlook and behaviour will do justice to us. The claim is that a prejudiced view subsumes a person under a social rubric in order to attribute a certain feature to her: 'She is an academic, and, as everyone knows, all academics are arrogant'. The person finds herself, as it were, like a butterfly pinned to a label and thus classified. An unprejudiced outlook, on the other hand, will treat that person as an individual. Instead of a label, it will provide an integral biographical account of that person for us.

A moral principle is implicit in this critique of prejudice: Everyone has the right to be judged as an individual. It is wrong to view someone with disfavour on the basis of a social classification. Disapproval, then, is allowed only on the basis of well-examined particular judgements.[10]

This critique of prejudice does not seem to be a particularly powerful one. When the anti-Semite says: All Jews are dishonest, the feeble objection is: But not *all* of them are like that! The refutation of prejudices is thus transformed into a matter of counting heads. The more there are, the more, it would seem, the anti-Semite is correct.

If it were true that generalizing is the crucial vice of prejudice, we would of course have to conclude that, even if its content is racist, we simply do not have any stronger objections to it. But the correctness of that account is doubtful; for it appears to have an implication that has no better logical basis than the one that it avoids, that is, the restriction of prejudices to negative views. Apparently, it is a just equally unjustified restriction to claim that all prejudices refer to whole *groups* of people. There seem to be prejudices against individuals too; some people are prejudiced against their neighbours. (Prejudices against groups may be socially more significant than prejudices against individuals, but that is another question – a question of finding certain things less interesting than others –; at present the point is rather why, as a matter of definition, there is any reason to exclude prejudices related to individuals.) In Mozart-da Ponte's *Cosi fan tutte* Ferrando and Guglielmo are both obviously prejudiced in favour of their respective fiancées, the individuals Dorabella and Fiordiligi, and not at all towards a group, such as all women, while the Enlightenment philosopher who subjects that prejudice to experimental testing, Alfonso, asserts a generalization which hardly could be more general: 'Così fan tutte'.[11]

Of course we could avoid the objection by returning to our starting point. The prejudicial character of prejudices had been located in generalizing. But making statements about whole groups is really only one way of generalizing. There are ways of generalizing about individuals that have nothing to do with groups. When I say 'Our neighbour never speaks the truth', that probably also manifests a prejudice. It seems to do so, however, because it generalizes ('never', implying an 'always' with regard to the opposite), not because it refers to a specific group – not even to the group of liars. But, as turns out, the criterion employed here does not really single out prejudices. For we do not also want to call the statement 'Our neighbour has always resided in our town' an expression of prejudice on the ground that it generalizes about every period of the neighbour's life.

So the objection has to be dealt with in a different way. A more promising strategy of defence would be this. Admittedly, a person may also be prejudiced against a particular individual, say his neighbour. Calling it a prejudice rather than a judgement, however, implies that he does not really know his neighbour. But if he does not know him as the particular individual he is, he can only classify him as a member of a group which he thinks he knows. This explanation seems to fit perfectly the original instance of the allegedly arrogant academic.

Clearly to classify in this way would be a flaw if it could be demonstrated that everyone has a right to be judged as an individual. But it is not clear how this could be demonstrated. Certainly there are contexts where individual assessment is essential; but there seem to be others where it is not. There is no obvious *a priori* argument that it is, in itself, wrong for a judgement to be directed against groups of people. Sometimes members of groups share certain features, and sometimes these features are harmful. As for the persons I have accused, Zola says in his admirable attack on the French military bureaucrats of his time, I do not know them; to me, they are mere entities, mere instances of the spirit of social malfeasance.[12] But for the anti-Semites who had victimized Dreyfus, this individual was a mere entity, a mere instance of the spirit of social malfeasance, too. We certainly do not want to include Zola on this ground under the same rubric as the anti-Semites. While both were concerned with whole bodies of people (and only derivatively with individuals), the difference which matters seems to be that, on the one hand, Zola was right, and, on the other hand, the anti-Semites were wrong in their respective attitudes towards the groups they accused.

28. That generalizing is the crucial vice of prejudice does not seem conclusive in itself (§ 27).

Neither does it seem consistent as a complaint by the Enlightenment, the major critic of prejudice. Here, after all, it is precisely the appeal to 'man in general' which is meant to supply a cure for 'prejudice'.[13] If the accusation is that generalizations often gloss over individual exceptions, it is hard to see how we could make sense of Enlightenment *humanism* with its vast claims concerning all mankind.

Nor is it clear how, in response to the complaint that making social generalizations about individuals is to fail to do them justice, we can deal with each other in better ways. In a rather shallow version, this ideal leads to a moral pedagogy which tries to get to know as much as possible about the individuals it is concerned with. The result will be effective, yet not necessarily desirable: mostly, it will consist in increased control over these individuals. Quite apart from this suspicion, knowledge of individuals does not ignore general categories; on the contrary, it is built on them. Whenever we help another person, we conceive of her as lacking in some respect that has been intelligible to us already. We classify her as a beggar, a prisoner, a sick person, and only on some basis of this kind will means be forthcoming to help her: money, liberation, drugs. The endless talks the psychoanalyst has with his individual patient are no exception; the therapy he aims at is grounded in a general apparatus of classes of mental disorders such as actual neuroses – neurasthenia, anxiety neurosis, hypochondria – transference neuroses – obsessional neurosis, conversion hysteria, anxiety hysteria – psychoses and so on, however these classifications may have been modified and supplemented since their original presentation.

An individual who conceives of himself as reduced to extremities which are radically unprecedented will also have to think of himself as radically isolated; nothing expresses his situation better than the words Heinrich von Kleist wrote on the day of his suicide: the truth is there was no help for me on earth.[14] As for this extremity, philosophy has no consolation to offer; nor did Kleist die because psychotherapy had not yet revealed itself.

29. Despair or inconsistency, then, appear to be the necessary concomitants of the protest against generalization in the name of individuality. No wonder, then, that scientific books which define prejudice as a generalized attitude themselves abound in classifications of prejudiced character types.

But perhaps theorists of prejudice have just been rather unfortunate in reasoning so inconsistently hitherto. New, self-critical theories of prejudice might be developed which would not contain any typologies of prejudiced people, but be confined to individual case studies. We might want to insist that every statement about a group runs the risk of doing injustice to its individual members, and that if time is too short to consider each individual as such, we simply have to suspend judgement.

Such insistence appears to be supported by the following consideration. There are prejudices towards things and prejudices towards persons. Someone might have a prejudice against butter, or a prejudice against intellectuals. Now it is clearly prejudice towards persons, not prejudice towards things that has aroused such extensive misgivings. This asymmetry calls for an explanation. If we pursue the course proposed above, it may help us to account for the difference.

It is clear from the start that the reason why one may be upset about a prejudice against intellectuals, but not about a prejudice against butter, cannot simply be a matter of falsity and truth. Manifestly, both of those prejudices can be false. A person holding the second of these prejudices might, for instance, say: Whatever looks like butter can only taste awful. But if she tried butter, she might in fact like it. In this case we assume the prejudice to be an error; so the asymmetry that concerns us must have some other cause, and there is an obvious candidate. We do not believe that the prejudice against butter, however erroneous it may be, shows any injustice towards an individual. It is not credible that the prejudice does some special injury to the third block of butter on the second shelf of the supermarket's cold-storage. An object offered for use or, in the present case, consumption, produced to satisfy a desire, may be replaced without loss by some other object possessing the same general character; conversely, if one rejects one such object it is, *ceteris paribus*, consistent to reject all such objects.

Injustice towards the individual, however, seems to be precisely the major reproach when someone is viewed with disfavour on the ground that he falls under some general social category, for instance, that of being an intellectual. In this case, the issue is not simply that a characteristic is attributed to some general class which happens not to possess it. Rather, the criticism is that one should not talk at all about intellectuals as if they were a general class. Prejudices against persons seem guilty of much more fundamental injustice than prejudices against things ever can be. And the reason for this seems to be that it is persons, not things which are, in an eminent sense, *individuals*. They are more than instantiations of something general. Subsumed under social, and hence general, characterizations, persons are reduced to something which does not exhaust them. They rightly feel injured in their self-esteem, even –

and this is remarkable – if they are proud of belonging to that class, *i.e.*, of being intellectuals, Iranians, Muslims or whatever the general characterization may be. The *resulting* difference between the examples is a moral difference; however, this moral difference appears to be only the consequence of a profound conceptual difference.

30. But there is reason for rejecting any critique of prejudice which accuses it of introducing social categories where only individual qualities matter. For the opposition of individual and society on which it is built is naïve. The naïveté is twofold: regarding the ascribed (§ 30) and the ascriber (§ 31).

The relevant opposition presents itself as if individuals existed apart from the way they are seen within society. But in fact individuality is itself a social product, a feature ascribed by others. Individuals are always and inevitably judged, appreciated or held in disdain, as bearers of certain social features. Individuality comes on the scene where there are different social circles (family, state, profession *etc.*). The more circles there are, the higher is the chance that others may have different and even contradictory expectations with regard to some human being, and hence see him or her in a differentiated way: that is, as an individual. Individuality, then, is so to speak the point at which different social circles intersect. A banker who confesses to being a convinced communist or a supermodel who holds a PhD in philosophy will easily be perceived as individuals; but not because what we say of them lies outside the bounds of the social. Attributions of individuality are not different in kind from attributions of general, social features; rather, they attribute *combinations* (in the case of *eccentric* individuality extremely rare combinations) of general and social features.[15]

31. But it is not only considerations about the object that raise doubts about the conception of individuality that underlies this critique of prejudice. Considerations about the judging subject also make it questionable. For we always judge others (and also ourselves), and hence also capture the individuality of others (and also of ourselves) by way of language which is inevitably a social product. Linguistic reference to particular phenomena is mediated through general terms. One may grasp a single object in one's hand, but one cannot mean anything and one cannot even say 'this' about it without using an abstract term applicable to other individuals.[16] In each and every case, language classifies.

As de Bonald has pointed out in his critique of the Enlightenment, language, necessarily employed in any articulate critique of prejudice, is not a neutral medium, but rather imbued with prejudice. Talkative as we are, we live on them and they live on us. According to de Bonald, the philosophers who have risen up with so much bitterness against what they call prejudices, ought to have started by ridding themselves of the language in which they were writing; for that is the first source of prejudices, and the one that contains all the rest.[17] Thus the dilemma de Bonald poses is, in a nutshell, this: A man free from prejudices wants to start from scratch. But where is scratch? Either it is after the acquisition of language, in which case it will not be free from prejudice. Or it is before language, in which case it may be free from prejudice, but nothing can be said. The project will never even get started, because nothing is left to define the point from which to move in the first place.

Even if we acknowledge that there are exceptions to every generalization in human life, we have also to acknowledge that we could not get along without generalizations. In understanding a sentence we extrapolate from the familiar to the unknown, from the past to the present. To ascribe meaning to a word is to generalize. Are we to conclude that it is a mistake to use language?

32. When de Bonald suggested that language is imbued with prejudice, he was in fact able to quote the Enlightenment itself in support; Enlighteners had made the same claim, though as a complaint about the imperfection of natural languages, while de Bonald used it as an argument in favour of prejudice. Regarding this divergence of interpretation, intellectual history has bestowed plausibility on de Bonald's conclusion. During the era of the Enlightenment, from Bacon (1620/22) to Condorcet (1793/94), philosophers had dreamt of an artificial universal language, founded upon rational principles and purified of the prejudices of the ages; by the end of the 18th century, however, that project had run into insurmountable difficulties.

Is this fact about the history of ideas decisive? Logically, one question is evidently prior to it, *viz.*, whether the shared premise of that entire dispute was sound in the first place. We might be puzzled by the idea that language itself could be 'imbued with prejudices'. For this claim looks as if it rested on a category mistake. Even if a language contains terms which *can* be used to express prejudice, such as the English verb 'to jew' which means 'to cheat' or 'overreach'[18], there is, we might want to object, nothing prejudiced *in the language*. Rather, the prejudice seems to lie in the *use* of language, or, as we might prefer to say, in the *user* of the language. It is just as easy to use a word like 'to jew' in a non-prejudiced way as in a prejudiced way; the former would be instantiated by uttering a sentence such as 'It is offensive to call an act of cheating "to jew"'.

This objection is not altogether pointless, but somewhat weak. For in uttering the sentence 'It is offensive to call an act of cheating "to jew"' we do not *use* the word 'to jew'; we merely mention it. Furthermore the point of this mention is that one should *not use* this word. The word 'to jew', as explained in a dictionary of the English language, does not merely happen to be usable in the service of prejudice; it embodies a prejudice.

The example also disproves another objection to de Bonald, *viz.*, that language could at most contain preformed *concepts*, not prejudiced *beliefs*. Whoever employs the concept 'to jew' is committed to believe in a connection between Jewishness and fraud; and generally, whoever employs, rather than merely mentions, a concept, is committed to a belief that it captures something in reality.

From the outset it would be a mistake to assume that learning our mother tongue consists in being informed of words, the atoms of language, and memorizing their dictionary meanings. A child cannot learn the signification of words without learning judgements, and, indeed, a whole way of life, along with them.[19] For a long period the child has to take those judgements, cognitive as well as evaluative, on trust. Within its native language, the child lives on prejudices.

We have thus moved already beyond the surface of language from which examples like 'to jew' can be drawn. For de Bonald digs deeper. What he is thinking of are in fact not such easily discoverable and to a certain degree trivial cases, but rather basic features, first, of language in general and, secondly, of specific families of languages, that we constantly take for granted. First, *e.g.*, when things are called by the same word a prejudice arises that they must all be of the same kind ('unum nomen – unum nominatum').[20] Secondly, a natural language embodies those distinctions which generations of speakers of that particular language have drawn; the language carries the prejudice that *these* are the relevant distinctions, not others that are not manifested in the language. This is obvious on the level of semantics; but it holds for the level of syntax, too. The grammar of Indo-European languages, *e.g.*, in its subject-predicate-structure contains a specific ontology not shared by some other families of languages, a way of looking at the world in one way rather than another. If there are nouns, adjectives and verbs in a language, we perceive the world as consisting of things, properties and actions; but possibly the world could be split up in other ways.

It may be admitted that though the language we are brought up to speak initially is something we have to accept without question, this does not have to be the case for the rest of our lives. Language can become an object of criticism. Otherwise not even the considerations presented here could have been formulated. But in order to criticize one prejudice inherent in language, we still have to presuppose a host of others.[21]

33. Any critique of prejudice, it seems, has to be rejected, because the critique seems to apply to language in general, while we cannot avoid using language in order to articulate that critique.

But this objection is subject to doubt. For the feature which gave rise to it was classification (§§ 25–31). This being the case, the objection seems simply to shift the problem. True, prejudice classifies and language classifies. That, however, is not really the issue. For it is not classification as such that hurts. It is hardly felt as prejudicial or humiliating to be subsumed as a pedestrian or as a taxpayer in a statistical survey. For such a classification leaves it open that many other, much more essential things may be said about a person who is an object of this survey. A generalization that expresses a prejudice, however, seems not to be so modest. The claim that 'the Germans' are cold and brutal is one about their essence, even if it is supplemented by the note that they are at the same time industrious and musically talented. A prejudice seems to be an abstraction that claims to exhaust the concrete phenomenon as far as it is relevant. Unlike the statistical classification, it seems to say something like this: 'You are black – or white – and that is all I need to know'.

34. The way in which prejudice has been critically assessed has changed significantly as a result of the previous considerations. The relevant defect now seems to be not so much generalization, which evidently can be quite harmless. Should the phrase '… and that is all I need to know' capture the critical feature of prejudice, then we are concerned not about generalization, but rather about abstraction and isolation of certain features.

But again abstraction and isolation are known to us as quite honourable ways of theorizing, as methodical safeguards of rationality. Abstraction and isolation are essential to the method of science. The more successfully natural scientists manage to isolate a factor and to explore just that one factor, the more precise are their results. Critics object that scientists do not care for the whole; but scientists know quite well that they *must not* care for 'the whole' and take every effort to exclude it. They shield their retorts and their thermometers as well as their entire laboratories.

Such proceedings, however, differ in an important respect from the stupid attitude that was characterized by the phrase '… and that is all I need to know'. What the sciences discover by virtue of abstraction and isolation is 'all they need to know' only at the time when they are exploring the particular question defined by the corresponding limits. They employ that method only because it is fruitful to treat just one thing at a time; but what they want to know is in principle everything – only it would be pointless to investigate it all at once.

Both statistical (§ 33) and, generally, scientific abstraction are employed with an awareness that the part they play is only a part. In prejudice, however, as William Hazlitt describes it, 'we see a part, and substitute it for the whole'.[22] Pronouncements such as 'Black people are ugly'[23] or 'Black is beautiful' declare the part about which they are explicit, colour of skin in the instances given, to be or, more exactly, to represent or to account for the whole. ('For the whole', since the words 'ugly' and 'beautiful' in those slogans are not intended in their narrow use as solely aesthetic predicates.)

'To abstract' literally means 'to draw off'. To do so is sometimes appropriate. The flaw of prejudice is not that it 'draws off'; rather, it might consist in stupidly forgetting at the same time that it does so.

35. 'Prejudices such as 'Black people are ugly' or 'Black is beautiful' declare the part about which they are explicit, colour of skin in the instances given, to be or, more exactly, to represent or to account for the whole' (§ 34).

But is it fair to present those two statements on the same level? Is it not crucial that the first is harmful and the second harmless or even beneficial? Are we allowed to ignore that all-important factor that distinguishes 'Black people are ugly' from 'Black is beautiful': *power*? The oppressors, saying the former, try to deprive the oppressed of their value; the oppressed, saying the latter, reassert their value against this act of deprivation.

The difference stressed here is important. But it is not a difference between prejudice and what is not prejudice. A prejudice, turned upside down, remains a prejudice. To alter minus into plus may change a lot, in particular the slogan's psychological impact – what was abhorrent becomes appealing –; but it does not change its epistemological status. If we proceed from 'All Muslims are violent' to 'No Muslim is violent', we pass from a grim outlook to a friendlier one; but such progress must not be mistaken for a *cognitive* advancement. *As a judgement* one may well be no better than the other.

The difference that power makes to prejudices is not a theoretical difference at all. It is a practical difference: a difference in effects. Power can turn that which does not yet do much mischief into disaster; for power is indeed also the power to cause harm. Prejudice may be encouraged by power, in particular towards expression in words and actions. An opportunistic anti-Semite who during the Weimar Republic would rarely have manifested his attitude towards

Jews verbally, and never in deeds, was instigated to do both under the Nazi rule. This rule, of course, institutionalized racial prejudice. Once institutionalized, prejudices cease to be merely subjective opinions. Obligation lends them an air of objectivity. They establish themselves as prerogatives. This is captured by Helvétius' succinct remark: 'Les préjugés des grands sont les lois des petits'.[24] The objectivity of institutionalized prejudice is derived from its power, as law, to form social reality according to itself. '[S]ince we cannot now apply laws fit to the people', Edmund Spenser says in his vindication of the English oppression of Ireland, 'we will apply the people and fit them to the laws'.[25] The reversed order suggested by Spenser mirrors the peculiarity expressed by the 'pre-' of prejudice. Once applied, however, political measures under specific aspects can make their objects be what they have defined them to be. What a private prejudice mostly accomplishes only in the mind of those who hold it – constant confirmation – (cf. § 77), is achieved as a matter of fact by institutionalized prejudice. The timeworn prejudice that Jews are filthy[26] actually became true under the appalling sanitary conditions of the Nazi concentration camps. Where power turns into violence, truth itself takes on a cynical aspect.

The violence by which oppressors enforce their abstractions makes their prejudices so much more terrible than those of the oppressed. But this does not prove that there is less *ressentiment* among the oppressed than among oppressors.[27] Again, to respond to the prejudices of their oppressors by counter-prejudices of the type 'Black is beautiful' may fulfil an important psychological function for the oppressed. Even that is no reason to contend that the latter are no prejudices. Prejudices may well very often fulfil important psychological functions for those who hold them.

36. The question of the relationship between prejudice and power (§ 35) is connected to the notion that prejudice is belief manifesting inequality and discrimination.

This at last is an error from which the 18th century was free and which has been cultivated only in the 20th century. The belief is now widespread that hatred and prejudice will fade away as soon as the equality of all is acknowledged. Thinkers and poets of the 18th century, by way of contrast, were lucidly aware of a, not at all uncommon, prejudice directed indiscriminately at all mankind;[28] this negative prejudice is perfectly egalitarian: a consistent misanthrope hates human beings as such, irrespective of gender, race, national origin, or creed. In accordance with the notorious (§ 33) slogan, he can say: 'You are human – and that is all I need to know'.

Unluckily for him, his prejudice is so egalitarian and indiscriminate that it extends to himself also, whether he wants it to do so or not. Timon, as the clairvoyance of Libanios represents him, could not bear his own shadow or his own mirror image, because they revealed a human shape; ultimately, he could not bear himself.[29] An enemy of the human race, being human himself, must in the end become hostile to himself, too; or rather, he must have been so in the first place, in order to become an enemy of all human beings, for there is no safer way to turn one's own life into misery.

37. Neither power and oppression (§ 35) nor inequality and discrimination (§ 36) define prejudice, though they can indeed go along with it in monstrous combinations. Whether a prejudice possesses one or all of those features, makes a most important difference; yet the difference is not that between what is prejudice and what is not. What has led us into this discussion, however, offers a rather more promising candidate for answering the question about the nature of prejudice. The phrase '... and that is all I need to know' (§ 33) proposes an apparently quite straightforward answer to the question 'What's wrong with prejudice?': Prejudices, the new approach suggests, are *stupid* (§ 34).

Stupidity as a characteristic of prejudice has been referred to already in some of the arguments considered. In particular the *prima-facie* plausibility of Kiesewetter's example of prejudice – 'All Jews are frauds' – (§ 22) depends on this characteristic rather than on the one singled out by Kiesewetter, *i.e.*, making a universal judgement where there is no universality. This is indeed common in cases where we hesitate to speak of prejudice. It is common because we must make concessions or even sacrifices not only on quantity when we consider ideas (§ 13), but also, in many cases, on quality as soon as we communicate them. We have to compromise between validity and appeal. A writer of aphorisms, for instance, if he understands the form he employs, will be prepared to favour the latter at the expense of the former.

Someone who is used to seeing himself in a mirror always forgets his own ugliness, says Nietzsche.[30] Is this a valid assertion? It might become one if we modify it, and say that that may happen sometimes, or perhaps often, but not always, since there will probably be some people who feel constantly reminded of their deformity by looking into a mirror. The more qualifications we add, the more accurate and unassailable we will be. Every further mitigation of a bold claim brings us closer to safety – and turns it into a banality. Every additional proviso to Nietzsche's aperçu on the stultifying effects of getting used to something rescues us from objections – and makes us more boring.

Pedantry is so tedious precisely because of its detailed accuracy. What it gains in validity, it loses in appeal. Nietzsche pronounces something to be universal truth[31] that is probably not universal. But what he says is anything but stupid. And it seems to be for this reason that we are reluctant to call it a prejudice.

So is prejudice characterized by stupidity? To assess this proposal, we need, to begin with, to know what stupidity is. But is stupidity capable of conceptual analysis at all? The question seems to be in place since we might think that 'stupidity' is not a concept, but an insult. This possible objection, however, is easily answered. True, the word 'stupid' is used as an insult. But why can't something be both an insult and a concept? Terms of abuse have their logic, too, and that this logic is beneath the dignity of philosophical analysis presupposes a lofty idea of philosophy that we do not have to share.

That 'stupidity' is used as an insult itself tells us something regarding its rationale. The word is used to attribute a shortcoming. Stupid people are believed to lack something that others who are not stupid possess. But what is this deficiency supposed to consist in?

38. We might think that stupid people lack knowledge. Stupidity, on this account, would be ignorance. Indeed, sometimes people say things like 'She is stupid. She does not even know how fashionably Princess Di was always dressed'. But such talk is misguided. Unlike stupidity, ignorance is compatible with full awareness of one's ignorance, and discontent at it – being ignorant, we simply may want to know more about what we are ignorant about, or we may even know that the subject matter is not worth knowing if, for instance, the relevant subject matter is Princess Di. Stupidity, by way of contrast, we generally attribute to others – and to ourselves only in retrospect: 'How *could* I be so stupid?'. If we were aware of doing or saying something stupid at the moment we do or say it, we would not do or say it at all.

Of course we can deliberately say something stupid in the service of a strategy, for instance in order to be underestimated. Under certain circumstances, an *air* of stupidity is the best policy. Sometimes we manage to make ourselves seem so foolish that nobody finds it worth the effort to oppose us. In this case, however, we are not stupid, but clever: we merely *pretend* stupidity.

Now real stupidity is perfectly compatible with having a great deal of information available. In this connection, quiz shows on television provide more evidence than we like to watch: people obviously can know a lot, indeed *everything*, about Olympic champions in clay pigeon shooting, marsupials or the biography of Buddy Holly, and still be stupid. Conversely, whatever we think of intelligence tests and their presuppositions, one respect in which they are clearly sound is that they do not simply examine whether the participants can reproduce information they have memorized.

Is a modified suggestion more plausible: that to be stupid is not to be ignorant but to be mistaken, not to lack knowledge, but to fail to hit upon the truth? For in intelligence tests people must at least be right, though certainly they cannot simply reproduce knowledge. On this account, to be stupid would mean to be in error. But there are ways of being right *and* stupid; for evidence of this we could return to the quiz show champions. Conversely, there are errors which would never have occurred to a stupid person, mistakes which could only arise in an intelligent mind. The history of ideas is, to a large extent, the chronicle of brilliant misunderstandings.

39. The previous argument has implied that stupidity is, to say the least, compatible with intellectual self-satisfaction. But does not being satisfied with one's own intellect presuppose that it works well and indeed no worse than that of others, so that one has no reason to envy them? We do not have reason to envy others when we are equal to them. But talk of stupidity as opposed to intelligence implies a significant inequality. A stupid person seems unequal to others in a respect where equality would be desirable: how could such a state be compatible with satisfaction?

The claim that stupidity is compatible with intellectual self-satisfaction cannot be correct, if what is taken to be a ground-breaking argument of modern philosophy has been sound. Descartes and Hobbes have inferred an equal distribution of intelligence among men from the fact that everyone is satisfied with his own intellect. Sound understanding, Descartes suggests, is the most equally distributed thing in the world. For each of us thinks himself so well endowed with it that even those who are the hardest to render content in all other respects are not in the habit of wanting more than they have. In this, Descartes argues, it is not likely that everyone is mistaken. It indicates rather that the capacity to judge well and to distinguish the true from the false, which is properly what one calls sound understanding or reason, is by nature equal in all men.[32] Hobbes guards his corresponding argument with numerous qualifications. He retains, however, the core of Descartes' reasoning: 'But this [*sc.* the contentment of all men with 'their own wit'] proveth rather that men are in that point equal, than unequal. For there is not ordinarily a greater sign of the equal distribution of any thing, than that every man is contented with his share'.[33]

Descartes' and Hobbes' argument infers a cause that is said to be uniform, *viz.*, equally distributed intelligence, from an effect that is said to be uniform, *viz.*, contentment. But this move is not convincing. When two people are content with the money they have, are we entitled to infer that money is equally distributed among them? Obviously not. One may be content with the little money he has got, because he is particularly unassuming, whereas the other, who asks a lot of life, may be content because he has plenty of money. For the present topic an inference of that kind is even less plausible. As a rule, human beings seem to be the more satisfied with the workings of their understanding, the more stupid they are. Of course this is just a contrary claim; as such it stands in need of explanation. But it is capable of being explained. For stupidity sets peculiar barriers to the understanding. It also prevents the understanding from understanding the barriers set to it.

Earlier we put the problem in the following way: A stupid person seems unequal to others in a respect where being equal to them would be desirable: how could such a state be compatible with contentment? The answer to this question is: It is compatible, if one does not apprehend the qualities one lacks. The condition for not apprehending them is plainly stupidity. In default of imagination, stupid minds easily evade awareness of unwelcome comparisons. Intelligent minds, on the other hand, each capable of conceiving of intelligence superior to their own, troubled by doubts and scruples, and insofar dissatisfied, are satisfied with themselves in another regard: they would not like to be in the place of the stupid. But then the source of *their* satisfaction is altogether different from that of the satisfaction of stupid people. If satisfaction with one's own intellect can have quite dissimilar sources, however, the inference to a common source, equal distribution of intelligence, is unwarranted. Descartes argues that it is not probable that *all* of us ('tous') are mistaken in our satisfaction concerning our intelligence. Of course it is not. But no such claim has to be made to oppose Descartes' conclusion. To do this, all that has to be claimed is that some are mistaken in this regard. And this is probable. In every other respect, after all, some are also mistaken.

40. The accounts of stupidity as ignorance or error (§ 38) characterize 'stupid' as a negative and comparative attribute, and it is this aspect to which they owe a trace of plausibility. Stupidity seems to be not seeing what others see, just as weakness is being unable to do what others can do. In cases where nobody can see and nobody can do, there will be no stupidity or weakness. But apart from this, those accounts do not offer a convincing answer to the question what it means to be stupid.

A more accurate understanding seems to be yielded by an English synonym for stupidity: narrowness of mind. In German, a similar understanding is expressed with slightly differing connotations by terms like 'Einfalt', 'Engstirnigkeit' (which comes closest to 'narrow-mindedness'), 'Beschränktheit', 'Borniertheit'; and other European languages explain stupidity in similar terms. A stupid man lacks not so much knowledge or truth, but broadness of perspective. If he lacks knowledge or the truth, then this seems to be rather a consequence of the latter deficit; and it is merely a possible, by no means a necessary, consequence of it.

To be stupid, on this account, is to look at the world from one's own limited perspective. Every perspective, however, is limited; for otherwise it would not be a perspective, *i.e.*, a *point* of view. Is, then, adopting a perspective stupid? It clearly is not stupid in itself. For if we do *not* adopt a point of view, we do not judge at all, either stupidly or intelligently.[34] Rather, we judge someone stupid if *few* ideas and *few* points of view form the basis of everything he says. By talking of 'few', the matter clearly becomes one of degree. Indeed there seems to be a continuum between stupidity and intelligence. A remark can be more or less intelligent, more or less stupid. Intelligent people are not different in *kind* from stupid ones. They simply have a *wider* horizon. To be stupid does not mean *not* to possess an intellect, but to possess an intellect that is sluggish, and familiar only with few forms, stagnating rather than extending its field. (And as a matter of course we manage to relativize our judgement according to age: A performance which would be classed as unintelligent, or at least as not particularly intelligent, in an adult may be considered highly intelligent in an infant. The astonishing wealth of ideas already mastered by a two-year-old boy would constitute a very narrow intellectual repertoire in a twenty-year-old man. But this is an intricate subject in itself, for *one* aspect of what we know as education actually consists in narrowing down rather than broadening perspectives.)

However limited an individual's points of view are, one feature, at least, always remains. These few or, in the extreme case, the one standpoint that this individual has adopted will be *his* standpoint. Stupid people can therefore be highly original. (Indeed, a link between originality and wisdom is not even probable (§ 11).) Since originality is sometimes instructive or amusing or both, stupidity can possess some merit. But usually it is annoying. The Greeks called someone who knew and cared only about what was his *own*, *i.e.*, τὸ ἴδιον, an idiot, ἰδιότης. Stupid people, if they are very stupid, are idiotic. (Of course we must not confuse them with egoists. If stupidity is egoism, then it is a kind of logical egoism that has to be distinguished from egoism in a moral sense – for the latter can clearly be pursued in very intelligent ways. In fact an egoist in the moral sense is well advised not to become an intellectual egoist: since he wants to make use of other people, he should be capable of imagining *their* points of view.)

Clearly, this account represents the relation between stupidity and ignorance more plausibly than the initial identification (§ 38). Stupidity has to do with a lack of knowledge only insofar as more knowledge can lead to – but does not have to lead to – an augmentation of points of view. Ignorance can enjoy a reciprocal association with stupidity, in the sense that ignorance begets stupidity which begets further ignorance.

41. There is, however, an objection to the account of stupidity as narrow-mindedness. Could it not happen that someone acts stupidly because he has, in a certain situation, *too many* points of view? We become neither prudent nor intelligent simply by multiplying perspectives. Every situation, particularly if it is supposed to lead to action, requires an immense reduction in complexity. We have to select a few points of view and to exclude a host of others. If we do not manage to do so, we will be less clear-headed not only than a person who has chosen few appropriate points of view but also than a stupid person who, without having chosen, simply happens to have few points of view. A narrow mind can clearly grasp the few ideas within its narrow horizon in a clear way, precisely because they are so few. Such a mind could be compared to a beggar who knows the year of issue of each of his few pennies. It will not be as rich as a mind that has too many points of view, but more lucid.

Kant, although he calls the stupid person a 'narrow-minded head' ('eingeschränkter Kopf'), defines stupidity as 'lack of judgement' ('Mangel an Urteilskraft'). This definition implies that a stupid person can have either not enough or too many points of view; for judgement yields the outlook *adequate* to a situation.[35] Certainly, to revise the account of stupidity as narrow-mindedness in this way would take into account the salient objection.

But the objection does not need to be taken into account. For it can be defused. Admittedly, as far as the description goes, the objection is correct. But the analysis it provides is inaccurate. For we have to distinguish *having* many standpoints from *applying* them. What is critical in the type of case mentioned is not having so many standpoints, but trying to apply them all at once when time is limited. Since this distinction has to be respected, it does not follow that broadness of mind is a form of stupidity just as narrowness of mind is one. What follows is that broadness of mind is not sufficient for prudence and intelligence, if these, in different respects, are opposed to stupidity. There may be many ways of being imprudent that fall short of positive stupidity; there may be many phenomena between or beyond being prudent and being stupid, *i.e.*, phenomena that do not fall into either of these two extreme categories. Even someone who does not merely have but even applies 'too many' points of view may well be neither prudent and intelligent nor stupid.

If we adopted Kant's move, this would result in a loss of discrimination. We want to distinguish the type of person to whom a great diversity of perspectives does not even occur and whom we call stupid, from the quite different type of person who is aware of such diversity, even though he may be thrown into confusion by it. If this kind of disorder takes on a systematic character, and becomes a more or less permanent frame of mind, the person affected is crazy. While stupid persons are characterized by lack of imagination, crazy people are disturbed by an abundance of fantasy.[36] The word 'stupid' is derived from the Latin 'stupeo', 'to be stiff'; imagination and fantasy, by way of contrast, are mobile. In crazy people they are so mobile that no one else is able to follow them; psychiatrists talk of 'fugue' or 'flight of ideas'. Craziness is hurried, stupidity slow. The stupid and the crazy differ more from each other than either of them from those we call 'normal'. Stupid persons have no 'wit' in the 18th century sense of the term, *i.e.*, they lack the ability to connect ideas which are far apart from each other.[37] Crazy people fall prey to an excess of this ability, *i.e.*, they connect ideas which are far apart from each other even when no one else can make sense of the connections.

Our conclusion must be that the objection put forward does not invalidate the account of stupidity as narrow-mindedness.

42. A person is stupid if *few* ideas form the basis of everything he says. But from this we must conclude that prejudices, though they certainly can be stupid, by no means have to be so. That prejudices can be stupid is trivial and does not constitute an objection: thoughts can be stupid but this is no argument against thinking. The crucial point is that prejudices are not inherently stupid. If prejudices are ideas about something formed before having examined it, there is nothing to preclude prejudices from being sophisticated. Such sophistication could, either by virtue of intuition or merely by chance, correspond to genuine complexity in the object of the prejudice. Of course, such correspondence is in no way necessary. There may, for instance, be theories that are far more complicated and multi-faceted than their subject matter requires, and that are so precisely because they are prejudices: their authors have been led by their love of complication, that *déformation professionnelle* of academics, rather than by an examination of what their theories are about. Sometimes, such theorists may be reluctant to give up their doctrines when they become aware how simple the objects of their

theorizing actually are – for they have put a lot of effort into their speculations and find it hard to admit that this was all in vain. But even that is not a proof of stupidity on their part, but rather of a kind of folly or, if they stick to this attitude throughout, craziness.

43. Maybe prejudices are not inherently stupid. But is it not true at least that prejudices represent us in a way that we dislike, just as we dislike to be represented stupidly? Our reaction seems to be the same in both cases, though different features may be responsible for the reaction.

In the case of prejudice, we are seen in a predetermined way. Reference to our reaction, then, suggests a new answer to the question 'What's wrong with prejudice?': We do not want to be seen in such a way, but rather as we are.

Even this claim, however, does not seem to be true. For often we do not want to be seen as we are. Rather, we want to be seen in a favourable light; and there is no guarantee that we will appear more favourably when seen as we are rather than when seen through the eyes of prejudice. It may well be the other way round. If someone has the prejudice that the Germans are great philosophers, he may well overestimate the present writer. (Prejudices can be positive; cf. § 26.) Conversely, we can hardly treat a person more offensively than to make her the exclusive object of our study, up to the point where even the last illusion about her has disappeared. The discontents with old acquaintances and the craving for new ones have much to do with fear that those who know us all too well may have a low opinion of us and with hope that those who know us less well may rate us higher.

When we pursue this line of reasoning, proceeding from the way in which people are viewed to the way they are treated, we arrive at the same result. When the Spaniards came to the 'New World', at least some of the indigenous people treated them in a way remarkably free from prejudice. In 1508 Puerto Rican Indians decided to find out whether Spaniards were mortal or not, by holding them under water to see whether they could be drowned. The Dutch artist Theodore de Bry depicted this remarkable experiment, which displays a truly scientific, open-minded spirit.[38] Being treated without prejudice need by no means be more pleasant than being treated with prejudice. Hence it cannot be this feature either which furnishes us with an answer to the question what is wrong with prejudice.

Notes

1 'Als ich einmal so durch die innere Stadt strich, stieß ich plötzlich auf eine Erscheinung in langem Kaftan mit schwarzen Locken. Ist dies auch ein Jude? war mein erster Gedanke. So sahen sie freilich in Linz nicht aus. Ich beobachtete den Mann verstohlen und vorsichtig, allein je länger ich in dieses fremde Gesicht starrte und forschend Zug um Zug prüfte, um so mehr wandelte sich in meinem Gehirn die erste Frage zu einer anderen Fassung: Ist dies auch ein Deutscher? [...] [D]aran, daß es sich hier nicht um Deutsche einer besonderen Konfession handelte, sondern um ein Volk für sich, konnte auch ich nicht mehr gut zweifeln; denn seit ich mich mit dieser Frage zu beschäftigen begonnen hatte, auf den Juden erst einmal aufmerksam wurde, erschien mir Wien in einem anderen Lichte als vorher. Wo immer ich ging, sah ich nun Juden, und je mehr ich sah, um so schärfer sonderten sie sich für das Auge von den anderen Menschen ab. Besonders die innere Stadt und die Bezirke nördlich des Donaukanals wimmelten von einem Volke, das schon äußerlich eine Ähnlichkeit mit dem deutschen nicht mehr besaß' (Hitler, *Mein Kampf*, pp. 59–60).

2 Note also the stress on rationality in this change: 'Wenn dadurch langsam auch meine Ansichten in bezug auf den Antisemitismus dem Wechsel der Zeit unterlagen, dann war dies wohl meine schwerste Wandlung überhaupt. Sie hat mir die meisten inneren seelischen Kämpfe gekostet, und erst nach monatelangem Ringen zwischen Verstand und Gefühl begann der Sieg sich auf die Seite des Verstandes zu schlagen. Zwei Jahre später war das Gefühl dem Verstande gefolgt, um von nun an dessen treuester Wächter und Warner zu sein. In der Zeit dieses bitteren Ringens zwischen seelischer Erziehung und kalter Vernunft hatte mir der Anschauungsunterricht der Wiener Straße unschätzbare Dienste geleistet' (ibid., p. 59).

3 Up to this point, Socrates recounts something close to what he had encountered himself when, testing the oracle from Delphi, he addressed everybody who called himself wise and found only false appearance (*Apology* 20d–23a); what follows in the *Phaedo* may explain why Socrates, in spite of this, did not become a hater of men.

4 'Ueber Vorurtheil', p. 351: 'Der Mensch muß, in so fern er ein *vernünftiges* Wesen ist, dahin streben, *sich allgemeine Sätze zu verschaffen, die ihm zu Principien dienen.* Die Vernunft strebt nehmlich dahin, alles aus Gründen zu erkennen, mit andern Worten, das Besondre aus dem Allgemeinen herzuleiten, und der Mensch wird also, um diesen Zweck zu erreichen, sich allgemeine Sätze verschaffen müssen. Dieß Streben nun, allgemeine Sätze zu haben, um sie als Principien der Erkenntnisse und der Urtheile zu brauchen, verleitet oft dazu, daß man Urtheile, die bey weitem noch nicht allgemein sein können, dennoch als allgemein ausspricht. Man findet, daß mehrern Dingen einer Art ein gewisses Merkmal zukomme, und dehnt es, um eine allgemeine Regel zu haben, auf die ganze Art aus; man sieht und erfährt, daß unter gewissen Umständen einigemal sich etwas zugetragen habe, und man setzt fest, daß dieß unter diesen Umständen sich immer zutragen werde. Man hat gefunden, daß mehrere Juden, niedergedrückt von Kummer und Elend, gleichsam ausgestoßen aus der menschlichen Gesellschaft, aller Erwerbsquellen beraubt, durch Wucher und Betrug sich zu ernähren streben, – und man spricht der Bequemlichkeit halber den Satz aus: Alle Juden sind Betrieger'. Hume, his general criticism of induction notwithstanding, seems to have claimed that prejudices generally are, or are based on rash generalizations, too. Cf. *Treatise*, pp. 146–7: 'A fourth unphilosophical species of probability is that deriv'd from general rules, which we rashly form to ourselves, and which are the source of what we properly call PREJUDICE. An *Irishman* cannot have wit, and a

Frenchman cannot have solidity; for which reason, tho' the conversation of the former in any instance be visibly very agreeable, and of the latter very judicious, we have entertain'd such a prejudice against them, that they must be dunces or fops in spite of sense and reason. Human nature is very subject to errors of this kind; and perhaps this nation as much as any other'.

5   *E.g.*, Shirer, *The Rise and Fall of the Third Reich*, p. 26, referring back to Olden, *Hitler*, p. 47.

6   *E.g.*, Toland, *Adolf Hitler*, pp. 45–6.

7   'Ueber Vorurtheil', p. 351: 'der Bequemlichkeit halber', p. 352: 'Solche allgemeine Sätze sind ein Polster für die faule Vernunft'. Kant, Kiesewetter's mentor, as early as in 1746 explained the emergence of prejudices, *i.a.*, by reference to indolence ('Bequemlichkeit') (*Gedanken von der wahren Schätzung der lebendigen Kräfte*, Vorrede, Nr. IV, p. 17). Cf. also du Marsais, *Essai sur les Préjugés*, vol. I, p. 7. Locke suggests that we have to account for prejudice by reference to inertia when he calls it a 'lazy anticipation' (*Of the Conduct of the Understanding*, § 10, p. 229). An account of this sort may be already implied in Descartes' critique of prejudice: 'præpostera & imbecillia sunt multorum judicia, ut magis a primum acceptis opinionibus, quantumvis falsis & a ratione alienis, persuadeantur, quàm a verâ & firmâ, sed posterius auditâ, ipsarum refutatione' (*Meditationes*, Præfatio ad lectorem, p. 9)

8   Cf. Nietzsche, *Menschliches, Allzumenschliches* I, § 32, p. 51.

9   *Confessions*, p. 630. Cf. ibid., p. 112: 'Les préjugés même qu'avoit conçûs la pauvre femme en faveur de mon mérite', p. 378: 'préjugés si favorables qui sembloient ne chercher qu'à m'applaudir'. Sailer in the chapter on prejudice in his *Vernunftlehre*, published in 1785, 1794 and 1830, speaks of '*prejudice for or against*' ('*Vorurtheil für oder wider*') something throughout (*e.g.*, pp. 118–19).

10 This criticism of prejudice was advanced by Wilhelm von Humboldt who made the concept of individuality central to his philosophy. 'Auch soll der Staat nicht gerade die Juden zu achten lehren, aber die inhumane und vorurtheilsvolle Denkungsart soll er aufheben, die einen Menschen nicht nach seinen eigenthümlichen Eigenschaften, sondern nach seiner Abstammung und Religion beurtheilt und ihn, gegen allen wahren Begriff von Menschenwürde, nicht wie ein Individuum, sondern wie zu einer Race gehörig und gewisse Eigenschaften gleichsam nothwendig mit ihr theilend ansieht' ('Über den Entwurf zu einer neuen Konstitution für die Juden', p. 99).

11 Mozart, *Così fan tutte*, II,13 (No. 30), p. 491.

12 This is a slightly more circumstantial version of Zola's elegant phrase: 'Ils ne sont pour moi que des entités, des esprits de malfaisance sociale' ('J'accuse', p. 931). Clearly, the second part of the sentence cannot be rendered literally. By 'esprits' Zola submits the individuals he has accused to an abstraction. He wishes to suggest that they merely represent and indicate something else, *viz.*, a state of institutional corruption. The way Zola's sentence is interpreted in the above translation captures that suggestion.

13 Hume, 'Of the Standard of Taste', p. 276.

14 'Brief an Ulrike von Kleist, 21 November 1811', p. 272: 'die Wahrheit ist, daß mir auf Erden nicht zu helfen war'.

15 Simmel, *Über sociale Differenzierung*, pp. 239–41; *Soziologie*, pp. 467–78.

16 Cf. Hegel, *Phänomenologie des Geistes*, pp. 82–92.

17 de Bonald, 'Pensées sur la morale', clmn. 1387: 'Les philosophes qui se sont élevés avec tant d'amertume contre ce qu'ils ont appelé des *préjugés*, auraient dû commencer par se défaire de la langue elle-même dans la-quelle ils écrivaient; car elle est le premier de nos *préjugés*, et il renferme tous les autres'. Cf. 'Sur les préjugés', clmn. 805.

18 *Oxford English Dictionary*, p. 577.

19 Barbauld, 'On prejudice', p. 326, and *passim*.

20 Hutcheson, *Essay on the Nature and Conduct of the Passions and Affections*, I, iii, 1, p. 58

21 On this subject, cf. also Herder, *Abhandlung über den Ursprung der Sprache*, pp. 152–3, and Nietzsche, *Morgenröthe* § 115, p. 107 ('Die Sprache und die Vorurtheile, auf denen die Sprache aufgebaut ist').

22 'Prejudice', p. 319.

23 Mozart, *Die Zauberflöte*, II,7 (No. 13), p. 221: 'weil ein Schwarzer häßlich ist!'.

24 *De l'Esprit*, p. 551.

25 *A view of the present state of Ireland*, pp. 141–2.

26 Cf. Corbin, *Le Miasme et la Jonquille*, p. 170.

27 Cf. Russell, 'The Superior Virtue of the Oppressed'.

28 That the opposite belief, that is, belief in the natural goodness of man, is a prejudice, too, and that it is so for the same reason, was, it has to be admitted, an insight reserved to the more disillusioned spirits of the age.

29 Τίμων ἐρῶν ' Ἀλκιβιάδου ἑαυτὸν προσαγγέλει.

30 *Menschliches, Allzumenschliches* II, *Der Wanderer und sein Schatten*, § 316, pp. 692–3: '*Sich zu überraschen wissen.* – Wer sich selber sehen will, so wie er ist, muss er verstehen, sich selber zu *überraschen*, mit der Fackel in der Hand. Denn es steht mit dem Geistigen so wie es mit dem Körperlichen steht: wer gewohnt ist, sich im Spiegel zu schauen, vergisst immer seine Hässlichkeit: erst durch den Maler bekommt er den Eindruck derselben wieder. Aber er gewöhnt sich auch an das Gemälde und vergisst seine Hässlichkeit zum zweiten Male. – Diess nach dem allgemeinen Gesetze, dass der Mensch das Unveränderlich-Hässliche *nicht erträgt*: es sei denn auf einen Augenblick; er vergisst es oder leugnet es in allen Fällen. – Die Moralisten müssen auf jenen Augenblick rechnen, um ihre Wahrheiten vorbringen zu dürfen'.

31 Notice the following phrases: 'immer', 'nach dem allgemeinen Gesetze', 'in allen Fällen'.

32 *Discours de la Méthode* I, 1, pp. 1–2: 'Le bon sens est la chose du monde la mieux partagée: car chacun pense en être si bien pourvu, que ceux même qui sont les plus difficiles à contenter en toute autre chose, n'ont point coutume d'en désirer plus qu'ils en ont. En quoi il n'est pas vraisemblable que tous se trompent; mais plutôt cela témoigne que la puissance de bien juger, et distinguer le vrai d'avec le faux, qui est proprement ce qu'on nomme le bon sens ou la raison, est naturellement égale en tous les hommes'.

33 *Leviathan* I,13, p. 111.

34 Cf. Chladenius, *Einleitung zur richtigen Auslegung*, §§ 309–17, pp. 187–95.

35 Kant, *Kritik der reinen Vernunft*, B 172–3, p. 185.

36 Jean Paul, 'Unterschied zwischen dem Narren und dem Dummen', p. 263: 'Das Übel des Dumkopfs besteht darin, daß er zu wenig Einbildungskraft hat; das des Narren, daß er zuviel hat'.

37 Jean Paul, 'Von der Dumheit', p. 267: 'Wiz ist Bemerkung des Verhältnisses zwischen entfernten Ideen […]. Bei dem Dummen ist iede Idee isolirt; alles ist bei ihm in Fächer abgeteilt und zwischen entfernten Ideen ist eine Kluft, über die er nicht hinüberkommen kan'.

38 Hanke, *The First Social Experiments in America*, pp. 68–9.

Chapter Three

On the Hermeneutic Vindication of Prejudice, and Why it Does not Succeed

44. We have run into difficulties with our attempts to explain what is wrong with prejudice. Perhaps the fault lies with the *conduct* of the examination, and we should simply have tried harder. But perhaps the fault, and the cause of our difficulties, lies in the *end* of the examination. After all, it is not clear that anything is wrong with prejudices as such. For even first-hand experience and genuine judgements seem to depend upon prejudice. This relationship appears to be twofold.

First, we can be guided by prejudices in a *positive* way: they can direct our attention towards something that would otherwise go unattended. (A broader and stronger version of this claim is notoriously endorsed by Burke; he asserts that we are thrown upon prejudices as a positive orientation of our existence as a whole: 'When ancient opinions and rules of life are taken away, the loss cannot possibly be estimated. From that moment we have no compass to govern us; nor can we know distinctly to what port we steer'.)[1]

But, secondly, guidance by prejudice can also be *negative*. We become aware of features of things precisely because they are not as we expected them to be. They strike us because they do not fit our prejudices. A crucial aspect of science is discovery, which involves novelty and surprise. Yet an empty mind, purged in the way suggested, *e.g.*, by Bacon,[2] could not be surprised.

Hence contrary to the anathema against prejudice as something we should not have or, if we do, should get rid of, prejudices on this twofold consideration are both necessary and (as a 'condition of' their 'possibility') more fundamental than judgements.

The capacity of prejudice to guide and focus attention is related to its economic aspect (§§ 12–17). The antithesis of judgement and prejudice, familiar from many Enlightenment treatises, suggested the following: Judgement means coming to a conclusion after considering all the factors, while prejudice implies jumping to a conclusion without considering them. But, according to the present objections, there will never be a time when all the factors have been considered. For everything has indefinitely many aspects. Since we cannot examine all of them, we are forced into a selection that is not based on a full examination of the object. It must be a prejudice that singles out the relevant factors.

45. To criticize prejudice as such, in the manner of numerous exponents of the Enlightenment, can be a hazardous business. For it exposes the critic to the suspicion that he resembles the child who considers her image in the mirror as something alien. In fact, the Enlightenment's claims regarding prejudice have been subjected to stricture of this kind. Hans-Georg Gadamer, in his major work *Wahrheit und Methode* of 1960, has accused the Enlightenment of a prejudice against all prejudices.[3]

According to Gadamer, every form of understanding necessarily involves some prejudice.[4] He sees 'prejudices' ('Vorurteile') as constitutive of experience and understanding,[5] the 'biases' that open up the world to us, or us to the world. Prejudices make judgements possible by directing our attention and thus have priority over them: *'the prejudices of the individual, far more than his judgements, constitute the historical reality of his being'*.[6] On this ground, Gadamer attempts a rehabilitation of prejudice.[7] He wishes to turn the critical theory of prejudice of the Enlightenment into a positive valuation.[8]

46. Gadamer's claim that the Enlightenment was prejudiced against prejudices was anticipated by, for example, Samuel Johnson and Friedrich Schlegel. Johnson said that anyone aspiring to be a 'smart, modern thinker' had to begin with 'a prejudice against prejudice',[9] and Schlegel asserted that the French abuse of prejudices was itself a prejudice.[10] At first hearing, this seems to be an odd reproach from thinkers like Johnson, Schlegel or Gadamer for whom being prejudiced is no fault but an inevitable feature of the human mind, – under this assumption, why should not the Enlightenment have a right to its special prejudice, too? But the formula of course aims to point out an inconsistency in Enlightenment thought. Someone who would be free from prejudice (as the Enlightenment claimed of itself)[11], would have to be so also with regard to prejudices.

What does Gadamer think the Enlightenment prejudice against prejudices amounts to? It amounts to the claim that prejudices must be false.[12]

The first thing to ask is under what conditions it is acceptable to attribute a view to 'the Enlightenment'. It would be a pedantic restriction to maintain that, given the broad and diversified character of this intellectual movement, it is never acceptable. We need such handy abbreviations for rhetorical purposes. It would amount to the same unwarranted restriction to demand that, if we were entitled to attribute a view to 'the Enlightenment', every minor exponent of that movement would have to have held it. For as far as interesting, substantial claims are concerned, there has hardly been any such *completely* undisputed view. So a claim attributed to 'the Enlightenment' cannot refer to a consensus without exception, but rather to a consensus among the most influential figures. Is it correct to describe the view that all prejudices must be false as a consensus of the latter type? It is not. For the falsity of all prejudices was a point of dispute among the most influential thinkers. The claim that all prejudices must be false was supported, on the one hand, by de Jeaucourt[13] and du Marsais.[14] On the other hand, the view was not upheld by Fontenelle,[15] Voltaire,[16] or Kant.[17] Therefore even if the falsity of prejudice was a prejudice, it is not justified to call it a prejudice of '*the*' Enlightenment. It is merely a prejudice of *some* authors of the Enlightenment. Let us turn to the most prominent example.

In the *Encyclopédie*, 'prejudice' is defined as a 'false judgement which the soul forms about the nature of things after an insufficient use of the intellectual faculties'.[18] Certainly, if the 'pre-' in 'prejudice' has any meaning, there must be some point in what the relative clause says: a prejudice has to be in some way incomplete as regards justification. The real problem is not the *differentia specifica*, but the *genus proximum* of that definition, 'faux jugement'. Why, according to Gadamer, should we reject this subsumption of prejudice under falsehood? Gadamer points out that before the Enlightenment the word 'prejudice', particularly in jurisprudence, had been used in a positive sense. Though this was the case, as an *argument* such reference is feeble. For that positive use of the word might have been introduced precisely to cover up for a dubious practice. In fact, as *Grimm's Wörterbuch* instructs us, prejudice was criticized as a misuse of judicial authority in Germany as early as 1538,[19] and it *might* after all have been precisely the merit of the Enlightenment to systematize the insight that something was wrong here – an insight that had previously been articulated only by isolated voices. Gadamer's contention does not provide a reason, but merely informs us what people believed once but do not believe any more. When there is a proposal to reform linguistic usage, as in the Enlightenment, in order to call for once things by their real names, there is no point in appealing to the very usage against which the proposal has been directed. Of course our ancestors could have known better than we. But that they actually did is precisely what requires argument. To report what they believed without providing such an argument is to beg the question.

Does it follow that all prejudices are false? It does not if we accept the premise of the following line of reasoning: Insofar as the world is as it is, independently of how we think it to be, a judgement I make *before* examining a subject matter may happen to be true of it just as it may also be false. So if there is an argument that is at the same time better than Gadamer's, simple and conclusive, why doesn't Gadamer employ it? Because he cannot, as an adherent of a kind of linguistic idealism, accept the premise that the world is as it is, independently of how we think it to be.[20] In short, Gadamer's conclusion follows from a premise he is committed to rejecting.

There is one last point that deserves to be examined. Is it true that the position Gadamer attacks actually instantiates a *prejudice*? Gadamer does not present an argument for this claim. But it might be supported by an argument that the universal ascription of *falsity* to prejudice is itself prejudiced. Since the term was reinterpreted by numerous Enlightenment authors, it looks as if whoever talks of prejudices (even if he admits his own prejudices) assumes his superiority over them. When I say to you: 'You are prejudiced', you get the impression that I am no longer discussing *with* you, but have started to talk *about* you.

What one person calls another's prejudices, are judgements, convictions, principles or articles of faith for the latter, and the converse probably holds also. Thus the reproach of prejudice can be shifted forwards and backwards, while both persons' thoughts remain the same. As soon as I have characterized your view as an expression of prejudice, I appear to have successfully shielded myself from your arguments. Thus the words 'prejudice' or 'prejudiced' themselves seem to have acquired a way of being prejudicial.[21]

In assessing this argument, however, two ideas have to be distinguished. First, it is true that if two people reproach each other with prejudice, no intellectual advance is made. The hunt for prejudice is self-righteous, and its only fruit is a sop to one's vanity (§§ 95–6). But from this it does not follow, secondly, that the Enlighteners Gadamer has in mind held a *prejudice* against prejudices. Rather, the argument is compatible with saying that some Enlighteners made an incorrect judgement, or incorrect judgements, about prejudice. And this, irrespective of our argument, is also a much more convincing claim as far as it concerns the way the relevant authors proceeded.

In terms of logic as well as in terms of intellectual history, the so-called prejudice against prejudices was not a prejudice at all. What several *philosophes* thought regarding prejudices was simply a false belief. This false belief was based on a confusion between the conditions of the truth of something and the conditions of finding out or knowing that it is true. Some Enlightenment authors, such as the Chevalier de Jeaucourt, confounded form and content: prejudice may be an inadequate form of belief (*if* it is inadequate to take something upon trust, rather than acquire it by reasoning), but its content may still be true. These authors committed the genetic fallacy in its negative version. Instead of proceeding with the proviso that the truth must be judged on its own merits, they concluded that since certain beliefs had been acquired in a specific way, they had to be false. This is indeed objectionable, but not in the way Gadamer objects to it. The authors concerned did not, as a mere expression of their own prejudice, stigmatize prejudice before they had inquired into it. Rather, they studied it in great detail, yet in the course of that study they made a logical mistake and thus arrived at a theory of prejudice that is not tenable. Of course one might not be interested in this. But then all one is interested in is rhetoric. For it is obviously so much more tempting to speak of a prejudice against prejudices than of a false belief about them.

To sum up, what Gadamer calls the Enlightenment's prejudice against prejudices is neither a prejudice nor can it be attributed to 'the' Enlightenment. That it is false does not follow from the reason given by Gadamer; indeed, it follows from a reason that Gadamer cannot consistently accept.

47. The characterization of the Enlightenment as prejudiced could, however, be defended along the following line. The Enlightenment attack on prejudice presented itself as a questioning of all authorities.[22] Such criticism had to make use of specific standards: those of reason. To question all authorities, the Enlightenment had to rely on the authority of reason. It did not overcome authority; it just substituted one authority for another.

This criticism can actually appeal to a self-interpretation of the Enlightenment. According to Condorcet, mankind has the choice between the authority of men ('l'autorité des hommes') and the authority of reason ('celle [*sc.* l'autorité] de la raison'). While the middle ages observed the former, Enlightenment, he suggests, is guided by the latter.[23] Though Condorcet means this laudatory, there is a less charitable interpretation of it. The Enlightenment could go to war against what it called prejudice only on the basis of a prejudice in favour of reason.

The examination of authorities by the Enlightenment, so the argument goes, produces an ever recurring circle. Every thought that questions an authority has to appeal to an authority itself. For all criticism presupposes a standard by which it criticizes. The criticism has to proceed in obedience to this standard. For if the criticism itself does not come up to the standard, how can it blame anything else for not doing so? In this sense the standard of criticism is higher than the criticism itself: it has authoritative status both for the subject and (according to the critic) for the object of criticism. Hence the criticism of authority voiced by the Enlightenment, far from rising above authority, was bound merely to pay tribute to a new authority.

But the analysis of thought implicit in this argument is unconvincing. For it is not feasible that thinking, before it proceeds, supplies itself with a normative basis in order to be able to proceed. Suppose that thinking seeks for a normative support of this kind: in that case it has already begun, is already proceeding, *ex hypothesi*, without such a norm. Suppose further that thinking then abides by this authoritative content: by what does it abide in this case? First it abides by an idea produced by itself, and secondly by its own thought that this content is unconditionally valid. There is no way of obeying an authority before one has thought and in order to become capable of thinking. For to obey an authority, one has to recognize it as an authority in the first place, and this cannot be achieved without thinking (§ 6).

48. The foregoing discussion has established only a single point against some exponents of the Enlightenment: When I make a judgement about something before examining it, I can, by chance, hit on the truth. Prejudices need not be false (§ 46). Does this negative point warrant Gadamer's positive rehabilitation of prejudice?

It is hard to see how it could. The *possibility* of truth that prejudices possess does not make good Gadamer's claim that all understanding is prejudiced. Certainly, it may be true, as Gadamer claims, that nothing is ever recognized if it is not encountered with certain expectations. But is it justified to label all such expectations with the specific term 'prejudice'? If its meaning is extended in such a way, prejudice can of course hardly fail to be, as Gadamer claims, inevitable. But the question is rather whether it is sensible to use a word that means a quite particular phenomenon in such a broad way.

The answer is that it is not sensible. For 'prejudice', as its name suggests, does not mean just any anticipation, but an anticipated *judgement*. The sense in which this holds needs of course to be clarified, and we shall do so now. What is a judgement? The concept originated from the sphere of law.[24] It is the judge who passes a judgement on the defendant. A judgement, again, is not just any opinion that someone holds, but a *decision*. A judgement *determines*. This equips us with a clearer understanding of the concept of prejudice. The first component of this word suggests that it is not (yet) a judgement, while the second suggests that it is one. A prejudice is and is not a judgement: Something is taken as decided, but the process of arriving at a decision has not really been run through. For a judgement presupposes that someone has considered and weighed the alternatives between which one

might waver in a given case. This has not happened in the case of prejudice.
Prejudice takes something as decided without ever making clear to itself the
reasons for the alternatives.

49. Gadamer is of course right that prejudice is a form of anticipation. But his
analysis is not helpful if we want to know – as we do – what form of anticipation
it is. Unlike Heidegger, who meticulously distinguishes between 'fore-having',
'fore-sight' and 'fore-conception',[25] and whom *Wahrheit und Methode* quotes
in support,[26] Gadamer's use of the term makes prejudice almost indistin-
guishable from preconception, presupposition, hypothesis, presumption,
presentiment, presage, premonition, foreboding, predilection, prepossession,
outlook, expectation or anticipation in general. Of course, it is far from clear
what precisely the fine distinctions between these attitudes are. This would
be well worth proper investigation. Certainly, those attitudes will be related
in manifold ways (cf. already § 32); but again, any relation presupposes a
distinction. It is, at any rate, remarkable that we possess such a subtle
terminology for our different ways of anticipating events, and there is no
good reason to use 'prejudice' as the melting pot in which their distinctions
are dissolved.

Gadamer's reason for maintaining that our understanding of a text is always
governed by prejudice is this: The base from which we approach it must always
be part of ourselves since it does not and cannot lie in the as yet indeterminate
text. But while it follows that we have to contribute something in order to get
to know anything, it does not follow that what we have to contribute has to be
a prejudice rather than simply an expectation. This is a significant conclusion,
too, but one that is crucially different from Gadamer's. To begin with, I shall
point out its significance; after that, I will elucidate the distinction between
prejudice and expectation that ought to be drawn by way of an example.

The fact that the attainment of knowledge presupposes expectations is
not a trivial one. This claim also has force against some Enlightenment tenets.
One of these has been that the way to attain knowledge is to be guided by the
nature of things themselves, not by what we ourselves bring along with us. It
is in this spirit that Montesquieu says in the preface to his *chef-d'œuvre* that
he has drawn his principles not from prejudice, but from the nature of things.[27]
The phrase is at the core of Enlightenment rhetoric: who would dare to oppose
the principle that, after all, the facts should be allowed to speak for themselves?
But facts do not speak for themselves at all; they *speak*, if, because and in so
far as we have lent them our language. According to Montesquieu, the wrong
approach to reality is mediate, the right one immediate. If getting to know

things presupposes expectations, however, it is mediated in any case, even if we get things right. But there are different ways in which it can be mediated, and it is still worth distinguishing expectation, as one such way, from prejudice, which is another.

An example may make this point clearer. When I start to read Fichte's *Wissenschaftslehre*, I might expect a treatise on the methodology of the sciences, because that is what I take the German word 'Wissenschaftslehre' to mean. What I find, however, is a theory of how subjectivity affirms itself as a primitive act of consciousness and constructs the objective world from appearances. As soon as I become aware of this, I retract my initial anticipation of the genre of the book. Now I either stop reading because I am disappointed, given that I expected to learn something about the way in which physics, chemistry or biology proceed, or, alternatively, become interested in the unexpected topic and go on reading. Gadamer calls anticipations of this sort prejudices. Of course he can call them whatever he likes. But the fact that I am willing to dismiss my anticipation as soon as I have a different experience appears to indicate that it is not the same as what is generally called prejudice: something which is upheld precisely against counter-evidence because it re-interprets that evidence in a way suitable to fit the original prejudice (§ 77). It may well be true that it is impossible for us to start any intellectual endeavour with *no* preconception; but we have to distinguish whether or not a preconception is held dogmatically, *i.e.*, as prejudice. My attitude with regard to Fichte's *Wissenschaftslehre* was no prejudice, but just an ordinary expectation, and if we want to *call* it a prejudice, we would have to introduce categories like 'prejudice type 1' and 'prejudice type 2' in order to save the insight that in it something different is at work than in the case of, for instance, anti-Semitism.

50. Gadamer's account of the rôle of prejudice in understanding is either false or, alternatively, coincides with what has been said above (§ 49) on the function of expectations. It is false if prejudice connotes an attitude that is upheld even when there is textual evidence to the contrary. For sometimes exegetes change their view of a text's meaning in the process of understanding and interpretation; Gadamer himself wishes to allow for this possibility.[28] If this possibility is taken seriously, prejudice simply means the stance that one adopts towards something when approaching it in order to understand. In this case the point worth making is this: Contrary to that *façon de parler*, it is an illusion that 'the facts speak for themselves'. We can avoid a misleading expression of this point by referring to expectations rather than to prejudices.

The example presented above (§ 49) was drawn from the way texts are read, in order to meet the *hermeneutic* vindication of prejudice on its own ground. We have to make a similar distinction, when we consider the way texts are written. For the way texts are written depends, though to an extent that varies, on the way texts are read.

Edward Gibbon's *Decline and Fall of the Roman Empire* could not have been written in the absence of any concern for the permanence of the British Empire, which when Gibbon wrote had just lost its north American colonies.[29] (Gibbon was a Member of Parliament from 1774 to 1783, and in 1779, between the publication of the first and the second volume of *The Decline and Fall*, composed his *Mémoire justificatif*, a state paper which replied to continental criticism of the British government's policy in the War of American Independence.) His current concern equipped Gibbon with questions to ask when confronting his ancient sources. It gave him a perspective on the historical material which differed from that of his predecessors and fellow-historians. Gibbon's perspective may have distorted his view of the Roman Empire in places; but it equipped him from the outset with a view of the problems of the durability of political orders.

The expectations someone has are circumscribed by his perspective. But just as there is reason to distinguish expectation from prejudice, there is reason to distinguish perspective from prejudice, too. Both are or involve ways of looking at things. But perspective stands to prejudice very much as, in speech, question stands to assertion. If I know someone's perspective, I do not yet know *what* he sees under his perspective, just as a question, granted that it is not of merely rhetorical character, leaves it open what the answer will be. If, on the other hand, someone tells me his prejudice, this tells me *what* he believes he has seen, the actual content of his belief. It is true that the distinction between questions and assertions is not absolute. Every assertion can be understood as an answer to a question. Questions specify the boundaries of what will count as a meaningful answer and what will not, *i.e.*, they define what sort of assertions are in place or out of place.[30] More accurately, the dependence is mutual: Statements have meanings as answers to questions, and questions follow previous answers. But none of this means there is no difference between questions and assertions. A relative distinction is still a distinction.

The bearing of this on our example is clear. Had Gibbon believed that the causes for the decline of the Roman Empire must have been the same as those of the crisis of the British Empire, that would have been a prejudice. But Gibbon did not hold that belief. The political changes he was familiar with from his own age enabled him to see similarities as well as differences in the past.

51. Clearly, Gadamer must not be taken to mean that we have to affirm prejudice blindly. Rather, he wishes to differentiate legitimate prejudices from all those numerous prejudices whose overcoming is the unquestioned task of critical reason. The problem of discerning 'true' prejudices, which enable us to understand, from 'false' prejudices, which lead to misunderstanding, is, Gadamer acknowledges, the central question of a truly historical hermeneutics.[31]

The passage which follows that acknowledgement cites authority as a source for legitimating prejudices.[32] But here the argument begs the question: one's prejudices are said to be grounded in recognized authority, but one's recognition of authority reflects one's prejudices. Apart from this *petitio principii*, Gadamer, as far as I can see, fails to give any account of how or why we are able to distinguish 'true' prejudices from 'false' ones other than the claim that we do in fact distinguish them.

When it is suggested that prejudices can guide and focus attention (§ 44), the problem remains that there are many different ways of doing this. Some of them may guide attention towards and focus it on factors which lead into a dead end. Nietzsche, apparently aware of this danger, suggested that a prejudice bestows on us a framework which we are entitled to cling to as long as we make progress within it rather than stagnate.[33]

But there is no evidence that Gadamer adopts this criterion either; rather, he does not seem to allow for such a notion of progress.[34] Nor is it clear that Nietzsche's suggestion solves the problem. The reason for this doubt is that some critical comparison with other prejudices seems required, if we do not want our talk of progress to be idle boasting. For what would 'progress' be worth, if, because of the framing prejudice, it went in the wrong direction? It would in truth be retrogression. However, as soon as we critically compare and assess prejudices, we have already moved beyond them: we have submitted them to *judgement*.

And even if that problem about direction could be settled, the difficulty would recur concerning the issue of degree. Progress is the process of gradually getting nearer to achieving or completing something. It must in some way admit of being quantified. This in turn requires comparisons. However, as soon as we start to compare different prejudices under the aspect of how much progress they yield, we are really free of them. What we do in this case is to collate hypotheses in order to find out which one promises the best cognitive output; for us they are not prejudices any more.

52. Gadamer thinks his main achievement was the discovery of prejudice as a source of world-disclosure. Some Enlightenment thinkers, however, regarded prejudice as something which blinds men to reality.[35]

The problem with these rival claims is that each of them seems to concentrate exclusively on one aspect of a two-sided phenomenon. On the one hand it is clear that a prejudice against someone can make me particularly attentive with regard to his weaknesses, and since these may be weaknesses that he actually has, not just ones that I fancy, it discloses a piece of reality to me. Hatred, an emotion often allied with prejudice, can sharpen sight. On the other hand, for precisely the same reason, I may be particularly inattentive to the strengths of the very same person, and in this regard prejudice conceals an aspect of reality from me. It is the same, just the other way round, with affections. The attitude of parents to their children is typically partial, guided by a positive prejudice. It is obvious that such love can blind. But does a mother understand her children better if she approaches them with the theoretical detachment of a scientist (if we assume, for the moment, that this would be a mind set free from prejudice)? To ask the question is to see its absurdity.

In Montesquieu's *Lettres persanes*, Rica's and Uzbek's view of Europe is at once revealing *and* contracted because they look at the western world with oriental prejudices – it is precisely this ironic balance that accounts for the humour of this literary and philosophical masterpiece. Prejudice, it seems, opens up some aspects of the world and conceals others.

That kind of structure is of course by no means specific to prejudice. It is familiar from a wide range of products of human intelligence, *e.g.*, conventions. An artistic genre, such as opera, is a set of conventions about how to organize artistic creativity. As such it manifests the contrary aspects of permission and prohibition. Every genre has a specific outlook on the world. It opens up ways of expression, both technical and spiritual, but it does so by determining at the same time what is permissible within these. A genre is a channel: it allows us to travel if and only if it defines at the same time the borders within which our ship has to move. When they are recognized, these borders do not pose a problem. An artistic genre, well applied, recognizes of all the possible contents of art only those which fit it. The story of *Così fan tutte* was suitable for an opera, but not for a song; 'Das Veilchen' was suitable for a song, but not as subject of an opera. If someone tries to press a content not suitable for a specific genre into that form, the result will be disappointing.

A similar structure can also be observed in tools. Tools are enabling precisely because of their respective limitations. A hammer cannot be used as a screwdriver. If it could it would not be suitable for hammering, *i.e.*, it would not be a hammer at all. For every tool there is only so much world as it has a grip on; but this limitation is the very condition for its having a grip on anything at all. It apprehends according to its grip; there is no such thing as a tool for all tasks.

The question is, however, whether prejudice is analogous to these phenomena, or can even be subsumed under them, in the sense that prejudices are a specific kind of convention or tool. If this could be claimed, Gadamer's case would be strengthened. As we saw, Gadamer claims that any understanding is necessarily prejudiced. Using the analogy of prejudices with tools, or even their subsumption under this category, it could be argued that the choice is not to see the world with or without prejudices. Rather, the choice is either to be confronted by the world without the benefit of these tools of the understanding and thus to be confronted by chaos, or to reach what understanding one can with the tools available.

53. But it seems that the analogy of prejudices with either conventions or tools, or even their subsumption under them, is not warranted.

A convention is, as the word implies, an agreement; when people revoke the agreement, when they start to disagree, the convention erodes. Again, when we do not want to use a tool any more, we decide accordingly and stop using it. But, by way of contrast, we do not abandon a prejudice because we want to abandon it; rather, it seems, we can discover that we had a prejudice only after getting rid of it. Prejudices, Thomas de Quincey points out, are not to be dispelled by a maxim, for in their serious manifestations they are something of which it does not even occur to us that it can be questioned: 'We laugh long and loud when we hear Des Cartes (great man as he was) laying it down amongst the golden rules for guiding his studies that he would guard himself against all 'prejudices'; because we know that, when a prejudice of any class whatever is seen *as* such, when it is recognised *for* a prejudice, from that moment it ceases to *be* a prejudice. Those are the true baffling prejudices for man, which he never suspects for prejudices'.[36]

As we have seen (§ 52), it is precisely the point of following conventions or using tools in a reasonable way to respect their limitations. To 'respect' a tool's limitations does not mean, imply or presuppose being *aware* of its limitations. To use a screwdriver appropriately, one does not have to *think* that it would be inappropriate to employ it for digging up soil. What is required is to *apply* the tool within the limits defined by the sort of instrument it is; what is not required is to be *conscious* of what is beyond these limits. But to apply a prejudice within limits that are properly defined one would already have to be beyond it. For that would require *judgement* with regard to its subject matter, and this is precisely the kind of achievement by contrast with which prejudice, in one respect,[37] is defined. In a nutshell: When, and only when a screwdriver is seen as a screwdriver, can it be used appropriately; but whenever a prejudice is seen as prejudice, it stops being a prejudice.

This is of course not to claim that prejudices are intrinsically boundless or unlimited. Many of them come with qualifications that restrict them to a specific range. But these boundaries do not seem to be set by the content of prejudices. Prejudices seem to allow their holders to draw up their own limits of tolerance. One anti-Semite believes that Jews should be excluded from higher education and marriage with non-Jewish persons, another believes that all of them should be deported to the near East, a third wants to kill them outright. One claims that those who have assimilated may stay, another that those are the more dangerous. Prejudices, it seems, have limitations, but what is characteristic of these limitations is their arbitrary character. Clearly this would not work for tools; for the hammer itself will not 'tolerate' the attempt to use it as a screwdriver.

(And the point is not only that the area of tolerance is extended at pleasure. What seems to make prejudice, or a certain kind of prejudices, so perfidious is that the high-handed way in which the limits of tolerance are defined is even used as an *argument* in favour of prejudice. Someone who has befriended one Jew, believes himself to be entitled all the more to disparage 'the Jews' (cf. § 77).)

It is certainly true that the world is incapable of being represented completely if represented from any one point of view, and incapable of being represented intelligibly if represented from all points of view at once. The mind does not simply reproduce in consciousness whatever is out there. We are able to listen to something only by not hearing everything. What we pay attention to always has to be less than all there is, or the case would not be one of attention at all. Selecting and ignoring are essential to perceiving. Something has to channel the direction of our senses as well as of our thoughts. But this something seems properly to be called expectation or perspective rather than prejudice (§§ 49–50).

54. To apply prejudices within properly defined borders, one would already have to have crossed them (§ 53, cf. § 17). This may alert us to an even more disturbing feature of these peculiar entities. Personal identity can be conceived of as a web, more or less stable, of prejudices along, of course, with memories

and stories, habits, predilections and other attitudes. In short, prejudices shape identities (though, certainly, they do not do so exclusively). I exist apart from my tools, at a distance from them, and may, if I have an interest in doing so, think of replacing them by others. But do I exist outside my prejudices? It is at least not evident what this 'I' might be, judge of what, in an important respect, makes it what it is.

This is not to deny that persons can distance themselves from at least some of their prejudices and that they do so sometimes. But precisely to have to distance oneself from something implies that the distance was not there in the first place, as it is in those cases where we consider which tools will help us achieve certain goals most efficiently.

Notes

1 *Reflections*, p. 153.
2 *Novum Organum*, aph. LXVIII, p. 179: 'Atque de Idolorum singulis generibus, eorumque apparatu jam diximus; quæ omnia constanti et solenni decreto sunt abneganda et renuncianda, et intellectus ab iis omnino liberandus est et expurgandus; ut non alius fere sit aditus ad regnum hominis, quod fundatur in scientiis, quam ad regnum cœlorum, *in quod, nisi sub persona infantis, intrare non datur*' (Bacon quotes Luc. 18, 17); aph. LXIX, p. 179: 'absolutis istis expiationibus et expurgationibus mentis'. Bacon's 'idolum' was later to become the French Enlightenment's 'préjugé'.
3 Gadamer, *Wahrheit und Methode*, p. 255: 'Es gibt nämlich sehr wohl auch ein Vorurteil der Aufklärung, das ihr Wesen trägt und bestimmt: Dies grundlegende Vorurteil der Aufklärung ist das Vorurteil gegen die Vorurteile überhaupt'.
4 Ibid., p. 254: 'Anerkennung der wesenhaften Vorurteilshaftigkeit alles Verstehens'.
5 Ibid., p. 261: 'Vorurteile als Bedingungen des Verstehens'.
6 Ibid.: '*Darum sind die Vorurteile des einzelnen weit mehr als seine Urteile die geschichtliche Wirklichkeit seines Seins*'.
7 Ibid.: 'Es bedarf einer grundsätzlichen Rehabilitierung des Begriffes des Vorurteils'.
8 Ibid.: 'die oben dargestellte Lehre von den Vorurteilen, die die Aufklärung in kritischer Absicht entwickelt hat, nunmehr ins Positive wenden'.
9 Boswell, *Life of Johnson*, p. 51. Cf. even Kant, *Logik Blomberg*, p. 169: 'man kann wircklich wiederum eine Art von Vorurtheilen wieder die vorurtheile selbst antreffen, wenn man nemlich so gleich geradezu alles dasjenige verwirft, was durch Vorurtheile entstanden ist'.
10 *Philosophische Lehrjahre* I, p. 117: 'Das französ.[ische] Schimpfen auf die Prejugés war selbst ein Prejugé'. Accent marks *sic*.
11 *E.g.*, Kant, *Kritik der Urteilskraft*, § 40, p. 390: '*Aufklärung* [...] Befreiung von Vorurteilen überhaupt'.
12 Gadamer, *Wahrheit und Methode*, p. 256.
13 Art. 'préjugé'.
14 *Essai sur les Préjugés*, vol. I, p. 153.
15 *Nouveaux Dialogues des Mortes*, pp. 334–44.

16 'Préjugés'.
17 *Logik*, p. 505.
18 Jeaucourt, Art. 'préjugé', p. 237: 'PRÉJUGÉ, s. m. *Logique*, faux jugement que l'ame porte de la nature des choses, après un exercise insuffisant des facultés intellectuelles'. Cf. du Marsais, *Essai sur les Préjugés*, vol. I, p. 153: 'Respecter les opinions reçues, c'est presque toujours respecter le mensonge'.
19 Meiszner, Art. 'Vorurteil', col. 1856, quotes his source as follows: 'eyn groszer miszbrauch an unsern heuptgerichten geübt, nemlich, das dieselbigen eynem jeden auff sein ersuchen, des gegentheils unerfordert und ohne alle rechtliche erkanntnisz der sachen, bescheidt, die sie vürurtheil gnent, mitgetheilt haben'.
20 Gadamer, *Wahrheit und Methode*, p. 419.
21 Consequently, an important rhetorical function that these words have acquired since the Enlightenment has been to forestall criticism by suggesting that, should there be any, there is only one possible explanation: the critics must be blinded by bias. Cf., *e.g.*, the final paragraph of the preface to d'Holbach's *Système de la Nature*: 'Près de descende au tombeau, que les années lui creusent depuis long-temps, l'auteur proteste de la façon la plus solennelle ne s'être proposé dans son travail que le bien des ses semblables. Sa seule ambition est de mériter les suffrages du petit nombre des partisans de la vérité, et des âmes honnêtes qui la cherchent sincèrement. Il n'écrit point pour ces hommes endurcis à la voix de la raison, qui ne jugent que d'après leurs vils intérêts ou leurs funestes préjugés: ses cendres froides ne craindront ni leurs clameurs ni leur ressentiment, si terribles pour ceux qui osent, de leur vivant, annoncer la vérite' (pp. XXXIII–XXXIV).
22 Gadamer, *Wahrheit und Methode*, pp. 261–3.
23 *Esquisse*, p. 175.
24 Cf. Aquinas, *Summa Theologica*, 2a2ae, qu. LX, art. 1, p. 145.
25 *Sein und Zeit*, § 32, pp. 150–3: '*Vorhabe*', '*Vorsicht*', '*Vorgriff*'.
26 Gadamer, *Wahrheit und Methode*, p. 254.
27 *De l'esprit des lois*, p. 84: 'Je n'ai point tiré mes principes de mes préjugés, mais de la nature des choses'.
28 *Wahrheit und Methode*, p. 366.
29 Gibbon's work was introduced as an example into the discussion of prejudice by Collingwood, 'Can historians be impartial?', p. 211.
30 Cf. Kant, *Kritik der reinen Vernunft*, 'Vorrede zur zweiten Auflage', B XIII, p. 23.
31 *Wahrheit und Methode*, p. 261: 'Damit wird die für eine wahrhaft geschichtliche Hermeneutik zentrale Frage, ihre erkenntnistheoretische Grundfrage, formulierbar: Worin soll die Legitimität von Vorurteilen ihren Grund finden? Was unterscheidet legitime Vorurteile von all den unzähligen Vorurteilen, deren Überwindung das unbestreitbare Anliegen der kritischen Vernunft ist?'. Cf. also Gadamer, 'Semantik und Hermeneutik', pp. 181–2.
32 *Wahrheit und Methode*, pp. 261–4.
33 Nietzsche, 'Vom Nutzen und Nachtheil', § 1, p. 256: 'wenn wir nur wenigstens innerhalb dieser Vorurtheile fortschreiten und nicht stillestehen!'.
34 *Wahrheit und Methode*, p. 280: 'Verstehen ist in Wahrheit kein Besserverstehen, weder im Sinne des sachlichen Besserwissens durch deutlichere Begriffe, noch im Sinne der grundsätzlichen Überlegenheit, die das Bewußte über das Unbewußte der Produktion besitzt'.

35 Early instances were La Bruyère who compared a person subject to prejudice ('[u]n homme sujet à se laisser prévenir') to a blind man ('un aveugle') (*Les Caractères*, p. 23), and Spinoza (*Tractatus de intellectus emendatione*, p. 18: 'animo occæcatos [...] à præjudiciorum causâ').

36 'Philosophy of Herodotus', p. 132.

37 The reason for this reservation has been given in § 48.

Chapter Four

On the Paradox of Recommending Prejudices, and the Ways in which it can be Circumvented

55. The hermeneutic vindication of prejudice has not succeeded. But possibly it contains an element that we have missed so far – an element that did not originate in hermeneutics, but has been borrowed by it from the tradition.

When Gadamer attributed disclosing power to prejudice, he might have had in mind an idea about the relationship between knowledge and *time* that can be traced back to contemporary critics of the Enlightenment.[1] We have already touched on this idea at an earlier stage. It was implicit in de Bonald's argument about prejudice and language (§§ 31–2). Whenever we utter a sentence the past speaks through us. This is true, however revolutionary the words may sound. For if the sentence is understandable, it cannot avoid using concepts that others before us have developed and that we have adopted from them. This is acknowledged in affirmative views of prejudice: the 'pre-' of prejudice is the *past*.

According to these views, the Enlightenment rejection of prejudice was the logical and historical consequence of an epistemology that linked knowledge with *presence*; any claim should be given just that degree of credence which the present evidence warrants. True, *i.e.*, experimental knowledge, says Thomas Sprat in his *History of the Royal-Society of London*, is about the 'present', about 'what is before us' and thus conforms 'to the *Design* of *Nature* it self': for nature 'has plac'd the *Eies*, the chief *instruments* of *observation*, not in our *Backs*, but in our *Foreheads*'.[2] The nexus between knowledge and presence seems to have been shared by both camps within the new philosophy of the 17th century, empiricism and rationalism. It is already clearly exhibited in the first of Descartes' four rules of method.[3] And the *Port-Royal Logic*, in a chapter explaining the criteria of 'clarté' and 'distinction' set up in that rule, associates the past with prejudiced error, the present with unprejudiced insight.[4]

The objection to that step was advanced with formidable rhetorical effect by Burke: 'You see, Sir, that in this enlightened age I am bold enough to confess, that we are generally men of untaught feelings; that instead of casting away all our old prejudices, we cherish them to a very considerable degree, and, to take more shame to ourselves, we cherish them because they are prejudices; and the longer they have lasted, and the more generally they have prevailed, the more we cherish them. We are afraid to put men to live and trade each on his own private stock of reason; because we suspect that the stock in each man is small, and that the individuals would do better to avail themselves of the general bank and capital of nations and of ages. Many of our men of speculation, instead of exploding general prejudices, employ their sagacity to discover the latent wisdom which prevails in them. If they find what they seek, and they seldom fail, they think it more wise to continue the prejudice'.[5]

When Burke says that the British cherish their prejudices 'because they are prejudices', the deliberate tautology seems to indicate that in his view there is no need for any argument in favour of them. But this impression is deceptive. For immediately Burke goes on to offer a reason for respecting prejudices that is not a tautology: prejudices manifest the accumulated experience of innumerable ancestors, and, as a consequence, have served those who have relied on them well. Prejudiced people are advised in the best possible way, that is, by reality itself.[6] When Burke calls them 'untaught' at the same time, he merely wishes to drive home the polemical point that they have never listened to Enlightenment doctrinaires; they have not listened, Burke implies, because they received infinitely better teaching. Contrary to du Marsais's claim that they lack thorough acquaintance with the world (§ 2), on Burke's account those who rely on prejudice have discovered the richest source of such acquaintance, that is, the entire human past.[7]

The new is seldom good, Burke maintains, because the good is new only for a short time. And 'those things, which engage us merely by their novelty, cannot attach us for any length of time'.[8] The only desire they satisfy is curiosity, and 'curiosity is the most superficial of all the affections'.[9] A proper understanding of prejudice warrants, Burke suggests, 'sullen resistance to innovation'[10] and, conversely, a 'powerful prepossession towards antiquity'.[11] Innovation is bound up with the notion of discovery, which is precisely what is ruled out by prejudice: prejudiced people do not make discoveries and indeed do not need to make discoveries, because, as the 'pre-' indicates, they know it all already: 'We know that *we* have made no discoveries; and we think that no discoveries are to be made, in morality'.[12]

56. Awe, not contempt, Burke concludes, is the stand we ought to take towards prejudice: 'a profound reverence for the wisdom of our ancestors'.[13] In the

end prejudice will always prove wiser than its enlightened critic. Therefore, instead of 'discovery', the proper attitude is 'imitation'.[14] The feature of time which is crucial to Burke's argument involves the contrast of 'old' and 'new'.[15]

These, however, are vexed categories. For whatever is now old was once new. Everything ripe was once sour. Indeed, some of the things Burke approved of in the Britain of 1790 had been revolutionary in the 17th century, driving out sanctified traditions. Hence some of the things justified on Burke's principle could not have commenced on this very principle in the first place. But if they had not commenced, trivially Burke could not have appreciated them at all. Cherishing the establishment of today *is* cherishing the innovations of yesterday. (And to say that the institutions embodying the relevant political prejudices have 'grown', not been 'made', requires us to forget how many heads had to be chopped off in the Tower for them to 'grow' – something that is among the things that people *make*.)

57. Of course the point of something's being old in Burke is that it has lasted long, and the weak point of being new that it is possibly frail, since it has not yet undergone the test of time.

But it is not credible that 'duration'[16] as such manifests value. A stone that has lasted long is not on this ground more exquisite than a swiftly fading rose; it is just different. The best things in human life are possibly fleeting. Admittedly, these general remarks do not take into account the political and historical context in which Burke raises the issue; but the point still stands. Institutions like torture have endured; does this prove any 'wisdom' in them worthy to be 'cherished' beyond the dubious wisdom of sheer efficiency?

The most we should be willing to say is that what has not been turned down in the course of time may be worth *a closer look*; but this is not enough for Burke: in fact it is even in tension with his claim (§ 58).

58. Burke's criticism of the 'enlightened age' suggests that the elimination of prejudice is temporally provincial. Purging the mind of prejudice throws it back on the mathematical point of the present, that flickering moment in time, while the wealth of the past is forgotten. Whereas the Enlightenment had claimed that prejudice was parochial and reason universal, Burke asserted that the kind of reason advocated by the Enlightenment and its epistemology – one bound to presence (§ 55) – was parochial, and prejudice communal (§ 10), if not universal,[17] quite apart from being infinitely richer and more substantial. Hence the 'spirit of innovation' that the Enlightenment had linked to what it had defined as reason is seen by Burke as the result of 'confined

views'.[18] In rejecting prejudice, and thus disavowing the past, human virtue, says Burke, reduces itself to 'a series of unconnected acts',[19] each act occuring in a discontinuous and incomprehensible present.

Yet this is a caricature. Someone who tries to avoid prejudice is not, if he wants to remain consistent, debarred from, as Burke puts it, 'avail[ing]' himself 'of the general bank and capital of nations and of ages'. He will merely avoid buying sight unseen from this shop. Of course, Burke himself does not want to recommend that kind of acquisition from the past either. For he also suggests that the riches of the past have to be 'sought' and 'found' in the first place: in other words, they must come to *presence*. But nothing else is required from someone who wants to avoid prejudice. Such a person does not have to reject the past, as Burke wants to make us believe, but to examine it. For, in the first place, how could anyone '*discover* the latent wisdom which prevails in them', that is, in prejudices, without inquiring into them? Secondly, even if one could, one should not. The wisdom embodied in prejudice is wisdom not only of, but, for the same reason, about past worlds. Hence we are left with the task of finding out whether the present and future worlds in which we live or will live are sufficiently similar to past worlds in which we don't live, before we espouse those past ideas. We do not need to change what *is* good, but we sometimes need to change what merely *was once* good. To believe that both kinds of things must converge would mean to indulge in fond hope. The conservative dictum according to which the institutions the conservative approves of have 'passed the test of time' is unduly euphemistic; what precisely they have passed is the test of *their* time. Thirdly, the most annoying feature of the past is that there is so much of it. 'In history a great volume is unrolled for our instruction', Burke assures us.[20] But the message it conveys is by no means plain. If it contains counsel – and this is Burke's suggestion -, then this counsel is often contradictory. History contains everything and furnishes examples of everything. What is more, history is constantly rewritten. There is no way of telling what may yet become part of history.[21] But even if we restrict ourselves, as we must, to history as it presents itself now, and, within this picture, as Burke suggests, to what has lasted long and prevailed widely, there is still a host of things highly diverse in character. It may be an overstatement to say that history therefore teaches nothing. But it is not an overstatement to say that where we face incompatible advice, there is no such thing as simple acceptance. For to accept one piece of advice would mean to reject the other. Hence what is required is informed choice. And this, again, calls for inquiry.

Such an inquiry, on the other hand, can of course take into account the fact that an idea is not merely the invention of one man or one generation, but has been produced, elaborated and approved of by many successive generations. We may regard this as an indication of value (but surely not more than a weak indication, § 57); what has not been turned down in the course of time may be worth a closer look. The crucial point is, however, that even such a charitable approach is already beyond uncritical acceptance. But a prejudice, critically examined, isn't a prejudice any more. Burke, though he prided himself on 'not being illuminated by a single ray of this new-sprung modern light',[22] was not sufficiently unenlightened to be able to repudiate Enlightenment thought as unwarranted. A mere difference in tone – and of course Burke uses warmer words when he talks about the past than most authors of the Enlightenment – does not establish a difference in substance.

59. To re-establish the primacy of the past over the present (which allegedly the Enlightenment had perversely attempted to turn upside down), Burke invokes the two related ideas of *precedent*[23] and *tradition*.[24]

'Precedent' literally means a thing which has gone before. But in its crucial legal meaning, what has 'gone before' is relevant only in so far as it has been fixed in form of a judgement. Common law and equity, as in the legal systems of England and the United States, are founded on the body of precedents established by the courts. As a previous judgement by others that we adopt, relying on their authority, precedent becomes a cognate of what Burke calls 'prejudice' (§ 10).

A judicial precedent is a judgement or decision of a court, usually recorded in a law report, that is cited as an authority for reaching a decision in the same manner or on the same principle in subsequent cases. By reference to precedent it is thus claimed that something should be done in a certain way now because it was so done in the past. Such a claim seems to stand in need of argument(s). For it makes perfect sense to ask *why* something should be done in the same way now as it was done in the past. Voltaire once claimed that such a practice, adopted as a universal principle, was inherently irrational, because it would contravene the irresistible movement of time.[25] But if we consider the domain where the institute of precedent originated, that of law, there appear to be at least three good reasons for it, one functional, one functional as well as moral, and one entirely moral. (That the idea of precedent can and ought to be *transferred* subsequently from the legal sphere to other realms of human life, as Burke implies, might of course require further argument.)

The first of those reasons is one of economy; it suggests a division of labour. Thinking things through that have already been thought through can be a waste of time, whenever the results of previous thought are conveniently available, *e.g.*, in the form of law reports. Since it means that those who have to make decisions do not have to consider each and every question completely anew, relying on precedent spares their energy to some degree, and enables them to utilize the wisdom of their predecessors. (This argument is a version of what has earlier been called 'the economic justification of prejudice' (§ 12).)

The second reason for the practice of following precedent is functional, as was the previous one, but also moral. An important social function of law is to stabilize expectations. Stable expectations are a precondition of cooperation in many sectors of society. Nothing in the world could provide absolute stability. But sanctions against those who do not fulfil legitimate expectations and compensation for those whose legitimate expectations have been disappointed provide relative stability, if such sanctions and compensations can themselves be expected. This last condition is satisfied by respecting precedent. (One might argue that it would also be satisfied by statute; but while written laws certainly stabilize expectations, too, it is clear that no legislator could foresee all eventualities which life might bring with it.) The practice of deciding disputes on the basis of earlier decisions makes the law and social life in so far as it is governed by it predictable, which is of functional value. At the same time, respecting precedent is to respect the legitimate expectations of citizens, which is of moral import. This second reason may easily appear to beg the question. It seems to presuppose the very practice it is meant to justify; for people would have no reason to form relevant expectations, if a legal system did not acknowledge the principle of precedent in the first place. This circle can only be avoided if, as the first step of the argument, it is established independently that what we call social life is generally possible only if stable expectations can be formed, and that it is possible under modern conditions in particular only if judicial decisions in line with earlier ones can be anticipated. Of course unexpected things will still happen in any society, and some of them will not, or not in everybody, cause anxiety and frustration, but surprise and joy. Yet it is clear that there is a degree of unpredictability in a social environment that deprives people of the opportunity to react rationally, and that it is precisely one purpose of instituting a legal sphere to prevent this degree ever being reached.

The third reason for precedent is entirely moral. It is a consideration of justice, understood as equality for equals. We want like cases to be treated alike. If one person did not serve a sentence of imprisonment for an act, then justice requires that others do not serve one either unless there is a relevant difference in the cases. To the same purpose, a rule obliging judges to respect past decisions forces them to put aside idiosyncrasies, *i.e.*, inclinations or disinclinations they may have as individuals. The uniformity noted under the second reason as an element of social stability and as a form of respect for legitimate expectations is also a matter of justice in that straightforward sense.

While these are reasons in favour of the principle of *stare decisis*, at the same time limits have to be set to it. A reasonable approval of that doctrine must not include a blank approval of past mistakes. Even if *communis error facit lex* (cf. § 67), an error may no longer be common as soon as it is discovered as such *and for that reason* no longer accepted by some. Other errors have been particular rather than common from the outset. If we do not want to perpetuate them forever, it must be possible to overrule precedents. In the words of Hobbes, 'if judges were to follow one another's judgments in precedent cases, all the justice in the world would at length depend upon the sentence of a few learned, or unlearned, ignorant men, and have nothing at all to do with the study of reason'.[26] In face of the functional and moral reasons that have been presented, it has to be noted that a practice of following precedent can be both dysfunctional and immoral. It will become dysfunctional when a sufficient number of members of a society insists that a certain way of conduct that used to be accepted must be discontinued. It can be immoral because the formal justice of the principle to treat like cases alike does not exhaust the idea of justice, and can be assessed in terms of a more substantive notion of justice. Harming a person when she does not deserve to be harmed is not warranted just because another person was so treated earlier in similar circumstances; in this way, precedent can conflict with and, on any defensible account, actually be rejected in response to considerations of justice.

By implication, precedent is nothing like a firm ground in the past which we could rely on without further reflection. There is no reason to believe that the idea of precedent renders the Enlightenment project of sifting past and present obsolete. The facts before a court are never exactly the same as those cited as a precedent. There is always a question whether or not the different facts which have been identified in a later case are sufficiently similar to those of the precedent to make the decision in the precedent case a guide to the decision in the later case.

In Hobbes' *Dialogue*, the Student of the Common Laws of England rightly says that a sense of justice that intends to treat like cases alike is worthless if it is not accompanied by 'a faculty of well distinguishing of dissimilitudes in such cases as common judgments think to be the same. A small circumstance may make a great alteration'.[27] What constitutes 'like treatment' for 'like cases' is in no way something given, but a matter of critical examination; it requires careful inquiry, guided by our present concerns, to determine which similarities are relevant and which differences do not warrant differential treatment.

To establish and appreciate something as a precedent requires a special kind of scrutiny. In many cases there are competing and conflicting precedents; a decision has to be made as to which one is going to count. 'The turbulent government of England, ever fluctuating between privilege and prerogative, would afford a variety of precedents, which might be pleaded on both sides', Hume says in his *History of England*.[28] Precedents do not simply exist; they are claimed and contested.

It is therefore clear that Burke requires something different from the arguments mentioned to establish the primacy of the past over the present. What he requires seems to be that the past is worthy of respect for no other reason than that it is the past.

But such a claim would be almost incomprehensible. What does it mean to honour the past for its own sake? Honour is a recognition of certain qualities, of excellence in the honoured. But simply to be located in time is hardly a quality. The least we want to say is that the case for something must be rather thin if it has no more in its favour than a previous date. Certainly the practice of following precedent does have more in its favour, as we have seen. But those forward-looking reasons for it, economy, stability and justice, though conditional, appear strong enough to render a backward-looking reason for precedent, deference to former times, downright superfluous.

One might want to reiterate at this point the reason Burke advances in favour of prejudice (§ 55): a precedent, like a prejudice and like the prevailing legal and social institutions, generally embodies in a concrete form a technique for dealing with contingency which has been found useful. But none of this removes the objection that duration does not in itself manifest value (§ 57).

60. It is at this stage that the idea of *tradition* (§ 59) enters the argument. For this idea seems to supply us with a counter-objection. The objection we were left with was that duration does not in itself manifest value. How, then, do we find out that something does manifest value? We evaluate it in the light of certain standards. And where do we get these standards from? We can hardly escape the conclusion that, at least in part, we receive them from tradition. We are, Burke suggests, the product of tradition. That being the case, the traditions that made us can never become the object of our criticism in their entirety. The argument, then, is that we must defer to the past we happen to have because it has made us who we are. Tradition is the context within which

our thinking, and hence also our criticizing, takes place. Should we ever approach the situation in which all our traditions should be made the object of our criticism, the subject of that criticism, we ourselves, would also disappear.

In his writings, Burke represents the tradition he is mostly concerned with, the political tradition of Britain, as coherent (though not uniform). As a matter of historical fact, however, traditions conflict, not only as between countries but within a country. There is, and was already in the 18th century, *e.g.*, first, a tradition of anti-Semitism, the one Burke himself belongs to,[29] but there is also, secondly, a tradition of philo-Semitism, and there is a third tradition of thought, called humanism, which claims that one should see the human being in the person one comes across rather than, in the present case, the Jew. The idea that we have to accept tradition as something simply given loses all clear meaning once the alternatives are recognized. Whatever the exact relationship between those three positions, it seems implausible that simply because a man has been brought up in one of them, he could not end up in another one. Is Burke, against all credibility, committed to maintaining that this could not occur since his respective tradition made the man 'who he is'? It seems that Burke is not so committed although there is at least a suggestion in his work that someone who radically breaks with his own tradition *betrays* it.[30] But what Burke is really committed to is that, however relentlessly a man examines some feature of his tradition, he inevitably presupposes other features of it at the same time.

A difficulty with the claim that we are the 'products of tradition' seems to be that, as even the fiercest traditionalist has to admit, we are not *only* products of tradition. However, if we are also the products of other things, a competition of authorities arises, and it is not clear why 'the past' should always get the upper hand. Clearly, the traditionalist would not be impressed by the objection that we are also products of biology, so that according to his logic we ought to be filled with devotion towards nature. He would argue that while it is true that biology also 'makes us who we are', this has to be supplemented by the qualification: '*viz.*, animals'. But the explicit interest of the traditionalist is what has made us into beings capable of judgement, and to this question his answer is: our historical past. That this answer to the more specific question is exhaustive, is, however, not evident either. For 'who we are' in this sense is by no means something fixed, and one of the chief ways in which we develop our identities is surely through criticism of our own past.

Indeed, the traditionalist argument itself indicates what its own limits are. It makes the point that not everything can be criticized at once. All that follows is that those who want to criticize have to do so sequentially, taking up one feature supplied by the tradition after the other. Enlightenment may well be a piecemeal endeavour, laborious and in need of staying-power. But this is no objection to it. It would be unreasonable to require anything that has a historical dimension to it to be successful in one fell swoop.

This answer could well provoke another move: While many features of a tradition may be criticized, it must contain a core which cannot be repudiated, because it constitutes the identity of the culture in which alone that criticism makes sense. If that core were questioned effectively, the tradition and the culture which depends on it – the one we ourselves belong to – would no longer be *that* tradition. But to assume that the culture must in its core remain the same is to beg the question. Radical changes, *i.e.*, changes concerning what had been considered the core of a culture's values, have happened in history – it is plausible, *e.g.*, to conceive of the Christianization of Europe as such a transformation – and while it may in such a case be a sensible question whether the change has been beneficial for the people who have undergone it, we must not *presuppose* that it cannot have been so. For such a presupposition would render the plea for tradition circular.

The argument from tradition is not suited to establish the primacy of the past over the present. It ultimately rests on a misunderstanding of what a tradition is. A tradition is not an ancient entity preserved throughout the ages. It is a temporal sequence of exemplary figures; and exemplarity is not an inherent characteristic of certain persons who once existed. Exemplarity is the result of a posterity's way of speaking about such persons. This does not mean that this way of speaking is arbitrary or that it would make equal sense to speak about anybody as an example; but it means that what is decisive is not the past as such but what we see in it. A tradition is not something in bygone time; it is, rather, a consensus in the present. The normative power of precedent depends on how it is conceived and understood *now*, not on its factual character *heretofore*; and so it is with tradition.

To assert a tradition is to attempt to forge a consensus among a present generation that others and itself should be seen in a certain light. Traditions are construed from the perspective of the living, which emerges from their needs and intentions. In literature, *e.g.*, *we* dismiss certain authors who fancied themselves very important in their own times, regarding themselves as the true and exclusive heirs to a great tradition, and *we* elevate others who were considered marginal, idiosyncratic, and not in any way linked with acknowledged mastership in their own days, far above the anonymity they have in fact suffered from in the historical past. Sometimes people of former times – artists or thinkers, for instance – are represented as 'a tradition' who did not even know of each other by name. The perfectly legitimate point of this is that seeing them in this way has a value *for us*. Hence the phenomenon of tradition, far from establishing a primacy of the past over the present, marks a primacy of the present over the past.

61. The objection to Burke has been that even the conservative who exhorts us to rely on tradition must himself examine it (§ 58). There appear to be two strategies of response to this objection. Though both aim at defending Burke, it is not clear that they supplement each other; they could more easily be read as alternatives.

As a *first* strategy of response it could be said that Burke need not rule out the possibility of people dismissing some traditions and accepting others (§ 60). Along this line, however, difficulties remain. While Burke claims that prejudices manifest accumulated wisdom (§ 55), the critical suggestion has been that he is bound to *show* that they do not manifest accumulated folly. Yet on the conservative account – and this constitutes the *second* strategy of response – this is precisely what he need not do.

For, so the argument goes along this line, we ought to have a prejudice in favour of *existing* institutions. The argument, like most of Burke's ideas, was developed in a political context. The belief that institutions and prejudices have something to do with each other was shared by both their apologists and their critics. Burke maintained that established institutions embody sound prejudices; Rousseau sought to distinguish the man of nature from the factitious and chimerical man whom institutions and prejudices have substituted for the former ('distinguer la realité de l'apparence, et l'homme de la nature de l'homme factice et fantasmal que nos institutions et nos préjugés lui ont substitué'[31]). For the purposes of the present argument, however, it would be more accurate to speak of a '*presumption*' with regard to institutions rather than a prejudice.

Burke calls the presumption for what is established 'another ground of authority in the constitution of the human mind': 'It is a presumption in favour of any settled scheme of government against any untried project, that a nation has long existed and flourished under it'.[32] No one, it is inferred, is required to defend the existing institutions. As for any suggestion that they should be altered, the burden of proof rests on those who propose the alteration, not with those who are satisfied with the *status quo*. Hence the latter, unlike the former, are exempt from investigating the existing state of affairs. Since change is not a good in itself, those who urge one should show a reason for it.[33] Change for change's sake would be either a pointless waste of time and effort, or a dangerous undertaking, or both. After all, things are swiftly destroyed, but take a long time to grow once more. Of the British parliament, Burke said: 'It required a great length of time, very considerable industry and perseverance, no vulgar policy, the union of many men and many tempers, and the concurrence of events which do not happen every day, to build up an independent house of commons. Its demolition was accomplished in a moment; and it was the work of ordinary hands. But to construct, is a matter of skill; to demolish, force and fury are sufficient'.[34] In the words of an admirer of Burke, only a child or a madman is needed to burn a town; but to rebuild it, architects, materials, workmen, money, and, above all, time are necessary.[35]

'Rage and phrensy will pull down more in half an hour, than prudence, deliberation, and foresight can build up in an hundred years', says Burke himself, in *Reflections on the Revolution in France*.[36] The conservative presumption is thus a measure of caution: a known good is not lightly to be surrendered for an unknown better. (Montaigne maintained that even an evil, if only it was very old and very well-known, was always more bearable than an evil that was new and untried.)[37] So, Burke concludes, 'it is with infinite caution that any man ought to venture upon pulling down an edifice, which has answered in any tolerable degree for ages the common purposes of society, or on building it up again, without having models and patterns of approved utility before his eyes'.[38] It is for this reason that the conservative regards himself entitled to say: 'I am right, as long as you cannot prove that I am wrong'.

62. The conservative presumption is that the burden of argument for change always lies on the party asking for it. It is, however, not altogether clear that the idea works in the ahistorical fashion in which it has been presented (§ 61).

For it seems to be the case that modern societies cannot exist without constant revolution. Innovation is the battle-cry of each and every entrepreneur. Uninterrupted disturbance of all social conditions, everlasting uncertainty and agitation distinguish the bourgeois epoch from all earlier ones, say Marx and Engels in their famous, by no means outdated, diagnosis. All fixed, fast-frozen relations, with their train of ancient and venerable ideas and opinions, are swept away, all new-formed ones become antiquated before they can ossify; all that is solid melts into air.[39]

The survival of modern societies seems to depend on the permanently accelerating invention of new technologies of production and communication, and the conquest of new markets. This in turn requires, at an equally accelerating rate, ever changing political, legal and social arrangements. On this account, a conservative presumption may have been appropriate in traditional societies – at least among those interested in sustaining them – but it would be out of place in modern societies – even among those interested in sustaining them.

In the context of modern societies, then, it is unlikely that anything which just stays as it is will be functional. This might support an actual shift in the burden of proof, institutionalizing the Enlightenment's challenge to past customs. In a modern society, then, whenever we want to keep something unaltered, it needs to be shown that, against all the odds, this is feasible.

63. The pace of modern societies seems to have rendered the conservative presumption obsolete. But the conservative may simply consider all the specifically modern circumstances mentioned (§ 62) as part of the disease he wishes to cure.

On this radical account, the reasons that have been adduced fall indeed flat; the only problem its advocate faces is whether he can still be called conservative. He seems to have turned into a reactionary, and it is doubtful whether Burke would have endorsed that response. After all, Burke was not a despiser of modernity, and he acknowledged that modern societies, precisely in the interest of their preservation, require alteration: 'A state without the means of some change is without the means of its conservation'.[40] Burke was conservative only in so far as that relation constituted, on his account, the sole justification of deliberate change: 'I would not exclude alteration neither; but even when I changed, it should be to preserve'.[41]

Is there any alternative available? An argument for conservatism which does not aspire to abolish modernity could perhaps run like this: Precisely *because* modernity is in any case so ruthless in doing away with all traditions, these ought to be guarded by a presumption against innovation, very much as species of animals and plants receive special protection because the industrial and agricultural exploitation of nature has resulted in making many species extinct.

64. We shall therefore drop the objection that the conservative allocation of *onera probandi* is anachronistic. This allocation now looks fairly reasonable. We must, however, be entirely clear regarding its status. The presumption does not provide a concrete reason in favour of any existing institution. It is not exactly the kind of thing that can carry weight as an argument. Rather, the presumption merely predetermines which party, if there is to be an argument, must lead the attack.

In other words, sound as a presumption in favour of the familiar and against the unfamiliar, in favour of the actual and against the possible, may be, it is not sufficient at all stages when we are engaged in finding out what to do. The sober point of it is that no one needs to give reasons in defending an existing institution until some solid argument is adduced against it; but of course as soon as such an argument is produced, it has to be taken seriously, and the proper way to do this is to consider it, *i.e.*, to try to understand, assess, and answer it. Allocating the burden of proof is a move at the beginning of the game, not its end. In particular, it is not a reason for refusing to attend to criticism. If burdens of proof are to function properly, *i.e.*, if putting them on the opponent is not just a trick to render one's own position secure, it must be possible that they are met. Otherwise their only upshot will be to block discussion: The conservatives will appeal to the presumed allocation of the *onus probandi*, the progressives to their arguments; each side is sure that the burden of proof now lies upon the other. The demand on the other side to take up the burden of proof and thus permit the argument to proceed is precisely what prevents the argument from proceeding.

When someone has built his case – against the *status quo* and in favour of change – the burden of argument is shifted. Otherwise no change could ever be successfully proposed, something that, as previously conceded (§ 63), even conservatives wish to do sometimes. If nothing else, at least they want to cure people of their mania for innovation. Burke's defence of prejudice was part and parcel of a political agenda: 'My whole politicks, at present, centre in one point; and to this the merit or demerit of every measure (with me) is referrible; that is, what will most promote or depress the cause of Jacobinism. What is Jacobinism? It is an attempt (hitherto but too successful) to eradicate prejudice out of the minds of men, for the purpose of putting all power and authority into the hands of the persons capable of occasionally enlightening the minds of the people'.[42] It is an unsatisfactory definition of a conservative to characterize him as someone who desires to conserve; after all, conservatives also have rubbish bins in front of their houses, literally as well as figuratively, and thus show by their actions that they do not conserve everything. Conservatism is rendered intelligible only by some understanding that the things it desires to conserve are worthwhile.

So once the advocate of innovation has argued that the suggested innovation entitles us to *hope* for certain things, he can only be countered by an account of what we ought to *fear* from it, *viz.*, the loss of certain things which have existed for some time and are to be replaced by the innovation. The conservative must be clear about what he has to lose. When it is argued that what he considers a loss would not really be one, he must be able to *show* that it really would be one. This, however, cannot be done unless he has articulated the specific merits of the institutions that have come down to us, and can point to what he considers their 'profound and extensive wisdom'.[43]

The conservative might still be well advised to look twice at the claims of the would-be innovator, but when he looks, and looks again, he has already embarked on an investigation of the matter. A prejudice in favour of the *status quo* that would rule out even this possibility would, it seems, deserve to be dismissed as stubborn.

65. Even if there were varieties of it that possessed some merit, prejudice undeniably also covers some flagrant manifestations of dullness. Though we have rejected the idea that prejudices *must* be stupid (§ 42), it is evident that some of them are. While it may be worth looking out for 'latent wisdom' where we encounter ideas handed down to us from the past (§ 58), these ideas sometimes turn out to be born of a hopeless tradition of ignorance. As Socrates, a hero of the Enlightenment, discovered, the things and concepts one most often uses are often the ones one knows least about; one is unable to take them in because they are always before one's eyes. One does not hear what goes without saying, and one hardly listens to what is always being said. Blind- and deafness to the ordinary is a recurrent theme in Plato's early dialogues. At the beginning of *Republic* I, morals are a closed book to Cephalus because they are so familiar. Thrasymachus is able to pass a genuine judgement on morals rather than reproduce the traditional prejudice, precisely because he sees it from a distance; however mistaken Socrates may find Thrasymachus's position, it is obvious that he appreciates it as infinitely more engaging than that of Cephalus.

What is more, prejudices sometimes contradict one another. If some are valid it has to be the case that some others are not. Hence no indiscriminate apologia for prejudice could possibly be acceptable. But if they are to discriminate, the apologists of prejudice need a criterion. For they must be able to answer the question: Which prejudices should we have?

This is clearly reflected in the British tradition of vindicating prejudice which runs parallel to the French Enlightenment's attack on it. In his essay 'Of Moral Prejudices', Hume talks of 'useful Byasses'.[44] Lord Chesterfield, in an article 'On Prejudices', asks with regard to '[t]he bulk of mankind': 'Will not honest instinct prompt, and wholesome prejudices guide them, much better than half reasoning?'.[45] Burke, in the passage on prejudice we have cited from his *Reflections*, asserts: 'Through just prejudice, his [man's] duty becomes a part of his nature'.[46] Talk of 'useful Byasses', however, presupposes an unbiased examination of such bias. And if the bias has been shown to be reasonable, it is no mere bias any more. Again Chesterfield and Burke are of course right that not *any* prejudice will do if advocacy of prejudice is to be credible; but if it has been labelled 'wholesome' or 'just' it is implied that the prejudice has been assessed, *i.e.*, made subject to a *judgement*, not merely to a further prejudice. Since the criteria of utility, wholesomeness and justness are *applied* to prejudice, they cannot be derived from the sphere of prejudice. For if they were derived from prejudices themselves, we would have to know that *those* prejudices were sound. And this, of course, would immediately lead into a regress.

The advocates of prejudices must not themselves hold them *as prejudices*. They must have made genuine judgements about their contents. For, if they are to arrive at something deserving the name of a recommendation, they must have inquired into them. A recommendation, if it is more than the expression of a whim, has to be based on reasons. Hence a recommendation of prejudice is paradoxical. As soon as it has been recommended, it can no longer be prejudice. If the recommendation of a prejudice is not groundless, it has undergone examination and has thus become a proper judgement rather than a prejudice. He who illuminates the darkness to show how good it is destroys it.

66. Hume at least may have been impressed by such considerations, since he withdrew his essay, preferring to be known as the author of views which followed the mainstream of Enlightenment: 'It is well known, that in all questions, submitted to the understanding, prejudice is destructive of sound judgment, and perverts all operations of the intellectual faculties'.[47] This conclusion is understandable, if we assume that affirmation of prejudice involves a contradiction. But it may not be inevitable. For there seem to be ways round the paradox that a recommended prejudice ceases to be a prejudice.

First of all we have to distinguish between recommendations of prejudice in general and recommendations of particular prejudices. If someone is to recommend particular prejudices, it seems necessary that he has examined their particular content. Here we are confronted with the paradox. For if he has done so, they cease to be prejudices. If, on the other hand, someone makes a general recommendation of prejudice, the paradox does not arise. Of course such a recommendation has to be based on some examination of prejudice in general. For if it is a recommendation, it needs to be based on some reason. The reason may be that we cannot do without prejudice if we are to get on with our lives. Or it may be that prejudices or communal sentiments are the

cement necessary for social stability. Such broad claims make no reference to
particular prejudices. Accordingly, they do not imply that any particular
prejudices have been examined. So they do not transform prejudices into
judgements, and hence avoid the paradox.

The phrase 'general recommendation of prejudice' cannot, of course, be
taken to mean a *universal* recommendation of prejudices (but cf. § 67). As
Hume, Chesterfield and Burke recognized, the claim that *all* prejudices are
reasonable is unacceptable. We cannot get round the fact that the term
'prejudice' also covers some forms of stupidity which no rational person would
wish to recommend. Therefore some selection among prejudices seems
necessary, and it is hard to see how that could be achieved without becoming
more specific. Proceeding towards particulars, however, will entangle us in
the paradox. Hence a general recommendation of prejudice will have to confine
itself to this: 'There is a limit to the number of things you can afford to question
and these need to be balanced by other things you take for granted. Therefore
you need some prejudices – but I cannot tell you which ones to adopt'. Now
certainly, this is not a *very* interesting claim. But nor is it a completely
insignificant one.

General recommendations of prejudice have something in common with
Tertullian's dictum about Christ's incarnation, 'certum est, quia impossibile'.[48]
The dictum is remarkable; but it is, in a crucial regard, precariously vague.
Tertullian implies that divine matters will appear absurd to human reason,
since they reach far beyond it. Even if, for the sake of argument, we concede
this, it does not tell us why on earth, of all the impossibilities we could think
of, we ought to believe precisely the Christian one. The situation is analogous:
An intriguing claim is put forward, but at the very centre of it there is a gap,
which cannot be filled without giving up what is intriguing about it.

67. A general recommendation of prejudice might, however, be accompanied
with the claim that the content of prejudices does not matter – if only they
satisfy one condition; they have to exemplify, in the words of Duclos, 'la loi
du commun des hommes' (§ 10).

Duclos' words refer us to jurisprudence. In the reasoning of this discipline,
communis error facit ius (cf. § 59) is a phrase that has a long standing. It was
coined on *Dig.* 1.14.3 with reference to an example cited by Ulpian (*Sabinus*,
l. 38): a runaway slave named Barbarius Philippus not only succeeded in
living the normal life of a freeborn citizen, he was even appointed *praetor*
and actually held this public office. The question was raised whether the edicts
and decrees he had issued as *praetor* were invalid. Ulpian argued that none of

his acts had to be declared null and void, because the entire legal community had acted in good faith. Following this lead, Pascal claims in his *Pensées* that, when we do not know the truth about something, it is a good thing that there should be a common error to fix the minds of men, as, for example, when we attribute the change of seasons, the progress of illnesses, *etc.*, to the moon.[49]

Pascal does not explicitly refer to prejudices in this fragment. But some of the errors he talks about could very well be prejudices. Whether or not he thought so, it is not hard to imagine *some*body having that view.

It also has to be noted that Pascal, unlike Duclos, Burke, and Hazlitt (§ 10), regards the communal character of prejudice merely as a means to put a stop to useless curiosity ('curiosité inutile'). Since disagreement gives rise to investigations into the objects of disagreement, only a common error will guard us from curiosity: this is the only reason why Pascal finds it attractive.

In our assessment of this position, we must distinguish two questions: whether it is self-contradictory, and whether it is false. Only if the answer to the first question is yes, will Pascal's thesis exemplify the paradox of recommending prejudices (§ 65). Since the second question is also important, we shall have to look into it as well.

First, there is certainly nothing inconsistent about asserting that an error, if, because and in so far as it is common, fulfils a certain function and is therefore good. The paradox of recommending prejudices arises from the presumption that, in order to recommend a prejudice, one has to check it – which transforms it into a judgement proper and thus ends its existence as a prejudice (§ 65). But there is no need for this in the present case. All one has to do is enquire whether the prejudice is common – for no more than that is asked for – and this does nothing to prevent its remaining a prejudice. Indeed, the whole point of Pascal's position is that one does not need to look at particulars.

There is nothing self-contradictory in Ulpian's judgement in the case of Barbarius Philippus – indeed, it seems a perfectly reasonable solution. But would every case of error be so inoffensive? It has to be admitted that the peculiar prudence of jurisprudence has always been to consider it more important that cases be settled, than that they be settled right; it is the former, not the latter, on which political rulers are prepared to spend vast sums of money. But this is merely an explanation, not a justification.

So what, secondly, about justification? Is the position endorsed by Pascal right? Let us consider a case which seems to be covered by Pascal's claim, yet which has far weightier implications than Pascal's own example, people's opinions about the moon.

During the first half of the 17th century, the practice of killing those women who were called witches prevailed throughout the Christian world. (The 'witches' of Continental Europe and Scotland were burnt, while those of England were hanged.) To fulfil God's commandment to Moses – 'thou shalt not suffer a witch to live' (*Exodus*, 22:18) – was an object of great moment for the Protestant reformers, for the popes and saints of the Counter-Reformation, and for leading intellectuals, such as Jean Bodin, alike. The people of Clermont were convinced that a disease Pascal suffered from at the age of twelve months had resulted from a spell cast by a woman who had made a secret pact with the Devil, and Blaise's father sent for the alleged witch, threatening her with death unless she transferred the evil spell to a black cat.[50] It may have been a common prejudice at that time that there were witches and that they had to be killed. It is imaginable that even those accused of witchcraft shared in that prejudice. Did things become worse when this common error was contested? They were clearly better for those who, as a consequence, were not killed, and they were not obviously worse for all the rest. If there are no witches, witchcraft can do no harm; if the harm is merely imaginary, burning witches does not help and hence not burning those women does not make things worse. The conclusion to be drawn from this counter-example, then, is that Pascal's position is unacceptable.

Pascal seems to suggest that consensus as such is good. 'As such' does not here mean 'in itself'. As noted above, in Pascal's view consensus is good not as an end, but merely as a means: it fixes the minds of people, thus warding off restless curiosity, 'curiosité inquiète'. But Pascal seems to maintain that consensus 'as such' is good in the sense of being so irrespective of what it is consensus about. This, however, is a mistake. Consensus is good if it is consensus about upholding a good state of affairs or abolishing a bad one; it is bad if it is consensus about upholding a bad state of affairs or abolishing a good one. And if the avoidance of vain curiosity was the only good Pascal considered, it might be objected that this is inadequate since there were other goods at stake at the same time.

There is, however, a difficulty with this argument. The counter-example implied that we know there is no such thing as witchcraft. While that may be a reasonable assumption, it seems to do injustice to Pascal. For as Pascal explicitly says, he is thinking of cases where we do not know the truth about something: 'Lorsqu'on ne sait pas la vérité d'un chose ...'. Clearly there remains an ambiguity in these words. During the 17th century disagreement arose about alleged witches, their effects and their treatment. Pascal's words could be interpreted as endorsing the view that such disagreement was worse than consensus, even if that consensus referred to an error. But the context of his remark is a negative verdict on man's curiosity about things which he cannot know: 'choses qu'il ne peut savoir'. While it seems proper to say that in the 17th century the vast majority of people in Europe *did not* know the truth about witchcraft, *viz.*, that it was something merely imaginary, it might be going too far to contend that they *could not* have known this. But if they could have known, Pascal would not have been committed to approving a consensus that seems utterly abhorrent. On a charitable interpretation, his claim 'When we do not know the truth about something, it is a good thing that there should be a common error to fix the minds of men' must be rendered as 'When we cannot know the truth about something, it is a good thing that there should be a common error to fix the minds of men'; and there is at least no obvious example that would prove him wrong. At most it remains odd to speak of 'error' at all where its opposite, knowledge, is, *ex hypothesi*, not even possible.

But, even if we leave open the question of truth or falsity, the fact alone that Pascal's apology for common error is not self-contradictory provides a counter-instance to the claim that recommending prejudices is inherently illogical (§ 65).

68. The paradox that a prejudice ceases to be a prejudice as soon as it is recommended can be avoided in the case of general recommendations of prejudice (§ 66). But Chesterfield at any rate does not merely wish to sanction prejudice in this general way. He discusses *particular* prejudices in his essay and recommends them. Is there a way round the paradox even in this case?

When we recommend something we claim that it is good *for others*. We do not have to hold that it is good for ourselves, too. Chesterfield seems to make precisely this distinction. For he says that prejudices are good for 'the bulk of mankind'. But he did not count himself among the bulk of mankind. So he says that prejudices are good for others. Certainly, these prejudices are examined in his discussion, and are hence transformed into judgements. But they are so transformed only for him (and for us, when we study his essay). They remain prejudices for those who have them. And this, Chesterfield adds, is nothing we have to deplore. To put it in contemporary parlance, Chesterfield takes the attitude of a sociologist who describes how prejudices perform a function in the maintenance of society – perhaps, as a kind of second nature, they take on an imperative rôle in people's lives merely because they get so used to them (probably the weakest form of a general recommendation of prejudice, § 66), or perhaps there is some reason deriving from the actual content of the prejudices (a recommendation that refers to particular qualities of them).

Chesterfield is considerably more frank than the sociologists who have to sell the same sentiment as 'theory'. 'The herd of mankind can hardly be said to think; their notions are almost all adoptive; and, in general, I believe it is better that it should be so, as such common prejudices contribute more to order and quiet than their own separate reasonings would do, uncultivated and unimproved as they are. We have many of those useful prejudices in this country, which I shall be very sorry to see removed'.[51] Chesterfield avoids the paradox by distinguishing different strata within society. Though he too wants the society of which he is a member to be maintained, Chesterfield himself does not share the prejudices whose function for society's maintenance he analyses. We may call this an *external* recommendation of prejudice. It can include far more significant claims than a merely general recommendation of prejudice.

It is worth noting how slight the difference is between an external justification of prejudice and the account of prejudice, associated with a number of Enlightenment figures, against which the justification is directed. In fact the authors of those competing doctrines hardly disagreed in their findings. They dissented merely in their attitude to these findings. Radical Enlightenment writers, particularly in France, claimed that prejudices are nothing but the conventional lies of a given society. (It goes without saying that exaggeration is indispensable to polemics.) And as radicals they were not interested in the maintenance of the society they lived in. Satisfied neither with its political and economic order nor with its religious legitimation, they concluded that both that society and its constitutive prejudices should be abandoned. Chesterfield, and others who proposed external justifications, did not really disagree that prejudices, or at least many prejudices, were the conventional lies of a given society, though they would not have presented the matter in so many words. However they *were*, particularly in Britain, interested in the maintenance of the society they lived in, and largely satisfied with its political and economic order.

The slightness of the difference is not surprising. For an external view of the society one lives in seems to be itself an enlightenment achievement (first clearly manifested by the Greek enlightenment, the Sophistic movement).

To be close to the position one is attacking can be considered a weakness as well as a strength. On the one hand, it can be seen as the half-hearted posture of a man who, conceding the premises, shrinks back from the radical conclusions. On the other hand, it can be seen as reflecting the logical force of an argument which shows that the conclusion of the opponent does not follow even if we grant him his premises. In the present case, however, both suggestions would be misleading. The conclusions did not diverge because the case had been argued in a weaker or stronger way, but rather because of different interests in different situations. (Or, to put it another way, in the light of interests even the first, the critical interpretation could have been turned into a compliment: it has often been admired as the political prudence manifested in English history to have broken off without hesitation almost any theory's spearhead before it hurt.)

A position that is *logically* opposed to external justifications of particular prejudices is external criticism of prejudices in general. Such a negative assessment of prejudices in terms of utility has been presented by du Marsais,[52] as well as by Kant. Some people, Kant says, seek to excuse letting prejudices stand on the ground that disadvantages would arise from rooting them out. But, Kant claims, these disadvantages should be accepted. For subsequently they will bring all the more good.[53] This is a comparative empirical claim. It weighs two sets of effects and informs us which one, in the long run, will bring the greater benefit. But the argument required to redeem such a claim has in fact not been tendered. It is a mere assertion.

69. One way of putting the paradox of recommending prejudices (§ 65) is this: The defenders of prejudice need to be clear-headed not to believe in them, but if they are so clear-headed, shouldn't we expect them to be enemies of prejudice? The answer, as regards external recommendations of prejudice, has been that this depends on their value-rankings – whether they attach more value to the adequate justification of our beliefs, or to something like social cohesion, which they think the flourishing of certain prejudices promotes (§ 68).

There is one external recommendation of prejudice that appears to be of particular moment. What gives rise to it is the doubt whether it is desirable, or even at all possible, that children should be brought up on the principle that all prejudices have to be abandoned. If this doubt is justified, then human society either should not or could not reproduce itself and continue to exist in accordance with that enlightened principle. This recommendation of prejudice was developed with critical intent; it was designed to rebut a particular account of education that dates back to the very beginnings of the British Enlightenment. In order to understand that recommendation fully, it would seem advisable to quote the condemnation of prejudice to which it forms a response.

In 1661, Joseph Glanvill complained: 'ANother genuine derivation of this *selfish fondness*, by reason of which we miscarry of *Science*, is the almost insuperable *prejudice* of *Custom*, and *Education*: by which our minds are encumber'd, and the most are held in a *Fatal Ignorance*. Now could a man be composed to such an advantage of constitution, that it should not at all adulterate the images of his mind; yet this *second nature* would alter the *crasis* of the Understanding, and render it as obnoxious to aberrances, as now. And though in the former regard, the *Soul* were a pure ἄγραφον γραμματεῖον; yet *custom* and *education* will so blot and scrible on't, as almost to incapacitate it for after-impressions. Thus we judge all things by our *anticipations*; and condemn or applaud them, as they agree or differ from our education-preposseßions'.[54] Glanvill's more celebrated contemporary John Locke thought he knew how to overcome the evil the former had considered 'almost insuperable'. Unlike most Enlightenment authors who meditated on an effective 'manner of rooting out the prejudices of education',[55] Locke considered how one could prevent such prejudices coming up in the first place. According to him, we should not receive any principles 'till we are fully convinced, as rational creatures, of their solidity, truth, and certainty'.[56] Acting against this imperative is, Locke suggests, to be guilty of an act of imposition, one of 'the common and most general miscarriages which I think men should avoid, or rectify, in a right conduct of their understandings, and should be particularly taken care of in education'.[57] This statement seems to imply that the right pedagogy consists in keeping the mind free from all opinions until it is able to give a reason for them.

A spiritual heir of Glanvill and Locke was encountered a century later by Samuel Taylor Coleridge in the person of his friend John Thelwall. Reporting his dispute with Thelwall, Coleridge suggested a striking analogy against Locke's implicit claim that freedom from prejudice is a state of mind desirable in children: 'Thelwall thought it very unfair to prejudice a child's mind by inculcating any opinions before it should have come to years of discretion and be able to choose for itself. I showed him my garden and told him it was my botanical garden. "How so?" said he – "it is covered with nothing but weeds". "O" I replied – "that is only because it has not yet come to its age of discretion and choice. The weeds, you see, have taken the liberty to grow, and I thought it unfair in me to prejudice the soil towards roses or strawberries"'.[58]

Thelwall, with his enlightened conception of education, seems to have considered it intolerant and tyrannical to instil prejudices into the tender mind of a child. Reason appears to have been the only foundation for holding something true admitted by him; consequently where a child could not reason, it would have to suspend belief. What Coleridge advanced against this conception was, of course, an image, not an argument. But the image is meant to suggest an argument. The argument is this: Suspension of judgement, that highly sophisticated technique of scepticism, is not an option for a child. The place meant to be reserved empty until the 'age of discretion and choice' has arrived, will be occupied by wild and random fancies, those weeds of the infant's mind.

Coleridge implies that if the mind, left to itself, will not wait until it is capable of making itself into a blossoming garden, then the parents have no rational alternative; they must impart their own beliefs which, for the child, will be prejudices.[59] There remains, of course, a question: When we do so, how can we be sure that our beliefs are the seeds of roses and strawberries rather than of weeds? Perhaps we are not sure. But this is an empty doubt. For the alternative of suspending judgement when bringing up a child is not open to us. We have to take a stand; otherwise the child will not be brought up at all.

If we interpret Coleridge in this way, however, we have already moved to the stronger claim indicated at the beginning of this discussion. Coleridge's image merely suggests that striving to keep children's minds free from prejudice is not desirable, because they will be uncultivated. He does not imply that it is impossible. Meadows left to themselves, 'covered with nothing but weeds', do after all exist. They may flourish in their own, natural way. Whether a child's mind can flourish without prejudice is less clear.

A child learns by believing her parents, or the adults who rear her; doubt comes later.[60] All of us do and must begin with a body of accepted beliefs. For it does not and cannot occur to us to doubt any one proposition unless we see some conflict between it and some other of our accepted beliefs.

Whatever we tell a child seriously is, for the child, a prejudice to begin with; the faculty of criticism cannot be the first to develop. A positive relationship to many things in the world is the precondition of the first negation of a thing. The child cannot immediately assess, doubt or criticize the thing she is taught; for that could only mean that she was incapable of learning it.[61] Without trust in and credulity towards those who cherish her in her early years, a child will not merely be, as Coleridge suggests, uncultivated; it would be lost, unable to learn her parents' language (§ 32). (In *Some Thoughts concerning Education*, Locke had to go beyond his critical principle, and tried to give positive advice; no wonder, then, that that book abounds with the prejudices of 17th century England 'to be wrought into the mind, as early as may be'.)[62]

The recommendation of prejudice we have derived from Coleridge is external: it explains why adults are right in seeing prejudice as a necessary frame of mind for children. The necessity asserted is provisional. Prejudice is held to be something that can either be transformed into genuine judgement or revoked as error, as soon as we are adults.

70. The link between prejudice and childhood (§ 69), it must be noted, makes its approbation sound rather restrained or even condescending. For does it not imply that prejudice is infantile?

But the message of Coleridge's image not only applies to children; it holds just as much for an adult when she learns something new, say the art of painting. Doubt and critical judgement cannot be the first step for an adult in such a situation either. When the art is passed on to us by example from master to pupil – and there is no other way of passing it on to us – we have to start by absorbing, as we are told, the way things are done, the prejudices of the profession. And since our teacher once did the same herself, we embark, and must embark, on a tradition to begin with, however radically we may depart from it later on. Otherwise learning would not take place at all; we would not even become beginners, but would be left with the poverty of intellect and skill of rank incompetents. The reason for this is not that the knowledge of fine art is esoteric and ethereal – indeed, we may or may not think that this is the case. Letting oneself absorb the prejudices of the *métier* would also be required for the initiation into more obviously exoteric and banal activities such as cooking. Within the domain of learning complex activities, of getting acquainted with ways of doing things that require skill, this external recommendation may well stand universally.

But again, as in the education of children, the need for prejudice derived from that observation is merely provisional; otherwise we might, as Joshua Reynolds cautioned, really become childish: 'Prejudice is generally used in a bad sense, to imply a predilection not founded on reason or nature, in favour of a particular manner, and therefore ought to be opposed with all our force; but totally to eradicate in advanced age what has so much assisted us in our youth, is a point to which we cannot hope to arrive. The difficulty of conquering this prejudice is to be considered in the number of those causes which makes excellence so very rare. Whoever would make a happy progress in any art or science, must begin by having great confidence in, and even prejudice in favour of, his instructor; but to continue to think him infallible, would be continuing for ever in a state of infancy'.[63]

71. Whereas it seemed originally that *any* recommendation of prejudice is inconsistent, it now appears that only an *internal* approval of prejudice is impossible. But even that seems to be subject to doubt. A counter-example appears to be provided by what is called creativity. The manifestation of creativity seems possible only where someone is fully concentrated on a particular problem. One must devote oneself to one's work as if there was nothing else in the world. The field that can be tilled by one person at a time in a way approaching perfection is extremely limited. Since it is quite obviously not true that there *is* nothing else in the world apart from one's work, the view a creative mind is often bound to take is that whatever else there may be is unimportant.

Devoting all its energy to its chosen field, the creative mind cannot fully appreciate other fields. Erudition, tolerance and understanding are not always and everywhere a grace; they might reduce someone who had the endowment of a poet into a scholar or critic. One cannot have too much talent, but one can have a talent too much. In its attempt to understand the opinions and diverse perspectives of everyone else, the mind can lose the constancy it needs for great achievements, and go astray. A creative mind needs to protect itself against this danger. The only object of its attention may, in a sense, seem to be itself – but of an attention of such intensity that no ordinary egoist is capable of. (So it 'may seem' in the internal perspective – a semblance which is part of the artists' myth of originality (§ 11). From an external perspective, every work of art is rightly found to depend on prior works and the prior expectations of its audience. But the fact that, in one respect, even the most creative artist works with an imagery of which some is inherited by no means diminishes his need, in other respects, to shield himself from influences that would threaten his creativity.)

At earlier points of the argument (§§ 13, 41) it was shown that there are not only failures of dullness, of seeing too little or too slowly, but also failures of sharpness and quickness, when we are swamped with irrelevant detail. Just as we may not be aware of what we should see, we may also be aware of too much and of what we should not be noticing at all. The latter trouble may be particularly acute for creative minds.

In order to maximize the intensity of his attention an artist at work must minimize distraction and disturbance from competing endeavours, often by ignoring them, but sometimes, when they are considered importunate, by rejecting them outright. In letters and conversations of persons of great creativity, such as Goethe, we find strikingly dismissive or even abusive remarks about the endeavours of others. Furthermore, we may assume that such a person is fully aware of not having studied those endeavours. In that case, his or her unappreciative attitude is, as the person is aware, mere prejudice. Yet this person also knows that failure to appreciate those endeavours is a condition of his or her own creativity. On this ground, such a person might say to him- or herself: It is good that I am prejudiced; for otherwise I could not be creative.[64] There is at least no obvious sense in which this is absurd. On the contrary. It does justice to the human spirit's intricate character; it is always possible that not knowing and not appreciating something releases rather than inhibits us. A link between a belief and an interest is not in itself objectionable (§ 75). Such a link can even be seen, and was so seen by Burke, as the peculiar blessing of prejudice compared with theoretical judgement: 'prejudice, with its reason, has a motive to give action to that reason, and an affection which will give it permanence'.[65]

Hence it seems that internal approval of prejudice is also possible.

72. Have our last remarks gone too far? It would seem that just as the external justification of prejudice was possible only on the basis of a distinction between the persons who hold a prejudice and the person who examines this prejudice, so an internal approval of a prejudice is possible only if we distinguish its truth from its benefit. For what has not been established in the example of the internal approval of prejudice (§ 71) is that the endeavours of others are really worth nothing. Whether that is the case or not can be distinguished from the question whether it is beneficial (in the sense of being a condition of creativity) to believe that they are worth nothing. This distinction clearly cannot apply from an internal perspective.[66] For then the belief which is a condition of the person's creativity would dissolve. From an external perspective, however, this distinction must be drawn.

Functionalist justifications of prejudice generally present evidence that prejudices are needed. But they must not conclude from this evidence that they are true; there could very well be a need for errors. The conclusion mentioned clearly requires the assumption that there is a benevolent and truthful Providence which ensures that whatever is needed is true; and this is just not credible.

Yet there seem to be cases where those two things cannot be kept apart. These are the cases for which Virgil coined the phrase 'possunt, quia posse videntur':[67] 'they are able to do it because they deem themselves to be able to do it'. To believe that I can jump over the chasm between those rocks may be a mere prejudice. For I have not checked my physical powers; I simply trust that I can do it. Precisely this belief, however, might enable me to do it. Had I doubted it, I could not have done it. The 'will to believe' can be self-verifying.

In fact, this point seems to apply to internal *and* external justifications of prejudice. Chesterfield gives an example of the latter that can be interpreted in this way. An anecdote told by Addison in the *Spectator* of 20 May 1712 had included the following passage: 'Sir ROGER obliged the Waterman to give us the History of his Right Leg, and hearing that he had left it at *La Hogue*, with many Particulars which passed in that glorious Action, the Knight in the Triumph of his Heart made several Reflections on the Greatness of the *British* Nation; as, that one Englishman could beat three *Frenchmen*; that we cou'd never be in Danger of Popery so long as we took care of our Fleet; that the *Thames* was the noblest River in *Europe*; that *London-Bridge* was a greater Piece of Work than any of the Seven Wonders of the World; with many other honest Prejudices which naturally cleave to the Heart of a true *Englishman*'.[68] Chesterfield calls the first of Sir Roger's reflections 'an instance of a common prejudice in this country, which is the result of error, and which yet I believe no man in his senses would desire should be exposed or removed'. For, so this justification of prejudice goes, unreason, well used, becomes reasonable.

The common man in England, Chesterfield suggests, 'is thoroughly convinced, as his forefathers were for many centuries, that one Englishman can beat three Frenchmen; and, in that persuasion, he would by no means decline the trial. Now, though in my own private opinion, deduced from physical principles, I am apt to believe that one Englishman could beat no more than two Frenchmen of equal strength and size with himself, I should however be very unwilling to undeceive him of that useful and sanguine error, which certainly made his countrymen triumph in the fields of Poictiers and Crecy'.[69] Though it is clear why Chesterfield calls the prejudice an error – on grounds of a prior examination, 'deduced from physical principles' – he clearly indicates a sense in which it is not an error, but a truth. In so far as the British soldiers actually won 'in the fields of Poictiers and Crecy', and in so far as the relevant proportion held true at these places, one Englishman *could* beat three Frenchmen. Furthermore their belief that they could played a causal role in bringing about this result: it 'made' them succeed.

73. But the example might reinforce a suspicion that may already have arisen when the external justification of prejudice was first expounded (§ 68). External justifications of prejudice assert that prejudices are good – for others. The justification is based on a knowledge that one does not want to impart, and if it is made public, then it is in the well-founded hope that not everybody will read it. If the soldier realized that his self-assurance was mere prejudice, he might start to doubt and even abandon it, and, as a consequence, the ruling

class could no longer use him so readily as cannon-fodder. Chesterfield certainly enlightens us; but he cannot intend to enlighten those he enlightens us about. For thus enlightened they would cease to function in the service of those others, like Chesterfield, who want to have them at their disposal. The consistent attitude of someone who has discovered how prejudices work to his own advantage, and approves of this relationship, seems to be to draw profit from one's own dishonesty. Chesterfield's lesson on how to exploit the nexus between confidence and the readiness to take risks seems to reveal something more general: External justifications of prejudice seem to be elitist and cynical.[70]

But we need to know whether external justifications of prejudice *are* inherently elitist and cynical, or whether they merely *can be* elitist and cynical, but need not be so. The first alternative would certainly have to be taken seriously, even though it is not in itself an argument. For elitism and cynicism might be acceptable; nothing has been put forward so far which shows that they are not. The second alternative – that external justifications of prejudice *can* be elitist and cynical – would be trivial. For beliefs and opinions can also be elitist and cynical; but that is hardly a reason for contending that we should not have beliefs or opinions.

Now external justifications of prejudice can be elitist, but they need not be so. They are elitist, whenever they presuppose, with approval, a hierarchy of social strata. This presupposition is, for instance, clearly present in Chesterfield's talk of 'the bulk' or 'the herd of mankind', or in the defence of prejudice that Frederick II, King of Prussia, presented in 1770 in the form of an attack on du Marsais: prejudices are the reason of the people.[71] Such talk is elitist in that it subjects the masses to what is claimed to be the deserved contempt of a superior caste.

But class or caste, the feature that incurs the suspicion of elitism, is only one sort of factor that may give rise to a difference between external and internal points of view. The difference between parents and children (§ 69), though it is, among other things, also a difference in social status and hence power, does not really incur that suspicion. To constitute a difference between external and internal points of view, a difference in *time* will do as well. When, face to face with the cathedral of Amiens, a friend asked Heine why no one was capable of creating such buildings today, he answered that the people of those times had convictions, while we moderns have merely opinions. But opinion, Heine added, was inadequate for the erection of a gothic cathedral.[72] Without the firm conviction of medieval men that they were building for God, cathedral architecture could never have achieved the heights it did. As an enlightened atheist, Heine thought of those Christian convictions as prejudices. So reflecting on the frame of mind that made the cathedrals possible, Heine arrived at an external recommendation of prejudice. Works of that kind required perseverance, and such perseverance presupposes the sort of tenacity peculiar to prejudices. The difference which makes the recommendation external is not the result of social stratification, but historical distance.

Perhaps we can still hear a tone of condescension in Heine's remarks, though it is not captured by the word 'elitism'. But there is an external justification of prejudice that presupposes neither social hierarchy nor any kind of patronage. It is based on the fact that there is a division of labour not only in what we do, but also in what we know. Every profession has first-hand experience of some things which other professions know about only at second hand. Although the professions can be in a hierarchy, they need not be. One expert can rely on another in one respect, and the other on the first in another respect, without their forming an order of merit. Neither of them is 'better'; they simply know different things. Therefore external justifications of prejudice need not be elitist or condescending.

74. The concept of cynicism is not as straightforward as those of elitism and condescension. Of course, we are not talking about the followers of Diogenes in this context.[73] The German language now appropriately distinguishes between 'kynisch' and 'zynisch', and it is patently the latter we are here concerned with. Even that is rather a vague idea, but one element of it is captured by the word 'contemptuous'. Now clearly using men as cannon-fodder is cynical in this sense. But again external justifications of prejudice need not be like that.

Imagine someone who believes that she is, in spite of minor discomforts, generally strong and healthy. Her doctor, however, knows that she has cancer. But the doctor does not object to the patient's belief. For he also knows that by virtue of that belief, the patient may master her disease. In such a case, the physician justifies a prejudice. We do not have to claim that this conduct shares *nothing* with a case of sending soldiers into battle exploiting their unfounded self-assurance. In both cases there is an asymmetry of knowledge that is consciously and deliberately upheld by the person superior in insight. Here as there, one party appears, to a degree, blindly obedient to the instruction of the other. The physician's behaviour is certainly paternalistic. But it is in no way contemptuous. We may perfectly consistently suppose that, should he ever get into the same situation, the physician would wish to be treated by others in the same way as he treats his patient and that this wish would not be

Rethinking Prejudice

the result of self-contempt. There would be nothing odd or even contradictory in such an attitude.

The concept of paternalism is of course derived from the relationship of a father to his child who again does not need to be cynical when he instils prejudices into the child's mind (§ 69). As long as the word 'cynicism' does not mean a genuine concern for the well-being of another human being – and surely this has not been the point that has bothered us here, though Diogenes's 'cynicism' emerged from such a concern – we have to conclude that external justifications of prejudice need not be cynical either.

Notes

1   Cf. Gadamer, *Wahrheit und Methode*, pp. 260, 264–7, 269–75.
2   III, xi, p. 338. Cf. Glanvill, *The Vanity of Dogmatizing*, p. 138.
3   Descartes, *Discours de la Méthode*, II,7, p. 18: 'Le premier était de ne recevoir jamais aucune chose pour vraie, que je ne la connusse évidemment être telle: c'est-à-dire, d'éviter soigneusement la précipitation et la prévention; et de ne comprendre rien de plus en mes jugements, que ce qui se présenterait si clairement et si distinctement à mon esprit, que je n'eusse aucune occasion de le mettre en doute'. Descartes wished, however, to exempt morality from this rule (cf. ibid., III, 1–3, pp. 22– 5; *Principia Philosophiae* I, 3, p. 5). La Bruyère seems to have been the first to suggest that we should extend Descartes' first rule of method from his domain, metaphysics and science, to our views of other human beings (*Les Caractères*, p. 24).
4   Arnauld and Nicole, *La Logique ou L'Art de penser*, I, 9, p. 107.
5   Burke, *Reflections*, p. 168; cf. § 10. Burke's argument was anticipated by Herder: '[W]enn man alle diese Bilder und Vorurtheile (praejudicata) als Vorurtheile (praeiudicia) und leere Idole zerstören will: so hat man freilich die leichte Arbeit der Gothen in Italien oder der Perser in Ägypten; allein man behält auch nichts als eine Wüste nach. Man hat sich eben damit selbst von der Beihülfe aller Jahrhunderte der Väter entblößet, und steht nackend da, um aus dem kleinen Haufen von Materialien, die man selbst zusammengetragen, und von willkührlichen Worten, die man etwa selbst untersuchet, ein Systemchen aufzuführen, das jenem Werk der Jahrhunderte so gleicht, als die kleinen Tempel, die die Verehrer der Diana sich machen ließen, dem grossen Wundergebäu zu Ephesus' (*Abhandlung über den Ursprung der Sprache*, p. 153).
6   Cf. Burke, *Reflections*, p. 79.
7   Cf. also Gibbon, *Memoirs*, p. 4: 'The Satirist may laugh, the Philosopher may preach: but reason herself will respect the prejudices and habits which have been consecrated by the experience of mankind'.
8   Burke, *A Philosophical Enquiry*, pp. 121–2.
9   Ibid., p. 122.
10 *Reflections*, p. 166.
11 Ibid., p. 76.
12 Ibid., p. 166.

13 'Speech on Moving his Resolutions', p. 81.
14 Burke, *Reflections*, p. 83.
15 Ibid., p. 169; cf. § 55.
16 Burke, *Reflections*, p. 169.
17 Burke stresses that a sound political constitution is not made up of 'the rights of man'; on the contrary, 'it is made by the *peculiar* circumstances, occasions, tempers, dispositions, and moral, civil, and social habitudes of the people' ('On the Reform of the Representation in the House of Commons', p. 97; emphasis added). Cf. *Reflections*, p. 36.
18 *Reflections*, p. 78. Cf. ibid., p. 65, and 'On the Reform of the Representation in the House of Commons', pp. 96–7.
19 *Reflections*, p. 168.
20 Ibid., p. 258.
21 Nietzsche, *Die fröhliche Wissenschaft*, § 34, p. 404: 'Es ist gar nicht abzusehen, was Alles einmal noch Geschichte sein wird'.
22 *Reflections*, p. 147.
23 *Reflections*, pp. 75, 119.
24 Ibid., pp. 55, 75–6, 78–81, 83–4, 166–7, 181, 183–5, 436–7.
25 *Essai sur les mœurs et l'esprit des nations*, ch. lxxxv, p. 79: 'C'est donc une idée bien vaine, un travail bien ingrat, de vouloir tout rappeler aux usages antiques, et de vouloir fixer cette roue que le temps fait tourner d'un mouvement irrésistible'.
26 *Dialogue between a Philosopher and a Student of the Common Laws of England*, p. 86.
27 Ibid.
28 Ch. xlviii, p. 580.
29 *Reflections*, pp. 102, 104, 113, 163.
30 Ibid., pp. 30, 60–1, 65–6, 81–5, 181–5.
31 *Rousseau juge de Jean Jaques*, p. 728.
32 'On the Reform of the Representation in the House of Commons', p. 96.
33 Whately, *Elements of Rhetoric,* p. 114; cf. § 76. A stronger conservative position doubts in advance that there could be any convincing argument for change, *e.g.* Montaigne, 'De la præsumption' [= *Essais* II, 17], p. 655: 'Et pourtant, selon mon humeur, és affaires publiques, il n'est aucun si mauvais train, pourveu qu'il aye de l'aage et de la constance, qui ne vaille mieux que le changement et le remuement'.
34 'A Representation to his Majesty', p. 136.
35 de Maistre, *Essai sur le principe générateur des constitutions politiques*, xxxviii, p. 274: 'Pour brûler une ville, il ne faut qu'un enfant ou un insensé; pour la rebâtir, il faut des architectes, des matériaux, des ouvriers, des millions, et surtout du temps'.
36 p. 303.
37 'De la vanité' [= *Essais* III,9], p. 959: 'le plus vieil et mieux cogneu mal est tousjours plus supportable que le mal recent et inexperimenté'.
38 *Reflections*, p. 125.
39 *Manifest der Kommunistischen Partei*, p. 465: 'Die Bourgeoisie kann nicht existieren, ohne die Produktionsinstrumente, also die Produktionsverhältnisse, also sämtliche gesellschaftlichen Verhältnisse fortwährend zu revolutionieren. Unveränderte Beibehaltung der alten Produktionsweise war dagegen die erste Existenzbedingung aller früheren industriellen Klassen. Die fortwährende Umwälzung der Produktion, die ununterbrochene Erschütterung aller gesellschaftlichen Zustände, die ewige Unsicherheit und Bewegung zeichnet die Bourgeoisepoche vor allen früheren aus. Alle festen eingerosteten Verhältnisse mit ihrem Gefolge von altehrwürdigen Vorstellungen und Anschauungen werden aufgelöst,

alle neugebildeten veralten, ehe sie verknöchern können. Alles Ständische und Stehende verdampft'. The dissolution of 'ancient and venerable ideas and opinions' which Marx and Engels are happy to witness *is* of course precisely the loss of prejudices and 'pleasing illusions' lamented by Burke: 'All the decent drapery of life is to be rudely torn off. All the superadded ideas, furnished from the wardrobe of a moral imagination, which the heart owns, and the understanding ratifies, as necessary to cover the defects of our naked, shivering nature, and to raise it to dignity in our own estimation, are to be exploded as a ridiculous, absurd, and antiquated fashion' (*Reflections*, p. 151). The same phenomenon is seen as historically transient by Marx and Engels, but as a perpetual requirement of human nature by Burke; this accounts for the difference in valuation.

40 *Reflections*, p. 59.
41 Ibid., p. 436.
42 'Letter to William Smith, 29 January 1795', p. 404.
43 Burke, *Reflections*, p. 176.
44 'There is another Humour, which may be observ'd in some Pretenders to Wisdom, and which, if not so pernicious as the idle petulant Humour above-mention'd, must, however, have a very bad Effect on those, who indulge it. I mean that grave philosophic Endeavour after Perfection, which, under the Pretext of reforming Prejudices and Errors, strikes at all the most endearing Sentiments of the Heart, and all the most useful Byasses and Instincts, which can govern a human Creature. The *Stoics* were remarkable for this Folly among the Antients; and I wish some of more venerable Characters in latter Times had not copy'd them too faithfully in this Particular. The virtuous and tender Sentiments, or Prejudices, if you will, have suffer'd mightily by these Reflections; while a certain sullen Pride or Contempt of Mankind has prevail'd in their Stead, and has been esteem'd the greatest Wisdom; tho' in Reality, it be the most egregious Folly of all others' (p. 371). For utility as justification of prejudice, cf. Voltaire's poem 'Il est des préjugés utiles', in his 'Lettre à Théodore Tronchin', p. 158.
45 p. 258.
46 p. 169. There is clearly a tension between this qualification of prejudice by 'just' and the assertion that the British value prejudices as such: 'we cherish them because they are prejudices' (p. 68; cf. § 55).
47 'Of the Standard of Taste', p. 277.
48 *De carne Christi*, 5. For an attempted rationalization of Tertullian's idea cf. Augustine's comparison of the stories of Jonah and Arion. Jonah, the Bible says, was swallowed by a 'great fish' and vomited out after three days (Jonah 2.1); Arion, having thrown himself overboard from a ship, according to a pagan myth, was safely supported by a dolphin which had been charmed by his music, and carried to the shore (Herodotus 1.23). 'Verum illud nostrum de Iona propheta incredibilius est. Plane incredibilius, quia mirabilius, et mirabilius quia potentius' (*De civitate Dei* I,14, p. 66). But if it is more incredible only because it is more miraculous, and more miraculous only because it manifests a greater power, then, Augustine suggests, it is ultimately more credible: hence 'Plane'. In other words, to quote Bayle's taunting phrase, with an omnipotent God among your premises, the more impossible a thing appears to be, the more credible it is ('il résulteroit de là que plus une chose paroit impossible, plus est elle digne de croiance') (Art. 'Jonas', p. 465). Cf. also Locke, *Essay*, IV,xviii,11, vol. III, p. 147.
49 Pascal, *Pensées*, frgm. 744*-926* (Lafuma), p. 409: 'Lorsqu'on ne sait pas la vérité d'un chose il est bon qu'il y ait une error commune qui fixe l'esprit des hommes comme par

exemple la lune à qui on attribue le changement des saisons, le progrès des maladies, etc.'.
Cf. frgm. 745*–926*, ibid.
50 Cf. Périer, 'Mémoire', pp. 59–61.
51 Chesterfield, 'Letter to his son, 7 February 1749', p. 1307.
52 *Essai sur les Préjugés*, vol. I, p. 23: 'il n'est point de préjugé qui ne produise tôt ou tard les
   effets les plus nuisibles et les plus étendus'; p. 43: 'il n'est point de préjugé qui n'ait des
   suites plus ou moins terribles pour la société'.
53 *Logik*, p. 511: 'Auch sucht man das Stehenlassen der Vorurteile damit zu entschuldigen,
   daß aus ihrer Ausrottung Nachteile entstehen würden. Aber man lasse diese Nachteile nur
   immer zu; – in der Folge werden sie desto mehr Gutes bringen'.
54 *The Vanity of Dogmatizing*, pp. 125–6; cf. Locke, *Essay*, IV, xx, 9, vol. III, pp. 165–6.
55 Hutcheson, *Inquiry concerning Beauty, Order, Harmony, Design*, VII,4, p. 85.
56 *Of the Conduct of the Understanding*, § 12, p. 231.
57 Ibid., p. 232.
58 *Table Talk*, p. 181.
59 Sailer, *Vernunftlehre*, p. 108: 'Auch die wichtigsten Wahrheiten, die die Kinder auf das
   Vaterwort hin glauben, sind im Grunde für Kinder Vorurtheile. Denn sie glauben nicht,
   weil sie die Wahrheiten einsehen, sondern weil sie der Vater für Wahrheiten ausgiebt. Also
   sind nicht alle Vorurtheile der Kinderstube giftige Pflanzen. Also giebt es heilsame
   Vorurtheile'.
60 Barbauld, 'On prejudice', pp. 323–4, 334–5.
61 Cf. ibid., p. 332: 'Without this principle of assent he [*sc.* a child] could never gain even the
   rudiments of knowledge'.
62 § 46, p. 36.
63 Reynolds, 'Notes on "The Art of Painting"', pp. 148–9. Apart from his argument from
   learning, Reynolds also defended prejudice, and with much more determination, on grounds
   of an aesthetics of taste, see his *Discourses on Art*, pp. 156, 180–82, 184.
64 Goethe might have had something like that in mind when he wrote in 1823: 'so läßt sich
   ein außerordentlicher Geist denken, der nicht allein irrt, sondern sogar Lust am Irrtum hat'
   (*Maximen und Reflexionen*, p. 531).
65 *Reflections*, p. 168. In a remarkable way, Burke assimilated his pre*judices* to pre*dilections*,
   or rather what would be the negative class corresponding to this term, as it were, to his
   'pre-aversions': 'The dislike I feel to revolutions' (ibid., p. 65), 'The very idea of the
   fabrication of a new government is enough to fill us with disgust and horror' (ibid., p. 75).
66 Cf. Nietzsche, *Menschliches, Allzumenschliches* I, § 34, pp. 53–5.
67 Virgil, *Aeneid*, V, l. 231, vol. II, p. 460.
68 No. 383, p. 198.
69 Chesterfield, 'On Prejudices', p. 260. As we should expect, Chesterfield believed that *some*
   prejudices are false, while some are true. Ibid., p. 257: 'A prejudice is by no means, though
   generally thought so, an error. On the contrary, it may be a most unquestioned truth, though
   it be still a prejudice in those who, without any examination, take it upon trust and entertain
   it by habit'.
70 Cf. Wieland, 'Etwas über die Vorurtheile überhaupt', p. 147. Riem, 'Ueber Aufklärung', p.
   315.
71 Anonymus [*i.e.*, Friedrich II., 'der Große'], *Examen de l'essai sur les préjugés*, p. 8: 'Les
   préjugés sont la raison du peuple'. Friedrich at once borrowed and, in a characteristic way,
   deviated from Voltaire; cf. Voltaire's 'Poëme sur la loi naturelle', pt. IV, p. 460: 'les préjugés

sont la raison des sots'. Friedrich's reasoning, supposed to save the common man from Enlightenment, was attacked by Diderot: 'Lettre sur l'Examen de l'essai sur les préjugés'.

72 Heine, 'Über die französische Bühne', p. 279: 'Als ich jüngst mit einem Freunde vor der Kathedrale zu Amiens stand, und mein Freund dieses Monument von felsenthürmender Riesenkraft und unermüdlich schnitzelnder Zwergsgeduld mit Schrecken und Mitleiden betrachtete, und mich endlich frug: wie es komme, daß wir heut zu Tage keine solchen Bauwerke mehr zu Stande bringen? antwortete ich ihm: "Theurer Alphonse, die Menschen in jener alten Zeit hatten Ueberzeugungen, wir Neueren haben nur Meinungen, und es gehört etwas mehr als eine bloße Meinung dazu, um so einen gothischen Dom aufzurichten"'.

73 Ancient cynicism was moral iconoclasm of prejudices. This meaning is still present in the younger Schlegel: 'Es giebt auch einen *moralischen* Witz, dessen Tendenz ist cynisch, nämlich zur Vertilgung der Vorurtheile' (*Philosophische Lehrjahre* I, p. 378).

Chapter Five

On Morality, Sadism, and Related Matters, or How to See that Prejudice is not to be Dispensed with

75. We have seen that the contradiction apparently inherent in the recommendation of prejudice (§ 65) can be circumvented (§§ 66–74). There may of course still be doubt about the particular advantages attributed to prejudices in the above arguments. For some of them involve predictions and statements of facts. But an examination of these is not the issue here. The issue is whether it is inconsistent to recommend prejudice in those ways, and there is no reason to think that it is. If such recommendations are ever flawed they are so on different grounds.

All justifications of prejudice, however, will be mere *ad hoc*-constructions, if the Enlightenment succeeded – as some of its exponents have claimed – in establishing a critical standard to condemn prejudice. The apologies are built on sand, if there is a clear, general answer to the question: What's wrong with prejudice?

Several answers were found wanting above. But John Locke assures us that he is offering the 'one mark whereby prejudice may be known. He that is strongly of any opinion must suppose (unless he be self-condemned) that his persuasion is built upon good grounds; and that his assent is no greater than what the evidence of the truth he holds forces him to; and that they are arguments, and not inclination, or fancy, that make him so confident and positive in his tenets. Now if, after all his profession, he cannot bear any opposition to his opinion, if he cannot so much as give a patient hearing, much less examine and weigh the arguments on the other side, does he not plainly confess it is prejudice governs him? and it is not the evidence of truth, but some lazy anticipation, some beloved presumption, that he desires to rest undisturbed in. For, if what he holds be, as he gives out, well fenced with evidence, and he sees it to be true, what need he fear to put it to the proof? If his opinion be settled upon a firm foundation, if the arguments that support it, and have obtained his assent, be clear, good, and convincing, why should he be shy to have it tried whether they be proof or not? He whose assent goes beyond this evidence, owes this excess of his adherence only to prejudice, and does in effect own it, when he refuses to hear what is offered against it; declaring thereby that it is not evidence he seeks, but the quiet enjoyment of the opinion he is fond of, with a forward condemnation of all that may stand in opposition to it, unheard and unexamined; which, what is it but prejudice?'.[1]

Locke's analysis shares some features with criticisms of prejudice that have been considered earlier and have turned out to be unsuccessful. But it contains an element that goes beyond them. For Locke to call something a prejudice is not yet warranted if it is just unexamined. Certainly also on Locke's account, a prejudiced person is more interested in his belief than in truth. (Locke does not employ the term 'interest', but he calls the biased man's presumption 'beloved', contends 'that he desires to rest undisturbed in' it, and that 'he seeks [...] the quiet enjoyment of the opinion he is fond of"; and these attitudes are either themselves cases of what can be called interest, or at least they indicate that an interest is involved.) Consequently, a prejudiced person is unable to reconsider her belief in a disinterested way. But it is also the case that sound minds do not reconsider many of their beliefs; therefore the crucial indication whether a belief is a prejudice or not is given by the negative case, when the holder of the belief faces opposition to it, but cannot stand it. For something to be a prejudice, in Locke's view, it is not enough that it be second hand, or that the reasons *in favour of* it are weak. Locke's positive and promising point is that a refusal to consider the arguments *against* it makes it a prejudice. Presenting our objections to someone who has taken his stand, we assume that we can get in through a door, but what we believed to be a door turns out to be a wall: this is what, according to Locke, proves the stand taken to involve a prejudice.

If this point could be vindicated, it might even be strong enough to reestablish some version of the claim that recommendations of prejudices are contradictory (§ 65) – or at least what has been termed 'internal' recommendations of prejudice (§ 71). For a person cannot consciously be prejudiced in Locke's sense, *i.e.*, resist the correction of her beliefs in full self-awareness. (This is to draw a consequence from, rather than to interpret Locke's text; but at least the phrases 'he cannot so much as give a patient hearing', 'to rest undisturbed', and the word 'quiet' in the phrase 'the quiet enjoyment of the opinion he is fond of' are instructive.) To be prejudiced in the sense of resisting the correction of one's beliefs cannot be a conscious act, because it would be a contradiction to hold a certain belief and to admit at the same time that the opposite belief is based on stronger reasons. For in the extreme case that would mean to concede that the opposite belief is true. But that is impossible, for no one can *hold* a belief and believe at the same time that this belief is false. Beliefs aim at truth: To say 'I believe that so and so' carries a claim that 'so and so' is true. To believe that so and so is one and the same as to believe that that thing is true. Therefore the extreme case, imagined as a case of full self-awareness, would simply mean that the person would begin to hold the belief opposed to the one she used to hold. But if the prejudices cannot be conscious *qua prejudices* in Locke's sense (though trivially their content has to be conscious), then the factors which have given rise to them cannot be conscious *qua such factors* either.[2]

The factors giving rise to prejudices were above identified as interests. Of course I can be, and often am, aware of the fact that I have certain interests. Furthermore, even the fact that a belief is combined with an interest does not make it a prejudice; such a suggestion neither reflects Locke's criterion nor offers a tenable criterion for prejudices – quite apart from questions of exegesis. For these two things clearly do not preclude each other: that I am interested in a belief, and that, as I have found out, there are good, or even the best reasons for it. The point is that the answer to the question why I stick to the belief has to refer to these reasons, not to the interest. Hence I can be aware that I have an interest in a belief; but I cannot knowingly stick to a certain belief only because I have got an interest in it.

76. We criticized Gadamer above for obscuring the distinction between prejudice and presumption (§ 49). As a matter of terminology, it is evident that Locke does not intend to distinguish these terms either. His phrase 'some beloved presumption' is used interchangeably with 'some beloved prejudice'.[3] (Again, he obviously does not wish to separate prejudice from anticipation.)[4] Locke's reason for introducing the term 'presumption' may well be stylistic variation. But, terminology apart, Locke's systematic contribution seems to allow us precisely to draw a dividing line between prejudice and presumption (cf. §§ 61, 64).

As the common prefix indicates, presumptions share with prejudices that they are made in advance (cf. § 1). But whereas people who hold a certain prejudice are convinced that what they hold is true, presuming rules out knowledge. Furthermore, according to the line taken by Locke, prejudices try to remain impervious to refutation; presumptions, on the other hand, signal that they can be contested and overturned. They are tentative; a working hypothesis, for instance, may well be introduced by the remark 'Let us presume that ...'. A presumption is recognized as defeasible, though the one who makes it believes that it has not been defeated.

Like prejudice, presumption was originally a legal term.[5] Unlike prejudice, however, the domain of presumption is the law of evidence. "A presumption' means a rule of law that Courts and judges shall draw a particular inference from a particular fact, or from particular evidence, unless and until the truth of such inference is disproved'.[6] The model example is the presumption of innocence in the courtroom: 'quilibet praesumatur bonus, donec probetur contrarium', 'innocent until proved guilty'. The phrase 'until proved guilty', on the one hand, marks the difference from prejudices as Locke conceives them; for the latter are said to be maintained even when it has been shown that the opposite of what they claim is true. On the other hand, the presumption of innocence is upheld, and bound to be upheld, until the accused has been finally convicted, even if none believes him to be innocent and if there is in fact plenty of evidence at hand that he is not. Does this remove the difference between a presumption and a prejudice, as Locke describes it?

The rationale for the presumption of innocence is not that, as a matter of fact, people who have been put on trial have usually been found to be innocent. The opposite may very well be true; as a matter of fact, people who are committed for trial (though *presumed* to be innocent) are *presumably* guilty. Insofar a *praesumptio juris*, very much like a prejudice as portrayed by Locke, is sustained in the presence of contrary evidence. But this seeming likeness of presumption and prejudice is only fit to draw our attention to a more fundamental difference between them. While Locke wants to alert us to a contradiction between the prejudiced person's beliefs and the available evidence this person stubbornly ignores, there is no contradiction between the presumption of innocence in the courtroom and the evidence already available that the defendant is not innocent; for the presumption does not make a point of fact at all, but a point of procedure, though the procedure may of course also be one for arguing about facts. A presumption is generally defined as 'such a *pre-occupation* of the ground, as implies that it must stand good till some sufficient reason is adduced against it; in short that the *Burden of proof* lies on the side of him who would dispute it'.[7] The point of a presumption, in general, is that parties to an argument are not all equally under obligation to prove their respective cases; the point of the presumption of innocence in particular is that it places the *onus probandi* on the prosecution (the plaintiff in civil cases, or the state, as surrogate plaintiff, in criminal cases), not on the defence.

So the presumption of innocence in the courtroom 'does not [...] mean that we are to *take for granted* he is innocent; for if that were the case, he would be entitled to immediate liberation: nor does it mean that it is antecedently *more likely than not* that he is innocent; or, that the majority of these brought to trial are so'.[8] If the rationale of this procedural norm is not a statistic showing that the average defendant is innocent, why, then, is a defendant presumed to be innocent? Let us consider this presumption in the light of its consequences.

To have a presumption on one's side is an advantage to the extent that defence is in general less exacting than attack. 'A body of troops may be perfectly adequate to the defence of a fortress against any attack that may be made on it; and yet, if ignorant of the advantage they possess, they sally forth into the open field to encounter the enemy, they may suffer a repulse. At any rate, even if strong enough to act on the offensive, they ought still to keep possession of their fortress. In like manner, if you have the 'Presumption' on your side, and can but *refute* all the arguments brought against you, you have, for the present at least, gained a victory: but if you abandon this position, by suffering this Presumption to be forgotten, which is in fact *leaving out one of, perhaps, your strongest arguments*, you may appear to be making a feeble attack, instead of a triumphant defense'.[9]

While it can be hard to demonstrate someone's guilt, it can be even harder for an innocent person to prove that she is innocent; after all, she has to talk about something that does not exist. 'Qui s'excuse, s'accuse': the actual effect could easily be the opposite of what was intended. 'Let any one imagine a perfectly unsupported accusation of some offence to be brought against himself; and then let him imagine himself – instead of replying (as of course he would do) by a simple denial, and a defiance of his accuser to prove the charge – setting himself to establish a negative – taking on himself the burden of proving his own innocence, by collecting all the circumstances indicative of it that he can muster: and the result would be, in many cases, that this evidence would fall far short of establishing a certainty, and might even have the effect of raising a suspicion against him; he having in fact kept out of sight the important circumstance, that these probabilities in one scale, though of no great weight perhaps in themselves, are to be weighed against absolutely nothing in the other scale'.[10]

Therefore, if innocence is presumed – *i.e.*, if the burden of proof rests with the accusers, not the accused – fewer persons standing trial will be convicted than would under the presumption of guilt. Hence fewer of the guilty will be punished, but so will be fewer of the innocent. Those who are not guilty are comparatively well secured against unwarranted punishment; but a number of those who have committed crimes but cannot be proved to have done so will go unpunished. Conversely, if guilt is presumed – *i.e.*, if the burden of proof is with the defence – more of the guilty will be convicted than would be under the presumption of innocence. Courts will be more effective in punishing the guilty, but at the same time they will also penalize more of those who have not committed the crimes they are arraigned for. We are thus left with two sets of consequences, and have to make a choice. 'It is better for ten guilty persons to escape than that one innocent suffer', wrote the most famous of English jurists, William Blackstone, in 1770.[11] 'Better' and 'worse' is made the yardstick here, while the idea we had to reject – a retrospective empirical survey of persons brought to court – was based on the thought that since it is a question of truth or falsity whether someone has committed an offence against law or not, presumptions of innocence or guilt must be a matter of truth and falsity, too. The presumption of innocence in the courtroom is based on fear of unjust conviction, *i.e.*, on something we *want* (in this case: something we want to avoid), rather than on something we *know*. But just as one can want many different things, so one can presume many things. The presumption of innocence is by no means necessarily true. A judicial system could be based on the presumption of guilt in the courtroom if, contrary to Blackstone, the interest that not one guilty should escape was found more important than the interest that the innocent should not suffer. Perhaps many judicial systems before the 18th century were like that, requiring the accused to prove their innocence.

The reason for choosing one presumption rather than another, then, is a conscious and explicit interest, a goal that one wishes to achieve. Now it has often been claimed that prejudices are based on interests, too (cf. § 75), but – and this makes all the difference – on interests which one would not avow, even to oneself. If, then, I were to say that the reason for choosing my prejudices (an odd phrase in itself!) was a certain interest, a goal that I wished to achieve, this would be tantamount to saying that they are merely wishful thinking (cf., however, §§ 71–72). Clearly I cannot admit that my reason for claiming that negroes lack intelligence is that I want to keep them in a low social position; rather, I must tell the story, if at all, the other way round: they should only do menial jobs because they are stupid.

77. Prejudices, unlike expectations or anticipations in general, are resistant to correction: this is the criterion proposed by Locke (§ 75). Though it has already shown up in the preceding discussion (§ 49), it has not yet been turned to account. It is worth noting, for a start, that an odd temporal logic has been attributed to prejudices. They have been characterized as hasty *and* lasting. The first aspect relates to the way prejudices come about, the second to the way they are held. Descartes may have had both aspects in mind when, in his

first rule of method, he distinguished, as well as connected, 'précipitation' and 'prévention'.[12] Prejudices are said to be formed quickly; but once they are there they turn out to be very persistent entities.[13] There are good reasons for doubting the former claim; the explanation of prejudice it involves is not tenable (§ 23). The latter claim, on the other hand, seems to be sound. Given what we have learnt about prejudices, can we account for their persistence?

Prejudice towards a class of people, we have seen, can be understood neither as incompatible with experience of them, nor as defined by insufficient experience of them; rather, prejudice determines what kind of experience someone is going to have with regard to these people (§ 19). If, as du Marsais had suggested, there was only prejudice where there was no experience (§ 2), we should expect that, as soon as experience enters, prejudice will disappear. Even on the account of prejudice as hasty generalization (§ 22) we should expect that as soon as more instances of a given class are experienced, one would become aware of one's hastiness and correct the generalization. It has in fact been argued that prejudice must vanish as soon as prejudiced persons are exposed to their targets.[14] But experience is not independent of the judgements available to a person. It presupposes thoughts, and would not exist without them. No experience simply mirrors reality 'as it is'. Not even the proceedings of empirical science constitute a counter-instance to this claim. Physics, setting up experiments to find out the properties of atomic particles 'by experience', started from an assumption which it owed to thought rather than any allegedly immediate experience: the assumption that there are atoms. Newton was convinced of the existence of forces, as presupposed in his law of universal gravitation, not because he had seen them, but because he believed that to deny them was to deny God; experimental research was then conducted on the basis of that presupposition, but it did not establish it in the first place.

Experience, scientific as well as common, is a result of discriminating essential from inessential aspects of reality. But reality does not supply us with this distinction. No one thing is more real than another. It is our judgement that links events together, so that they amount to an experience. Without judgement, we would arrive only at scattered notes aiming at an ever unattainable completeness. We would not reach what deserves the name experience. Hence to be based on judgements is not a defect of certain experiences. It is a constituent of all experience. William Hazlitt believed good prejudices could, at least very probably, be discerned from bad ones through the criterion of immediate sense experience: 'If I take a prejudice against a person from his face, I shall very probably be in the right; if I take a prejudice against a person from hearsay, I shall quite as probably be in the wrong'.[15] But the immediacy Hazlitt ascribes to the former case is illusory. Our way of seeing faces as, for instance, the faces of strangers or of those of our own tribe, is mediated through distinctions whose source amounts to no more than hearsay.

Experience is the person's judged confrontation with the world around him. We do not perceive an abstract spectrum of colours, but identify something at once as, *e.g.*, a garden. In a similar way, someone experiences 'German' or 'Jewish' people. As long as he has not revised his false belief about them (supposing that it is false which a prejudice need not be (§ 46)), it operates as his standard in experiencing the world. It is this feature which accounts for the persistence of prejudices. Prejudiced persons are notoriously able to incorporate new information into their prejudices. In this respect they are flexible and inflexible at the same time: flexible in their techniques of sustaining prejudice, and inflexible with respect to the prejudice itself.

The former aspect, flexibility, prevents us from regarding the prejudiced simply as dull or primitive. Actually, they can be quite sophisticated. We also have reason to oppose the *second* half of du Marsais's statement that a prejudiced person has neither experience nor reason ('n'a ni expérience ni raison').[16] Contrary to the conventional opposition of prejudice and reason, it seems that the more adroit someone is at reasoning, the more dangerous are his prejudices. When philosophers hold a prejudice, Fontenelle says, it is more difficult to cure them of it than it would be to cure ordinary people; for they not only stick to the prejudice itself, but also to the reasons they have constructed to support it.[17]

But even where prejudice is dull and primitive, we are not simply confronting a visceral state[18] that precedes all reason and resists all logical accounting. The most grotesque irrationalities of prejudice still have their meaning, their rules, their progression, and even their logic. Prejudice is, in particular, master of the logic of exception. It claims that exception proves the rule and never lapses into the hopeless venture of explaining how.[19] By avoiding this risky business, prejudice eludes the challenge that what it calls exceptions, far from confirming the old rule, may be early signs of a new rule, or even indicate that the relevant state of affairs is not governed by a rule at all.

Gustave Flaubert, in his *Dictionnaire des idées reçues*, gave examples of the logic of prejudice. When English women are mentioned as a topic of conversation, this sarcastic collection of prejudices recommends the reader to express surprise that some of them could have pretty children; when someone mentions negroes, correspondingly, it would be appropriate to express one's amazement that a number of them have been able to learn French.[20] Prejudice is not bound to generalization without exception. The last thing prejudiced people want to be is dogmatic; contempt for dogmatists is itself one of their major dogmas.[21] In admitting exceptions, the prejudiced man of modern times shows himself as humane and capable of learning – though of course not of learning that he should give up his prejudices. Rather, exceptions are their permanent confirmation; the constant argument to silence objections is: 'Still there are a few good ones all the same'. 'There are some decent people everywhere' insinuates: 'even in that group which otherwise is really worthless'. 'You are not like the others' is a variation on the refrain 'Basically they are all alike'. The willingness to differentiate is really a vehicle of intransigence. There is hardly a nationalist who could not refer to one 'good' foreigner; in fact some of his best friends are foreigners and this not only shows how scrupulously he thinks, but entitles him to issue his indictment against further infiltration of the country by foreigners.

There are of course other techniques for sustaining prejudice. The logic of rule and exception is often supplemented by a reference to *essence* (§ 33). Counterexamples never discourage an anti-Semite, because he is speaking of the 'nature' of 'the Jew'. If he gives examples himself they are supposed to illustrate this nature rather than to validate a general theory by empirical data. Nods and winks therefore seem integral to prejudiced discourse. The incidents mustered concerning 'the Jew', stories of fraud, seduction and infanticide that have varied but little for centuries, are not seriously meant as independent information upon which the case can be built; they merely illustrate once more what is already understood. They are anecdotes, not evidence.

But even where something is considered as evidence, we must recall that any evidence is evidence only if interpreted as such. Hence what would other-wise constitute counterevidence, actually becomes further supporting evidence for prejudice. We are thus confronted with reasoning of the following sort:

(1) Jews are deceitful.
(2) This man is a Jew.
(3) I have no grounds for believing that this man is deceitful.
(4) Hence, he is such a clever deceiver that even I do not realize how deceitful he is.
(5) The more decent a Jew appears, the more deceitful he is.

(The hope that prejudices will disappear when refuted is thus idle. The very notion of refutation is more intricate than assumed in such hope. What makes particular sorts of prejudices disappear is basically that they go out of fashion.)[22]

The common factor in these and similar techniques is that they display cleverness and stubbornness at the same time. Neither of these aspects could be explained if prejudice was based merely on lack of experience (§§ 2, 18) or incomplete experience (§ 22). They become intelligible if prejudice is rather a way of looking at things. For if I go on looking in the same way, even what is different will not force me to correct myself; rather, the way of looking will adapt it to itself.

78. We have seen that prejudices are attended by certain techniques to uphold them. In addition, some of the examples have made it clear that unwillingness to revise one's views in the light of contrary evidence can be irrational. (In this respect, prejudice mirrors authority which, as some Enlightenment writers have pointed out, is often its source (§ 6). Many societies have set up institutional devices for covering up failure so that the ruling authority *cannot* be wrong.)

What is not clear, however, is that an unwillingness to revise one's views in the light of contrary evidence *must* be irrational. Rather, there seem to be cases where it can be highly rational. Galilei declared how deeply he admired Copernicus who courageously insisted on the truth of his theory by deliberately ignoring, *i.a.*, the evidence from the brightness of Mars.[23] The sensible enquirer hangs on to a scientific theory in the face of conflicting evidence until he has a better *theory* (not just conflicting data) – and he is justified in doing so because the old theory allows him to make predictions which he could not make without it. Therefore resistance to correction cannot serve as a criterion responding to the question 'What's wrong with prejudice?'. The followers of Locke owe us a further criterion to determine under which circumstances it is wrong to be resistant to correction.

Of course this consideration does not do away with the evidence that resistance to correction may be a feature of prejudices. But that evidence does not establish that resistance to correction is the *criterion* of prejudice. For a criterion is more than a feature. It is a feature that enables us to single out a certain thing, or kind of thing, among other things, or kinds of things. Locke's proposal (§ 75) is supposed to do even more. The identification provided by his 'mark' is meant to be at the same time the recognition of a mistake. The criterion is supposed to answer two questions, both 'What is prejudice?' and 'What's wrong with prejudice?'.

But a twofold further reflection confirms that, as a criterion to determine the wrongness of prejudice, 'resistance to correction' fails. First of all, resistance as such neither proves that something is correct nor that it is incorrect. Perhaps our interlocutor is simply persistent. Whether someone is hard or soft in presenting a view cannot be a standard to assess its validity. Secondly, wrongness is simply presupposed in stating the criterion as 'resistance *to correction*'. What stands in need of correction is of course wrong. But this is to beg the question. For our question was: What's wrong with prejudice? The present answer comes down to: the fact that it is wrong (and does not stop being so). This answer instantiates what has been shown to be a false conception of prejudice held by some Enlightenment authors (§ 46).

79. The logical circularity of the proposal that has been considered, is, however, only a superficial aspect of a deeper and more substantive issue. We become aware of it as soon as we think about what it would be like *not* to be resistant to correction. Someone would *not* be resistant to correction if he was prepared to put (in principle each and every one of) his ideas to the test.[24] An enlightened world, which had accomplished its purpose of doing away with all prejudices, would be a world in which everything had been on the agenda.

Of course there is the pragmatic objection that we have neither time nor energy to put everything on the agenda (cf. the parallel, though not identical, objection in §§ 10, 12–13). But at this stage of the argument such an objection rather misses the point. For it presupposes that it would in principle be desirable to put everything on the agenda, whilst lamenting our lack of time and energy to do so. Considering where our reasoning has now arrived, it is precisely this presupposition of desirability that has to be called into question.

We take it to be an evil prejudice that the Australian Aborigines are subhuman. If the evil of prejudice consisted in its resistance to correction, we might easily conclude that what was wrong with this particular prejudice was that the individual who holds it had not gone to Australia, and had not subjected a representative group of Aborigines to experiments suitable to test his thesis.

But the evil of the prejudice does not lie in *this* omission. Indeed, it seems that the procedure which is supposed to remedy the prejudice might be worse than the prejudice itself, for it suggests transforming this very prejudice, a mere belief, into an action. Instead of merely holding an offensive view of Aborigines, the person is to go one step further and intervene in an insulting way in their lives.

On the other hand what we take to be the only decent view of Australian Aborigines is not one we would be willing to 'check' or 'put to the test', either. For that would require more or less the same offensive intervention in their lives. After all the issue is the same, and the claims are only distinguished in that one of them affirms what the other denies. But if the decent view is a prejudice, too, we have to conclude that racial prejudice has to be rejected, not because it is a prejudice, but because it is racist.

The problem of prejudice is a problem of order:[25] first things first, second things second, and not the other way round. To criticize something as prejudice, then, can be a fatal understatement in so far as it bears the implication that what was done before, should have been done afterwards, and if done afterwards, it would be in order. Our objection to Nazi anti-Semitism is not, or should not be, that the Nazis unfortunately did not do more empirical research on the behaviour of Jews – as if, had they done such research, we would have had to agree with them.

80. 'Racial prejudice has to be rejected, not because it is a prejudice, but because it is racist' (§ 79): Why, then, has it been so frequently rejected on the ground that it is a prejudice?

The attraction of this move is not hard to discern. It would allow to solve moral problems without much moral ado, that is, by a plain point about cognition: the person concerned has judged prematurely, instead of waiting for enough evidence to become available. The economy of thus transforming a whole complex of ethical problems into one apparently simple problem of epistemology is admirable. But the objection we are left with, once this transformation has been brought about, is not strong enough. In fact it plays down phenomena like racism. Of course these *are* prejudices. But that they are prejudices is a common feature they share with a host of innocuous and even reasonable attitudes. Hence the critical standard has to be derived from elsewhere: if the relevant phenomena can be criticized at all, there is no substitute for a genuine moral stance.

81. One logical as well as historical consequence of rejecting prejudice altogether, it has been suggested, would be to subject all human behaviour to scientific scrutiny and run it through a process of experimental testing. An example showed that this consequence might be undesirable (§ 79). But is the example conclusive, at least up to the point to which examples can be so at all? One might object that the claim about the Australian Aborigines is an evaluative one, for which there are no tests. Obviously, when the term 'subhuman' is employed, everything depends on a normative definition of what it is to be human. According to the chosen definition, any claim one cares to make could easily be proved or disproved. But in that case any additional experimental procedure would plainly be redundant.

This is true, but it does not affect the crucial point. For the point holds also in cases which are clearly empirical and decidable on the basis of scientific tests. It is, for instance, empirically not altogether impossible that human beings could be made less sensitive to pain, and thus even more efficient in warfare, if only they were tortured for a little while as babies. Though it would of course be a mere prejudice to believe that this is the case, assuming that no one has ever tested it, the same would obviously, on the same assumption, be true of the opposite belief. If lack of empirical support is a deficiency in the one case, it must also be so in the other. In so far as these are both questions of what is known, the same standards apply in each case. But, while it is clear that an unprejudiced view must require the test, the only humane intuition is that such torture must not take place. For, from the circumstance that the question is empirical and decidable on the basis of scientific tests, it does not follow that it is rightly treated as purely factual. Indeed, if a person were to regard the investigation in a purely factual light we would at once know a great deal about his values.

82. Enlighteners have sometimes held that the problem set out (§§ 79, 81) could not exist since, in the words of Thomas Sprat, '*Experiments*' are the proper cure for all '*moral* imperfections of human *Nature*'; for, he asks, 'What room can there be for low, and little *things* in a *mind* so usefully and successfully employd?'.[26] The answer is that there is always enough room for such things. The human mind, though finite, is not a box, nor are being 'useful' and 'successful' intrinsically moral qualities; after all, the questions remain, useful for whom? and, a success for whom? Sprat goes on: 'What anger, envy, hatred, or revenge can long torment his breast, whome not only the greatest, and noblest objects, but every sand, every pible, every grass, every earth, every fly can divert?'.[27] But perhaps the absence of such emotions is not enough to prevent harm once a will for knowledge at any price is at work. Sprat's arguments confuse objectivity with respect for other persons.

The idea of limits to curiosity was not a crude dream of certain church fathers to suppress the spirit of discovery in the middle ages, until some courageous spirits of modern times set the mind free. There have always been such limits, and there has been change only regarding *where* these limits have been drawn. The closest approach to a place offering an outlet for unlimited scientific curiosity was Auschwitz. At that Nazi extermination camp, famous German professors of medicine revelled in a virtually unbounded freedom of experimentation because there were no limits either to the supply of subjects or to what could be done to them.[28] As one of the most thorough historians of the holocaust puts it, 'it would have been hard to find so ideal a surgical laboratory'.[29] As in the imaginary concentration camps of the Marquis de Sade, themselves inspired by the spirit of experimentation (§ 89), nearly anything was permitted.[30] No wonder, then, that the man who established the system, *Reichsführer SS* Heinrich Himmler, 'an equally ardent critic of traditionalism and 'Christian' prejudices of establishment doctors, [...] could view human experimentation in concentration camps as a form of liberation from these constraints in the name of bold scientific innovation'.[31] Real science is objective and experimental, Himmler argued; hence, if medicine is to aspire to the status of a science, the consequences for its procedures have to be drawn.[32]

The example suggested above (§ 81), then, is no mere science-fiction scenario. Variants of it have become historical fact. However, we are not willing to learn anything from them apart from the lesson that such horror must never be repeated.

The fact of human vivisection in the death camps does not show, as some philosophers of history have inferred, that Nazism is a consequence of the Enlightenment. It is true that the establishment of human vivisection as a proper mode of experiment in the life sciences was an important Enlightenment project; the president of the Royal Academy of Sciences in Berlin demanded to use prisoners for this purpose in his letter *Sur le progrès des sciences* of 1752.[33] But to detect a similarity between an earlier idea and a later practice is not to explain the practice. It would be fallacious to take that observation as demonstrating a historical continuity. But there is no fallacy, as long as the function of that observation for the argument is not to trace anything to an alleged cause, but to alert us to the fact that the idea of limits to curiosity need not be a concern that only obscurantists can hit upon.

83. Yet the claims that have been advanced (§§ 79, 81, 82) are of course anything but uncontroversial. I shall examine two objections to them, quite different from each other.

The first objection says that the claims are inconsistent; the idea that there could be limits to examination seems to involve a contradiction, since before it can be accepted, it needs to be examined itself (§ 84).

The second objection argues that the claims are misdirected; they seem to be designed to take the ideal of open-mindedness so far that it can easily be dismissed as impracticable. What seems required for open-mindedness, on any reasonable interpretation, is not to test whatever can possibly be tested, but to be ready to correct one's own position when confronted with the results of tests which are pertinent (§ 85).

84. The first argument was put forward by the British 'Free-Thinkers' of the early 18th century. According to Anthony Collins the argument *'shows that there can be* no rational Restraint *upon* Thinking'.[34] The reasoning is this: 'ANY Restraint whatsoever from Reason on Thinking, is absurd in it self. No just Restraint can be put to my Thinking, but some Thought, some Proposition, or Argument, which shews me that it is not lawful for me to think on the Subject I propose to do'.[35] Whatever objection is presented to examining a matter, 'IT is evident this restraining Argument must be *thought freely on* or examin'd; for if I do not examine it, I cannot know that I ought to be restrain'd by it, but may proceed in my propos'd Enquiry'.[36] In the words of Shaftesbury: ''Tis our own thought which must restrain our thinking. And whether the restraining thought be just, how shall we ever judge, without examining it freely and out of all constraint?'.[37] An objection to examining a matter, however, is a thought against thinking. It presupposes what it denies: examining the matter in question. It therefore implies a contradiction.

There is clearly a point to this argument. It has to be considered successful, for instance, against the attempt by Christian theologians to convince us that reason has been spoilt by original sin. Even if these theologians manage to convince us of this claim, this result cannot be worth anything. For to become convinced is a matter of reason, and that, according to the claim, is spoilt. So if it is reason that approves of the claim, this can only throw suspicion on this very claim.[38]

The Freethinkers' objection draws on the fact that wherever an argument is presented, it will, *qua* argument, appeal to thinking. The contradiction exposed by the objection is bound to be made whenever the conclusion of an argument is: Don't think! As implied above there is no way of adopting even this maxim without thinking for oneself that it is a good thing to follow it (§ 6). But if this is the critical force of the Freethinkers' objection, its weakness becomes apparent as soon as it is applied to the claims that have been put forward above (§§ 79, 81, 82). For applied to them, the analysis of the relationship between restraint and what it restrains would not be specific enough.

When I say that I would not perform tests on Australian Aborigines in order to establish that they are not subhuman, because a test of this kind would intrude on those people, this of course requires thought. Even merely to suspect that a specific project would have unwelcome practical implications requires one to think about that matter. But it does not require more than that. In particular, it does not require that we actually perform any tests. A contradiction would result only if that requirement held. It does not hold since thought is capable of anticipation and of directing action in such a way that undesirable consequences are avoided. If it sometimes fails to do so, this is no disproof of that capacity. Rather, to speak of failure in this regard at all already presupposes that there is such a capacity. Of course the decision against certain kinds of tests remains, in conformity with the Freethinkers' argument, a *thought* about them. But this thought does not presuppose that one has carried through these tests. Otherwise, by analogy, one would have to kill someone in order to pass judgement on killing, because 'unless one had killed somebody, one would not really know what one is talking about'. As this example suggests, the underlying logic of the argument is spurious. For not only can we know about things that we have not done, we can even know about them better than those who do them; for some people do things and at the same time entertain illusions about what they do.

Therefore the first objection is not tenable. What it has vaguely described as 'examining the matter in question' in truth refers to two distinct things, and this dissolves the semblance of contradiction.

85. The second objection to the claims that have been advanced (§§ 79, 81, 82) admits that they are not inconsistent. But it challenges them for being misdirected. According to this criticism the claims that have been put forward are directed against a man of straw, for they overstretch the ideal of open-mindedness merely in order to reject it.

If the criterion of open-mindedness is our willingness to submit our views to examination, then we should take account of an ambiguity in the phrase. The weaker interpretation of such willingness would be that one is prepared to withdraw one's views whenever evidence that does not conform to them is present. The stronger interpretation would be that one would be prepared to carry out every possible test. Open-mindedness in the second, stronger sense would oblige us to action; open-mindedness in the former, weaker sense merely to *re*action. Now it seems that for obvious reasons – our capacities are finite – only open-mindedness in the weaker sense is a sensible aim. Hence, open-mindedness in the stronger sense could appropriately be called a man of straw. And it seems that this man of straw is the target of the present attack.

But this is not true. For in the area of fundamental moral beliefs we are neither open-minded in the stronger *nor* in the weaker sense. It is not merely that we refuse to realize those experiments we ourselves consider to be cruel. This certainly would be perfectly compatible with open-mindedness in the weaker sense. But if someone else had carried out those experiments, the costs of testing would already *have been* incurred and this could not be undone. Since open-mindedness in the weaker sense allows merely for reluctance to *incur* certain costs, but not for reluctance to consider any evidence present, the results of those experiments would have to be considered as a possible guide to our future action. But we are not willing to consider the results of torturing babies even if someone else has produced them. We are not open-minded on such issues even in the weaker sense.

86. 'We are not open-minded on such issues': but we might become so if we gave up all prejudices. In 1729, during the period of the early Enlightenment, Jonathan Swift's scathing satire 'A Modest Proposal for Preventing the Children of poor People in Ireland, from being a Burden to their Parents or Country; and for making them beneficial to the Publick' carried that idea to its logical conclusion. As Swift saw it, the exponents of the Enlightenment, 'under the Notions of weeding out Prejudices', liquidated 'Virtue, and common Honesty'.[39] While this claim may look fairly conventional, Swift was in truth uniquely radical in imagining what such liquidation could mean.

The Enlightenment, secularizing the Christian ideal of service, was, as Burke puts it, the age of 'all sorts of projects and projectors'.[40] Accordingly, the pretended author of Swift's satire develops a project to promote the general welfare. He writes as a private citizen without authority, hoping to correct and improve public opinion. What motivates him is the didactic impulse to set things right. To carry his project through, no other weapon is at his disposal than the genuine one of Enlightenment: good reasons addressed 'to the Publick'.[41] As a fully rational thinker, the projector has considered the possible alternatives to his recommendation, but has had to turn them down as impracticable;[42] his ideas are not half-baked. As a progressive thinker, the projector draws upon the most advanced scientific insights, those of the just emerging discipline of political economy; he rigorously pursues the discovery that people are the riches of a nation, backed by a careful statistical analysis of the population, and draws from it practically relevant conclusions. And as a sober person free from traditional prejudices and detached from merely affective scruples, the projector proposes, after meticulous examination of all relevant factors, as the most rational solution to the social problems of Ireland, the breeding of babies and their marketing as fresh meat.[43] Taken by itself, or seen in a different context, this suggestion would be just crudely disgusting. In the context in which Swift presents it, however, the impact it has is different: not disgust, but horror. For the pretended writer is not a beast lacking reason. The conclusion at which he arrives is precisely a result of applying the enlightening power of reason.

87. But perhaps we are wrong in closing our minds to such proposals, unusual and audacious as they may be. Perhaps everything should be discussed. For talking a matter over does not do any harm; only putting it into practice can do that.

In the first place, however, this objection seems to manifest plain ignorance of human affairs. A single word can destroy the ties between one person and another. Such harm is, unlike much other damage, irreparable. Once the word has been uttered, it can neither be unspoken nor recalled. Even if it is forgiven, things will never be the same.

Furthermore, the objection plays down the nexus between reasoning and acting. A divorce between the two, as conceived of in the objection, would certainly have suited the wishes of Enlightened absolutist monarchs of the 18th century. Frederick II of Prussia is cited with approval by Kant as having said that his subjects might reason as much as they wanted and about whatever they wanted, if only they continued to obey him.[44] But as Johann Georg Hamann observed, there is something wrong with this maxim. Wherever the thing we have to do is fixed in advance, reasoning about practical matters lacks its full seriousness.[45] We 'draw the conclusion' not only in words, but also in deeds, and we do so in the latter respect *because* we have done so in the former respect, if our words are seriously meant. We rightly call the subject matter of a discussion the 'agenda': 'what is to be done'.

Of course there are discussions which do not have any outcome; discussions which run idle. But the Enlightenment project of putting everything on the agenda could not have been satisfied with them. Apart from that, even discussions which do not result in action can do harm. Whenever a proposal is discussed, the sheer fact that it is discussed implies a value judgement, namely that it is, at least, *worth* discussion. When a group of people discusses the elimination of some of its members, this *does* something both to the subjects and to the objects of this discussion, whether or not the elimination is carried out. (And it does so, as has been stated before, in an irreversible way.) We owe such insights to the dark dénouement of the Enlightenment.

88. To put everything on the agenda is the logical consequence of the Enlightenment ideal of an open-mindedness which results from removing all prejudices; it has in fact been its historical consequence. Donatien-Alphonse-François, Marquis de Sade, who had learned the Enlightenment lesson regarding prejudices from d'Holbach, was the one who drew that consequence. The Enlightenment had brought the opportunity to consider everything without prejudice, de Sade realized. He was aware how his own efforts fitted into this

project.[46] De Sade, however, also believed that the Enlightenment had so far provided hardly more than that opportunity. Certainly, some progress towards the elimination of prejudice was apparent already.[47] But de Sade saw that the Enlightenment, contrary to its claim to dismiss *all* prejudices, had kept numerous taboos intact and even introduced new ones.

De Sade approved of the goal of what he perceived as the Enlightenment, but he considered the form taken by enlightenment in his time far from perfect. Against its inconsistency, de Sade reasserted what he took to be the Enlightenment's original claim: total freedom of mind. 'Encore un effort; puisque vous travaillez à détruire tous les préjugés, n'en laissez subsister aucun, s'il n'en faut qu'un seul pour les ramener tous'.[48] (When we take this as a claim made by de Sade, we have not forgotten that it is presented within a work of fiction. We ascribe such views to the author for convenience, not because we are certain that he identified himself with the words he put into the mouths of his literary figures, or, more precisely, of the executioners, as distinguished from the victims, among these figures. The question whether he did is of no consequence for us. What matters here is de Sade's work, in which a bold and important position is represented, not his person.)

One of the prejudices the 18th century Enlightenment had shrunk from scrutinizing was the wrongness of murder. Following the Enlightenment's ideals rather than their half-hearted realization, the holy torch of philosophical reason should enlighten our soul on this issue.[49] What de Sade recognized as the Enlightenment's merit in this respect was not a reasonable answer, but rather the right to look for one, as part of the freedom to put everything on the agenda: 'N'avons-nous pas acquis le droit de tout dire?'.[50] The boudoir in which murder is considered in the light of unprejudiced reason is surrounded by mirrors, so that everything can be seen ('tout soit en vue') from all sides and nothing can be hidden.[51] This is the spirit of de Sade's *œuvre* as a whole. His unique philosophical pornography describes how men and women become enlightened by putting everything on the agenda and losing their prejudices. Nothing is left out. Only when Juliette has tried out and acquired all vices, does she become knowledgeable and lucidly conscious; only at the end of the *120 journées de Sodome*, when everything has been said and done, is the libertine freed from prejudice and hence perfect.

Observed without prejudice,[52] murder is all right. A plain argument shows that not much can be wrong with it. De Sade's consideration is rational in a most straightforward sense: it transforms the problem into a matter of economy. De Sade endorses the labour theory of value. A worker estimates his work only on the basis of the effort and the time spent on its production. But the production of a human being is no effort for nature. And if the production of a human being is no great achievement, then the elimination of such a being cannot be a major wrong either. Even if we want to insist that the production of a human being is some effort for nature, then surely the production of an elephant is no less so, and, at least, killing human beings would be no worse than hunting elephants.

Every substance from which living beings are made is derived from the destruction of previous living beings anyway. If all bodies prevailed for eternity, nature could not create new ones. But if the eternal duration of living beings is impossible for nature, it follows that the elimination of such beings is one of their laws. To put it differently, wherever elimination is one of the conditions for something new to emerge, strictly speaking there is no elimination but only transformation. What seems to disappear is in truth merely converted into something new that could not have emerged otherwise. 'A dessein de conserver vos absurdes préjugés, oserez-vous me dire que la transmutation est une destruction?',[53] de Sade asks. To maintain that destruction takes place is nothing but a rationalization of the prejudice that something is wrong with murder. What we call destruction is just metamorphosis, change of form. But if there is no destruction in the first place, and cannot be any, it will be impossible to prove that anything is wrong with murder.[54]

There is, however, not only nothing *wrong* with murder; as every enlightened reader ('lecteur éclairé') has to appreciate, it is actually a necessary and a good thing. For it supplies that raw material which nature needs to create new things.[55] The prejudices that prevent us from seeing this, de Sade points out, are due to emotions;[56] but, as the Enlightenment's great insight has made eternally clear, the only relevant authority is reason and its product, argument.

89. *La philosophie dans le boudoir* describes a process of enlightenment. The persons who appear in it, and indeed in any work by de Sade, are not ordinary criminals who simply do what criminals do; they are distinguished by the fact that they permanently comment on and explain what they do. The subtitles of the philosophy in the boudoir, *Les instituteurs immoraux, Dialogues destinés à l'éducation des jeunes demoiselles*, are ironical only in part. In de Sade's fiction, Eugénie, a girl of fifteen, is the object of such education. Before she is undeceived about murder, Eugénie becomes enlightened on another subject: parents. The disenchanting explanation of their love is that, in exchange for it, parents want to be caressed when old. In truth, parents are simply worthless. Mere prejudice makes children believe that they have any value.[57] Unfortunately, some parents do not know that they are worthless. Madame de

Mistival, Eugénie's mother, is under the illusion of being responsible for her daughter, and comes to see what has happened to her. No prejudice – either about murder or the rôle of parents – is allowed to stand in the way of her treatment. This, highly appropriate for the enlightened actors, is up to date as regards the state of scientific and medical knowledge. A valet suffering from smallpox is ordered to infect Madame with the disease through sexual intercourse and it is Eugénie who sews up her mother's vagina to make certain that the contagion will not fail.[58] Freedom from prejudice had already been attained by Eugénie before this concluding scene; but the final act validates and authenticates that liberty. Even libertinage, Sade testifies at every turn, cannot do without rituals in which it affirms itself.

Compared, for instance, to *Les 120 journées de Sodome* or *L'Histoire de Juliette*, *La philosophie dans le boudoir* is harmless. It is, however, not the scale of the cruelties de Sade imagines which gives them significance, but their *raison d'être*. It was suggested earlier that one consequence of rejecting all prejudices is to subject the full range of human behaviour to scientific scrutiny and run it through a process of experimental testing (§§ 79, 81, 82). The methodical precision with which de Sade's actors arrange their orgies, as well as the completeness they aim at – nothing should be left unexamined – confirm this. These are scientific experiments. The divine Marquis' celebration of murder has the charm of a chemical laboratory: 'Et voilà donc ce que c'est que le meurtre: un peu de matière désorganisée, quelques changements dans les combinaisons, quelques molécules rompues et replongées dans le creuset de la nature, qui les rendra dans quelques jours sous une autre forme à la terre; et où donc est le mal à cela?'.[59] The actors are as sober and dispassionate as accurate researchers should be; their hearts must not be and are not involved.[60] Even their pleasure remains, in a peculiar way, cool. It is not enough for them to take pleasure in what they do; de Sade's characters must also remain capable of dissecting their own pleasure.

De Sade radicalizes the intentions of the *siècle des lumières* and draws its ultimate consequences. His work is both fulfilment and critique of the Enlightenment.

90. If it is not wrong to murder anyone, then it is not wrong to murder a murderer either.[61] But this bears a significant implication. When, because and in so far as the world is purified from all prejudices, even regarding murder, it is morally in a universal state of war. And conversely, when and in so far as the world is not in a universal state of war, this may be due to prejudices which, more kindly, are called our morality.

Our fundamental moral beliefs are prejudices in a well-circumscribed sense. Educated intuitions that they are, we received them from others. (As exponents of the Enlightenment rightly saw, authority is a major source of prejudice (§ 6).) They shape our identities (§ 54). They are formed before examination, and since we are not willing to subject them to examination, they are not mere presumptions. For such examination would already offend against the rules which they embody.

Consider the idea of human dignity. If we look at human beings in an unprejudiced way, we are bound to say that, on any defensible interpretation of the word, they behave sometimes, perhaps often, in unworthy, disgraceful and degrading ways. Whenever we say that all human beings possess dignity, we say that, whatever the empirical evidence, we are willing to regard them in a certain way which is independent of that evidence and will not be revised after considering it. There is nothing provisional or presumptive in this stance, as in making ourselves inconspicuous when we become aware of possibly violent youngsters in the street (§ 16). Where human dignity is concerned, we do not weigh up alternatives. If that moral idea has any worth at all, we have to assert it dogmatically, unimpressed by any empirical lack of dignity in human conduct. When we are said to have moral respect for humanity, the condition for rightly saying so is not that we should know the individuals of which humanity is composed. In fact it would not even be proper to say that, if we hold humanity in respect, we do so *in spite of* not knowing the individuals of which it is composed. (It might be closer to the truth to say that we respect humanity, if we do so, rather *because* we do not know the individuals of which it is composed, or, for that matter, deliberately ignore their peculiarities.) The moral belief in human dignity is, positively, a prejudice.

Such basic moral beliefs, then, are immune from refutation. However, they are not immune from refutation because they are final; they are final because they are immune from refutation. This means there is no mysterious metaphysical quality which renders them infallible; it is merely that, since the chain of reasons cannot go back *in infinitum*, it stops at some beliefs we take to be fundamental. On these we even insist, as in the example of belief in human dignity, however often they are proved wrong. They are ways of looking at the world rather than something which we read off from it.

91. Enlightenment, as its name suggests, divided the world into light and darkness. (The great exception was of course Leibniz, who described reality in terms of transitions rather than oppositions; but the 18th century Enlightenment was in part precisely a rejection of this metaphysics.) The

dark side, it was claimed, was populated by an indivisible alliance of 'prejudices and barbarism'.[62] Ranged against these remnants of the past, many of the *philosophes* saw with complacency the light of comprehensive humanitarianism beginning to dawn. But might there not be a barbaric freedom from prejudice, as well as humane prejudices?

One of the greatest spirits of the Enlightenment came close to this insight. In his *Dictionnaire philosophique* of 1764, Voltaire claims that there are some universal, necessary prejudices which embody virtue itself. In all countries, he says, children are taught to recognize a rewarding and avenging God; to respect and love their father and their mother; to look on theft as a crime, selfish lying as a vice, before they have any idea what vice and virtue are.[63]

The explanation shows that Voltaire attributes the normative qualities of universality and necessity to those prejudices on empirical grounds. But the 20th century saw the emergence of forms of communal life where children were brought up, for instance, not to respect and love their parents, but to distrust them and to denounce them to their youth group leader as soon as they expressed dissatisfaction with the political powers they were subject to. The moral beliefs mentioned by Voltaire are, as he says, prejudices; but they are not prejudices that stand out from other prejudices by normative standards such as universality and necessity.

92. The idea that fundamental moral beliefs should be unrevisable (§ 90) seems unwelcome to a historically enlightened mind. A historically enlightened mind, a product of the 19th and 20th century, is even more enlightened than an enlightened mind in the 18th century sense. The latter conceived reason as pure, purified even from the traces of history. The former sees reason in a historical perspective. For a historically enlightened mind, as for Burke (§§ 55, 58), the present, within the realm of time, is provincial – though it is held to be so not compared to the past, but compared to the future. Surely there are truths, including discoveries that current belief is in error, as yet undreamt of. The past, however, serves historical enlightenment as an analogon for speculation about the future. Many things we now consider immoral were moral at some place some time ago; so what is the guarantee that they will not change once more? Refusal to acknowledge this merely betrays the inability to conceive the unfamiliar, in short, a lack of imagination.

This view is particularly neat since it seems to allow us, in the present case at least, to have our cake and eat it. All our opinions are fleeting. Why could not our fundamental moral beliefs be in the same position as, for instance, Euclidean conceptions of space or Newtonian conceptions of time? At a given moment in our intellectual history, we cannot conceive of any acceptable alternative. But more inventive minds than our own come up with alternative theories which, to our surprise, we actually find more compelling. Knowing that this has happened so often in the past, we manage to reconcile two beliefs that previous generations had considered irreconcilable: we hold that our views are subject to revision even though we cannot remotely imagine what this revision could consist in. May we not say that this amounts to endorsement of our fundamental moral beliefs in the light of historical reflection rather than naïve dogmatism?

Relevant historical evidence seems available not only for the domain of natural science, but also for ethical intuitions. When the call to put everything on the agenda was first articulated by the Greek enlightenment of the fifth century BC, the Sophistic movement, Aristotle opposed it in a way that might strike us as both reactionary and naïve. In his *Topics*, he suggests that one should not debate every thesis that has been propounded. By way of example, Aristotle assures that someone who doubts whether the gods ought to be honoured and parents loved does not deserve an argument, but castigation.[64] Surely, the convergence with a spirit so different in kind and context as Voltaire on the relationship between parents and children (§ 91) is remarkable. The other instance, however, seems to lend strong plausibility to the claims of historical enlightenment. While Aristotle from his perspective could not even imagine that the *denial* of polytheism could be worth a verbal refutation, a few hundred years later it seemed incredible to people that the *assertion* of polytheism could be worth verbally refuting; only castigation would do, though of a more drastic kind than Aristotle would have recommended in the reverse case. For the Christians were certain that the gods Aristotle and all other pagans had talked of were in truth demons,[65] and with demons one does not reason; one has to fight them.

93. Aristotle's advice to punish those who doubt whether the gods later called pagan should be honoured, and the Christian persecution of those who continued to honour the same deities, both occasion a serious concern about prejudice. If I am not willing to treat some of the things I am convinced of as questions which are up for discussion, it may seem to follow that I will use force against those who are not convinced of the same things.

But it does not follow. Four things follow from that attitude. First, I will stick to some of the things I am convinced of. Secondly, I will not treat them as questions which are up for discussion. Thirdly, I will be morally incapable of doing or omitting certain things the doing or omission of which others would like to extort from me. I will be morally incapable of doing or omitting these things because they would run counter to my convictions.[66] What is more – and this is the fourth implication – it will not even come into my head that I would gain certain advantages by opening myself to the suggestions of those others; as Nietzsche says, a noble character is distinguished from a vulgar one in *not having at hand* a number of habits and points of view which the latter has.[67] But these four interrelated implications or consequences of my attitude cannot properly be called force or violence.

Antigone, in Sophocles' tragedy, is convinced that she ought to bury and mourn her brother. Nothing will shake her conviction. Antigone is not willing to treat it as a question which is up for discussion. This attitude is not just an example of the general truth that those who are certain of something are lazy disputants. For Antigone it would not merely be a waste of time to discuss her purpose. Rather, what is at stake for her is her integrity. To bury and mourn for her brother: this defines Antigone's point of no return beyond which she would never, under any circumstances, give in to the oppressor, even if it meant risking and losing her life. To treat this concern as a question which is up for discussion, Antigone is aware, would mean to betray the loyalties she is committed to; her resistance against it is genuinely moral. She realizes that to ponder upon it would be to search for reasons not (to be allowed) to act; Ismene's arguments at the beginning of the drama exemplify this. Antigone does not even listen to arguments – neither to her sister's prudential arguments, nor to Creon's reasons of state. She lets them both know that they may argue as much as they like; whatever they say, she must pay her respects to Polyneices. That she must do so, is, she says, the older law. It is an unwritten tradition of which none knows its origin in time (450–7). Antigone cannot give any reasons for it. She acts from piety. But the deceased – so enlightenment authors from at least Lucretius's time have objected – have no sensation and hence cannot gain any advantage from being treated with such reverence. On an enlightenment view, piety is just superstition. Only people who have never examined what the use of it is – which would have led them to the answer that it is of no use at all – can maintain that attitude. In so far as it lacks rational justification Antigone's conviction would, in modern, sober parlance, have to be called a prejudice.

The *observation* of some enlightenment authors that prejudice can blind people to reality cannot be swept aside, even though such metaphorical blindness, unlike the physical disability from which the metaphor is derived, does not simply happen to people (§ 6). Her prejudice makes Antigone, in a sense, shut her eyes when she comes across realities which she does not want to see. To be sure, from the beginning she is aware that Creon has the power and intends to kill her (72–6, 96–7). But at least she acts as if this did not make a difference. Antigone's prejudice tells her that she has to guard the dignity of Polyneices. Focusing all her attention on this duty, her prejudice leads her to ignore a great many aspects of the situation. This is as far as the enlightenment *observation* goes. The question is, however, whether this observation by itself establishes an *objection*. For, generally, Antigone's capacity to act at all, as well as, specifically, her stamina, the morality of her action are constituted precisely by that peculiar blindness. Moral character is revealed not only in the reasons one considers and in the deeds one does, but also in the deeds one does not do and – which is decisive – the reasons one does not even consider.

Unlike Antigone, who unswervingly sticks to her avowed principles, Creon politically adapts his principles to the requirements of staying in power. To have good sons, he declares, is what a man prays for (642–3). But he betrays the esteem for family bonds which he claims to stand for. The blood relationships he honours in those words are dismissed in his violent ban on paying respect to Polyneices, his orders to 'leave his corpse unburied, to be meat / For dogs and carrion crows, a ghastly sight' (205–6). That this discrepancy in Creon's character is the salient point of the tragedy is clear from the fact that it is punished by the curses of his son and wife, and the destruction of his family.

The claim that prejudices lead to violence is sometimes mediated by the idea of fanaticism.[68] Prejudiced people are fanatics, and fanatics are violent. But this argument does not establish the point. Antigone is literally a fanatic. All her thinking and feeling revolves round one single idea, the funeral of her brother. They are thus related to what the Latin language calls *fanum*, the site of the deity (cf. 450–60). The *fanum* furnishes her with the sort of certainty that is characteristic of fanatics. But though Antigone has thus rendered her position immune from criticism, she does not resort to violence. She does not thrust her conviction on other persons. In fact as soon as she realizes that Ismene's conviction is different, she tries to prevent her from participating in the action which follows from her, Antigone's, creed (69–71, 83). It is Creon who attempts to force his design on others, particularly on Antigone. His means are threats, and, where these fail, actual violence. Wherever the thought of violence enters Creon's mind, this unimaginative character becomes imaginative. His original edict decrees death by stoning (36), at another point he is going to have Antigone executed in front of Haemon, her bridegroom (760–61), finally he opts for burying her alive (773–6).

Indeed, the kind of moral resolution, exhibited by Antigone, not to give way to the violence which a power threatens to apply does not necessarily result in a situation where there is no violence. But this does not mean that such resolution is wrong, since there is nothing in the world that could guarantee such an outcome. The point is that moral resolution of that kind is not the source of violence. For Antigone would have preferred to bury her brother in peace. And, what is more, in certain situations it can be doubtful that there would be *any* limits to the use of force if there was not the moral resistance of those who will not yield to it.

The conclusion can be stated as follows, making use of an image that has been employed earlier with the opposite thrust. Prejudice has been censoriously characterized by the simile of a wall where one had expected to enter through a door (§ 75). But to be like a wall, as Antigone is towards Creon and his demands, can be a virtue. We neither could nor should permit everything to enter. And even where we are like doors, these will be closed and locked under certain circumstances. Certainly a locked door prejudices the situation of those who wish to enter. Yet this state may actually be better than having them enter.

94. But is Antigone not rendered self-righteous by her prejudice? Maybe she is. A prejudice can make someone self-complacent and self-righteous – but that depends very much on what prejudice it is, *i.e.*, on its content. There are prejudices which make men modest as there are others which render them arrogant. The belief that art is exclusively a matter of genius may be held as a genuine prejudice, and may cause the person who holds it to become humble; while he is a talented sculptor, he insists, on the basis of his prejudice, that he is not an artist at all, only a craftsman. However, the belief that everyone else is an idiot, a prejudice not altogether uncommon among men, is pure arrogance. Again, the pride of mankind, which resists the theory of descent from animals and establishes a great gulf between man and nature, is based according to Nietzsche on a prejudice as to what spirit is. This prejudice is relatively recent; during the long prehistoric period of mankind spirit was not held in honour as a privilege of man. Animism, on the contrary, rendered the spiritual common property; it was constituted by the belief that spirit exists everywhere. Thus spirit was seen as that which unites men with nature, not that which severs them from it; as a matter of course, human beings considered themselves as related to animals or trees. In this way, Nietzsche says, one schooled oneself in modesty – and this likewise was the result of a prejudice.[69]

So it is not the fact that something is a prejudice that accounts for complacency, but the content of what is held. Imputing prejudice to others, however, seems to have in itself an element of self-righteousness (§ 46). To assert that others have prejudices seems to presuppose that one is free from them oneself (for if I realized that my belief that the others were prejudiced was itself a prejudice, I would feel I ought to recant). This gives rise to the suspicion that the *chasse aux préjugés* conveys a peculiar, smug satisfaction; looking down upon the prejudices of his fellow men, the enemy of prejudice seems to attest himself how much higher he is than they. Indulging in his superiority, however, does not yet appear to be enough for him. The enemy of prejudice is not yet satisfied to know the truth; everyone else must be seen to accept his world-view as well. If this does not happen, then from his point of view there is a case for *justified* violence. It is true that the enemy of prejudice treats the prejudiced in this way because he considers himself right and his adversaries wrong; but that, inverting terms, may also be exactly what they say.

Lack of insight, acquired misconceptions, natural desires misdirected from birth and cultural perversions will form the chief barriers to agreement in practice, declares Eugen Dühring in his *Course in Philosophy as a strictly Scientific Weltanschauung and Way of Living*. If one acts in accordance with truth and science, he goes on, and the other in accordance with some superstition or prejudice ['Vorurtheil'] then agreement can come about only by chance, and as a rule mutual interference must occur. We will hardly ever succeed in settling such moral conflicts by way of genuine agreement, that is, by finally enlightening the mistaken party, even when malevolence plays originally no part in the matter. Dühring asserts that we have better chances for such an equalization by means of instruction when confronting whole groups of people rather than an individual. However, at a certain level of incompetence, brutality or perversity of character, he maintains, conflict is always inevitable. The infringement can take the form of unauthorized resistance, on the part of the ignorant or otherwise incompetent party, to the conduct of the other that is, in itself, authorized. The latter party is said thereupon to be entitled to force her way against the will of the former. It is not only children and madmen against whom, according to the enemy of prejudice, violence is the last resort. The character of entire natural groupings and whole culturally defined classes can make it an unavoidable necessity to subject their will, which is hostile because of its perversity, in order to lead it back to the ties held in common. Even in such cases the alien will is still recognized as having equal rights, Dühring claims, as though he wished to mock the victims of the imperialism he advocates. The perversity of the alien will's injurious and hostile activity, the author concludes, has called for an equalization, and if it is subjected to violence, this is only the harvest of the injustice it has itself sown.[70]

If we fear intolerance and violence there may well be one thing we would be well advised to fear even more than prejudice, that is, the hunting down of prejudice.

95. Among the enemies of prejudice, it was Locke who discovered the self-righteousness of imputing prejudice to others. Of course the question arises whether, once this discovery is made, one can remain an enemy of prejudice. Locke believed that one could; the therapy he suggests is designed to cure men at once of that self-righteousness *and* of their prejudices.

'Every one is forward to complain of the prejudices that mislead other men or parties, as if he were free, and had none of his own. This being objected on all sides, it is agreed that it is a fault and an hindrance to knowledge. What now is the cure? No other but this, that every man should let alone others' prejudices, and examine his own. Nobody is convinced of his by the accusation of another; he recriminates by the same rule, and is clear. The only way to remove this great cause of ignorance and error out of the world is, for every one impartially to examine himself'.[71]

But Locke's counsel is circular. Just as 'resistance to correction' as a criterion for prejudice begs the question (§ 78), so the advice that 'every one impartially […] examine himself' assumes, under the title of 'impartiality', the very freedom from prejudice it is claimed to bring about.[72]

96. The suggestion of self-righteousness, insofar as it is germane to the subject of prejudice, has led us into an excursus (§§ 94–5). We shall now return from this digression.

It was suggested above (§ 93) that fanaticism has sometimes been brought in as a mediatory link between conviction and violence. The other mediatory term designed to provide such a link has been intolerance.[73] We may then ask whether Antigone is intolerant. If this word implies that she forces her views upon others, she is not (§ 93). Yet does it follow that Antigone should be called tolerant? If this word means granting an equal right to all opinions, we must deny this also. Pluralism is a posture altogether alien to her. Antigone would not stake her life for her cause, if she believed that views contrary to her own deserved equal respect. Antigone holds Creon's decree to be literally intolerable.

But not only is Antigone convinced that she is right and Creon is wrong. She also holds that the matter about which she believes she is right is of the greatest moment. Yet it has to be admitted that we show tolerance only towards things which we are not particularly eager for or anxious about. Henri IV of France changed his religious denomination three times: 'As he had displayed such indifference about his own creed', says his admirer, the liberal historian Buckle, we find, accordingly, 'that he was the author of the first public act of toleration which any government promulgated in France since Christianity had been the religion of the country. Only five years after he had solemnly abjured Protestantism, he published the celebrated Edict of Nantes, by which, for the first time, a Catholic government granted to heretics a fair share of civil and religious rights'.[74] Henri's Leaguer enemies sensed his nonchalance well enough when, on the occasion of his conversion at St Denis on 25 July 1593, they attributed to him the irreverent quip that 'Paris is worth a Mass'; something Henri might have thought, but certainly would have been too prudent to say. The Edict of Nantes began to fall apart as soon as Henri was assassinated in 1610; for while Henri cared little about denomination (in religious, though not, of course, political matters), his subjects cared much. Indifference is the soil in which the plant of tolerance grows, and indifference is what Antigone lacks. For her it makes all the difference whether her brother is buried honourably or not.

However, Antigone is not the only one who lacks indifference. All of us do – at *some* point. Where people become serious, where things are at stake they really care about, they cease to be tolerant. As soon as the political power takes on the rôle of an umpire above the religious denominations, the claim to absolute recognition has shifted from the church to the state. Henri IV was serious about the state's power, which he ingeniously strengthened through religious toleration; consequently he was not at all tolerant towards those who tried to question it. In modern societies where money enters a matter, seriousness always enters as well.[75] Therefore no one tolerates the tolerance of a bank clerk who shows this virtue with regard to the figures on a bank account. But if this observation holds, the consternation is truly telling which meets the modest reflection that there are possibly some other serious things which actually deserve intolerance. The use of violence might be one of them. Refusal to participate in it, whenever it occurred in the totalitarian regimes of the 20th century, for instance, sprang not from indifference, but from firm conviction, from one of the 'préjugés', to quote Voltaire, 'qui sont la vertu même'.[76] The intolerable is the unbearable, and those few who resisted, *e.g.*, what was going on in the German death camps of the 1940s, felt that the operations there were unbearable and had to be stopped or, realizing that this was beyond their power, at least denounced.

97. Up to now we have seen no reason to believe that violence is the necessary result of firm conviction as such. Why then does the political history of the

20th century, in so far as it has been totalitarian, appear to be cogent proof of precisely that nexus?

In *Mein Kampf*, Adolf Hitler says: 'The lack of a great idea that creates something new means at all times a restriction of the fighting force. Belief in the right to apply even the most brutal weapons is always bound up with the existence of a fanatical faith in the necessity of the victory of a revolutionary new order on this earth. A movement that does not fight for the most exalted aims and ideals will, therefore, never avail itself of the ultimate weapon'.[77]

Hitler's remarks seem to confirm a close connection between conviction and violence. But it is worth paying attention to the difference between these remarks and the claim we have considered. For in that claim the primary element was conviction that certain moral ideals hold, whereas violence figured in second place, as a means. Yet Hitler's point is quite the opposite. His point is not that in order to realize an ideal, weapons are needed as means. It is the other way round. One needs an ideal to be capable of using the most brutal weapons. The status of ideals, then, is secondary. Hitler conceives of them as means to silence dissent and scruples. What is primary is the belief in the weapon, in violence itself. It is *this* belief, not moral conviction as such, from which violence follows.

98. The point that adherence to certain beliefs we are not willing to treat as questions up for discussion necessarily leads to violence has not been made. Hence it does not follow, as historical enlightenment (§ 92) claims for itself, that only if we relativize our convictions to our particular position and perspective, are we proof against violence. Antigone holds her conviction absolutely, yet though she is determined, she does not use violence on others (§ 93). Conversely, to relativize our convictions to our particular position and perspective can amount to a subtle, though unintentional, justification of violence.

Inconsistent Nazis deny the holocaust. Consistent Nazis approve of the holocaust. A naïve dogmatist in his moral prejudices is certain that it was abominable. A historically enlightened individual does not personally approve of the holocaust, either, but has to admit that in a few hundred years more inventive minds than his own could emerge and present new arguments in the light of which Auschwitz might be justified; not to acknowledge this would simply betray a lack of imagination (§ 92). This reply is not merely neat, as we said above about historical enlightenment; it is actually *too* neat to do justice to the phenomenon of morality. Morality insists that to keep an open mind can, in certain cases, be a crime. For what is at stake here is Antigone's twofold distinction: she is not capable of everything, and there is something about which she is serious. Of course what gives her moral stature and makes her, in the context in which she acts, a tragic figure is that she is serious about something which *is* serious. If it was not, we would rather be confronted with a comic figure: Don Quixote, not Antigone. But then, even reading Cervantes, are we so sure that it is Don Quixote who has gone mad, and not his time?

99. Historical enlightenment marks the self-surrender of European rationalism. In that tradition, reason stood for the capacity to transcend the limitations of time and place, to discount the effects of position and perspective. Historical enlightenment suggests that, although we cannot discount the effects of our historical position and perspective on our views, history will discount our views as having been effected by our position in it. But this reminder, abstract as it is, has to apply to every perspective equally, to that of the Nazi as much as to that of his opponent. They are all relative to their position in time; future history might and, as experience warns us, will actually supersede them all. The Enlightenment of the 18th century, whichever of its claims may not have been convincing, at least advanced concrete objections to specific concepts cherished by the tradition of theology and metaphysics. But historical enlightenment does not have any concrete objections to the concepts we use. It just asserts that they are historical, and this assertion is intended to mean that some day they too may be superseded. The historically enlightened mind insists that new arguments may always come up. Certainly they may. But this is not the issue. The issue is whether that is of so much moment. Are reasons as important as enlightened minds have believed?

According to a common Enlightenment scheme, prejudices are marked off from judgements by not being based on reasons. (This claim obviously had to be supplemented by a theory of what look like reasons but aren't reasons: *i.e.*, 'rationalization'; cf. § 77.) Consequently, the appeal to abandon all prejudices was associated with the requirement that we have reasons for everything we believe.[78]

This requirement is, however, subject to a dilemma. Either it can be met, in which case to meet it is devoid of merit; or it cannot be met. The first interpretation does not strengthen the case against prejudice, the second one strengthens the case in favour of it.

First, it is not possible to give a reason without referring to something particular and passing over many other things. Reasons particularize. This is hardly noticed before it hurts (and, as we shall see, normally it does not hurt but please). 'I love you.' 'Why?' Now a reason has to be given, and insofar as it is a reason, it will be something particular: 'Because your hair is beautiful.' 'That's all?' The reason is already the retraction of the avowed love. What hurts us in such a reasoning is the reduction which is needed for any reasoning; but it hurts us only as we realize that *we* must undergo it, too. What indeed can hurt more than to be reduced? Where completeness matters, as in love and friendship (for persons, as long as they are sound, consider themselves as wholes), reasons smell of insult. But as long as we reason, we cannot do any better. There is no such thing as a complete statement of reasons. Since all things in the world have indefinitely many aspects, we have to be selective when we refer to any of them in our reasoning. Paradoxically, however, it is precisely from this deficit that reasons draw their power. Their particularity constitutes their universal empire. Because statements of reasons may remain incomplete – and they may since they must – there are reasons for everything, and everything can serve as a reason. As soon as a culture has developed and propagated the practice of reasoning over several centuries, Hegel has observed, it will be simply raining reasons.[79] This proves useful in two ways: affirmatively as well as critically. The affirmative way is employed as we assert our interests. Reasons can be found and given for each of them, whatever it is. On the other hand, it is just as easy to see defects and incoherence in everything else; in this respect there will never be lack of proof either. Thus it is possible to have a reason for everything, but there is no merit in it, in particular no merit which would make a view that is backed by reasons in this inflationary sense in itself better than a prejudice that is not backed in this way.

There is a second, stricter interpretation of the requirement that we have reasons for everything we believe. If every judgement stands in need of a reason, then every judgement requires another judgement to which it has to be referred back. But this amounts to a contradiction. For if every insight is possible only by virtue of another one which is its ground, we would have to run through an infinite regress to arrive at any insight at all.[80] On this account, it would not be possible to give reasons at all. Of course, this is itself a reason. But on the present interpretation, the point has not been that reasons are worthless. Indeed, there may well be a sense in which they are essential. Rather, the point has been that, if some of our beliefs are based on reasons, there has to be something which is not based on reasons. We are able to reason in support of certain things and to prove certain things only if and because there are other things for which we do not have reasons or proof.

Every argument must start somewhere. Now the truth of your conclusion is only guaranteed, if (provided that you do not commit a logical error) your premises are true. If your premises were false, your conclusion could be false just as well as true; *ex falso quodlibet*, as the scholastics said. If you want to arrive at a true conclusion, you have to start from something which is not in doubt. If it is doubtful, your conclusion will be too. So you will not have made any progress. There is of course doubt which brings about progress: doubt that has consequences. This is the doubt which teaches you that something is not true. But if in this sense you doubt the premises of your argument, you are beginning a different argument with other premises, and the same logic as above applies. Again in a *reductio ad absurdum* you are not doing the opposite, but once more you apply the same logic, only backwards this time: you have to make sure that the conclusion is wrong; only on this basis you are entitled to infer that something must have been wrong with one or all of the premises.

Where do we get the premises of our arguments from? They may rest on a previous argument. But you can never prove your first statement or it would not be your first. As we have seen, for us to know anything to be true by means of reasons, there must be something we know without a reason. If a vicious infinite regress is to be avoided, Aristotle remarks in the final passage of his *Posterior Analytics*, there must be a starting point which is not subject to and, indeed, does not need proof: *intuition*, that is, an immediate grasp of truth.[81] But different people have different intuitions on the same subject. What are said to be 'evident truths' have not at all been evident to minds no less sane than those who had those intuitions. Of course this does not show that there is nothing deserving the name of intuition. But it suggests that intuitions, which vary according to what different people think, have experienced, believe and know, are mediate rather than immediate. The mediations have just been forgotten. Of course, something can be called an intuition only if it is not the outcome of a scrutiny of its object. But in that case, intuition is just a euphemism for prejudice. We call those prejudices that we are fond of intuitions, and we call those intuitions that we dislike prejudices; such choice of terms is a matter of rhetoric.

Some people become particularly devoted to their intuitions. Since they take them for illuminations, they can't resist bestowing on them the accolade of necessary truth. But in so far as intuitions are no more than prejudices that have been given a more imposing name, there is no guarantee that they are true. (The argument is the same as that which shows that nothing necessitates their being false, § 46.) They are, however, simply indispensable if we are to reason at all. Reasoning cannot proceed a single step without taking something for granted. Hence prejudice is not the obstacle to reason, as it has been represented by many Enlighteners. On the contrary, reason depends on prejudice. But conversely, prejudice, even when it is false, also depends on reason. The schematism of opposing reason to prejudice, to profess one of them in order to despise the other, is equally oblivious to their relations in both of its versions.

100. With the elimination of prejudice, the Enlightenment set itself a problem which is either insoluble, or leads to undesirable solutions. Does this mean that enlightenment rests on a mistake? Not necessarily, or at least not in every sense of the word 'mistake'. To achieve success with regard to one's goals does not always mean a success for oneself. For someone who solves a problem in a definite way renders himself, at least in this regard, superfluous. A more serious threat to the existence of the enlightenment could hardly be conceived of than the accomplished destruction of all prejudices.[82] Failure in achieving one's goals, on the other hand, can be used as a way of demonstrating the enduring necessity of what one proposes. Intellectual movements, not unlike their political counterparts, live in a kind of symbiosis with the problems they discover or invent; the alleged continuance of the problem is designed to prove that they are urgently needed. The consequent strategy, then, is to meet the failure to solve the alleged problem by 'more of the same' – in the present case, more enlightenment. As was suggested in the preface, there is no reason to believe that people in the 20th century had fewer (rather than merely different) prejudices than people had in the 18th century; but from an enlightenment perspective that is a reason only for acting as before but more so.

For this conclusion to seem rational, on the one hand, the semblance must be upheld that the difficulty is temporary, and that it will be overcome in the future. This semblance is intrinsic to the enlightenment project. To maintain it, the enlightenment has always been able to invoke its own good intentions. Any blame for its failure is to be laid on what constitutes the problem, *viz.*, prejudices, for these, instead of supporting their own abolition, are resistant to it (§ 77). On the other hand, the enlightenment is able to soften criticism with the acknowledgement that, up to a point, it has to tackle an insoluble problem; its strategy, therefore, is to treat the liberation from prejudice in the way that Kant, perfecting Enlightenment thought, calls the 'regulative use of ideas'.[83] A goal defined by a regulative idea is never to be thought of as accomplished. This concession from the outset at least lowers the possible merit of any competing approach. For, by implication, no one else will have solved the problem of prejudice either. In this twofold manner, both assertive *and* cautious, enlightenment stabilizes itself. As an attitude that knows how to draw success even from its failure, enlightenment may well turn out to be as tenacious as it claims prejudices to be.

Notes

1 *Of the Conduct of the Understanding*, § 10, pp. 229–30. For another important discussion of prejudice in Locke cf. 'A Third Letter for Toleration', pp. 297–9.
2 On this topic cf. the observations by Duclos: 'Ils [*sc.* les faux préjugés] naissent et croissent insensiblement par des circonstances fortuites, et se trouvent enfin généralement établis chez les hommes, sans qu'ils en aient aperçu les progrès. Il n'est pas étonnant que de fausses opinions se soient élevées à l'insu de ceux qui y sont le plus attaches' (*Considérations sur les mœurs*, p. 27).
3 § 38 of the *Conduct of the Understanding* (pp. 271–2), on 'Presumption', has nothing to say about its distinction from prejudice. Even when legal theory (Best) and rhetoric (Whately) had made available precise definitions of presumption, it was not uncommon for philosophers to talk as if there was not much of a difference between prejudice and presumption. Cf., *e.g.*, Peirce, 'The Order of Nature' (6.424.), p. 299: 'There are minds to whom every prejudice, every presumption, seems unfair'.
4 See *Of the Conduct of the Understanding*, § 26, p. 254.
5 Cf. Best, *A Treatise of Presumptions of Law and Fact.*
6 Stephen, *A Digest of the Law of Evidence*, pp. 3–4.
7 Whately, *Elements of Rhetoric*, p. 112.
8 Ibid., pp. 112–13.
9 Ibid., pp. 113–14; for a way in which this advantage can turn into a disadvantage cf. pp. 129–32.
10 Ibid., p. 114.
11 *Commentaries on the Laws of England*, p. 358.
12 *Discours de la Méthode*, II,7, p. 18.
13 Kant uses a German equivalent of 'persistence': 'Hartnäckigkeit der Vorurtheile' (*Reflexionen zur Logik*, Nr. 2546, p. 410). Cf. ibid., Nr. 2517, p. 402: 'Die Vorurtheile wiederstehen der Belehrung, indem sie 1. nicht wollen belehrt werden, 2. indem sie die Belehrung durch dasselbe Vorurtheil beurtheilen, welches hat sollen abgeschafft werden'.
14 This was the lesson Lessing intended to teach by his comedies *Der Misogyn* and *Die Juden.*
15 'Paragraphs on prejudice', p. 328. Hazlitt here falls short of his own insight, cf. § 10.
16 du Marsais, *Essai sur les Préjugés*, vol. I, p. 6. Cf. already Zollikofer, 'Neunter Discours', p. 66 (referring to the man of prejudice): 'Was ist aber wol unvernünfftiger, als sich selbst seiner Sinnen und der Vernunfft, welche der weiße Schöpffer dem Menschen nicht umsonst geschencket hat, berauben, und solche andern blindlings unterwerffen, die gleichfals Menschen, und folglich fallible sind?'.
17 Fontenelle, 'Histoire des oracles', p. 117: 'Quand les philosophes s'entêtent une fois d'un préjugé, ils sont plus incurables que le peuple même, parce qu'ils s'entêtent également et du préjugé et des fausses raisons dont ils le soutiennent'. Similarly Rousseau, *Confessions*, p. 285. For an objection to Fontenelle see Duclos, *Considérations sur les mœurs*, p. 27. On the philosophical rationalization of prejudice cf. also Nietzsche, *Jenseits von Gut und Böse*,

'Erstes Hauptstück: von den Vorurtheilen der Philosophen', §§ 1–23, pp. 15–39, particularly § 5, pp. 18–19.

18 Nietzsche, *Ecce homo*, 'Warum ich so klug bin', 1, p. 281: 'Alle Vorurtheile kommen aus den Eingeweiden'.

19 Flaubert, *Dictionnaire des idées reçues*, p. 172: 'Exception. Dites qu'elle 'confirme la règle'; ne vous risquez pas <à> expliquer comment'.

20 Ibid., p. 53: 'Anglaises. S'étonner de ce qu'elles ont de jolis enfants'; cf. p. 146; p. 102: 'nègres. s'étonner que leur salive soit blanche. – et de ce qu'ils parlent français'; cf. p. 198

21 Ibid., p. 72: 'Doctrinaires. Les mépriser [...] <<pr. quoi?>> <<on n'en sait rien>>'.

22 Duclos, *Considérations sur les mœurs*, pp. 27–8: 'Ce n'est pas la raison qui les proscrit, elles se succédent et périssent par la seule révolution des temps. Les unes font place aux autres, parceque notre esprit ne peut même embrasser qu'un nombre limité d'erreurs' (the economic explanation Duclos offers has its analogy in fashion, too).

23 Cf. *Dialogue Concerning the Two Chief World Systems*, p. 328.

24 Kant, *Kritik der reinen Vernunft*, 'Vorrede zur ersten Auflage', A 11, p. 13: 'Unser Zeitalter ist das eigentliche Zeitalter der Kritik, der sich *alles* unterwerfen muß' (emphasis added).

25 Spinoza, *Tractatus de intellectus emendatione*, p. 17: 'Ratio autem, cur in Naturæ inquisitione rarò contingat, ut debito ordine ea investigetur, est propter præjudicia'.

26 *History of the Royal-Society of London*, III, xiii, p. 344.

27 Ibid., p. 345.

28 Hilberg, *The Destruction of the European Jews*, pp. 600–9; Lifton, *The Nazi Doctors*, ch. 15: 'The Experimental Impulse', pp. 269–302, particularly pp. 301–2: 'Removal of Limits'; cf. Kater, *Das 'Ahnenerbe' der SS*, pp. 228, 231–4 on experiments with humans in the concentration camps Buchenwald, Natzweiler-Struthof, and Dachau.

29 Lifton, *The Nazi Doctors*, p. 295.

30 Ibid., p. 270: 'the Auschwitz principle that *anything is permitted*', p. 271: 'anything was possible'.

31 Ibid., p. 279.

32 'Letter to Reichsgesundheitsführer Dr. Leonardo Conti, 26 August 1942': 'Die Forderung, die im Rahmen einer anständigen Wissenschaft an jeden erhoben werden muß, daß nämlich exakte Versuche von objektiver Seite gemacht werden'; 'Letter to Reichsarzt-SS Dr. Ernst Grawitz, 30 September 1942': 'Wenn ein Problem untersucht werden soll, so hat dies wissenschaftlich zu geschehen, d.h. also wirklich ernsthaft in einer genauen, jeder Prüfung standhaltenden Versuchs-Anordnung – ohne Für und Wider – mit dem heiligen Ernst, etwas erforschen zu wollen' (Kater, *Das 'Ahnenerbe' der SS*, pp. 100 and 259).

33 *Briefe des Herrn von Maupertuis*, pp. 125– 9.

34 *A Discourse of Free-Thinking*, p. iii.

35 Ibid., p. 25.

36 Ibid., p. 26.

37 *Characteristics* VI,5,3, p. 342.

38 Cf. Rousseau, *Émile*, pp. 615–16: 'M'apprendre que ma raison me trompe, n'est-ce pas réfuter ce qu'elle m'aura dit pour vous? Quiconque veut récuser la raison doit convaincre sans se servir d'elle. Car, supposons qu'en raisonnant vous m'ayez convaincu; comment saurai-je si ce n'est point ma raison corrompue par le péché qui me fait acquiescer à ce que vous me dites?'.

39 'Thoughts on Various Subjects', p. 243.

40 *Reflections*, p. 242; cf. p. 91. Wary of that secularization, Burke was eager to point out that in his political proposals he, 'having no general apostolical mission' (ibid., pp. 33–4), was not pursuing yet another project.

41 Swift, 'Modest Proposal', pp. 109, 111.

42 Ibid., p. 110: 'As to my own Part, having turned my Thoughts for many Years, upon this important Subject, and maturely weighed the several *Schemes of other Projectors*, I have always found them grosly mistaken in their Computation'.

43 Ibid., p. 111.

44 'Was ist Aufklärung', p. 55: '*räsonniert*, so viel ihr wollt, und worüber ihr wollt; *aber gehorcht!*'.

45 This is the draw-back of Friedrich's and Kant's separation of the private use of reason ('Privatgebrauch der Vernunft') from its public use ('öffentlicher Gebrauch der Vernunft') ('Was ist Aufklärung?', p. 57): 'Was hilft mir das *Feyerkleid* der Freiheit, wenn ich daheim im Sclavenkittel' (Hamann, 'Brief an Christian Jacob Kraus', p. 22).

46 *La philosophie dans le boudoir*, p. 478: 'j'aurai contribué en quelque chose au progrès des lumières, et j'en serai content'.

47 Ibid., p. 479: 'Déjà nos préjugés se dissipent'.

48 Ibid., p. 483.

49 Ibid., p. 516: 'Daignons éclairer un instant notre âme du saint flambeau de la philosophie'. On the justification of murder in de Sade cf. also *L'Histoire de Juliette, Œuvres*, vol. IX, pp. 170–203. The Princess Borghese is singled out for torture and killing by Juliette because she was 'tenant encore à ses préjugés' (ibid., p. 419).

50 *La philosophie dans le boudoir*, p. 513.

51 Ibid., p. 387.

52 Ibid., pp. 513–14.

53 Ibid., p. 515.

54 Ibid.: 'il devient alors audessus des forces humaines de prouver qu'il puisse exister aucun crime dans la prétendue destruction d'une créature, de quelque âge, de quelque sexe, de quelque espèce que vous la supposiez'.

55 Ibid., pp. 515–16: 'Conduits plus avant encore par la série de nos conséquences, qui naissent toutes les unes des autres, il faudra convenir enfin que, loin de nuire à la nature, l'action que vous commettez, en variant les formes de ses différents ouvrages, est avantageuse pour elle, puisque vous lui fournissez par cette action la matière première de ses reconstructions, dont le travail lui deviendrait impracticable si vous n'anéantissiez pas'.

56 Ibid., p. 513: 'préjugés de l'amour-propre', p. 514: 'préjugés de notre orgueil', 'préjugés de l'orgueil'.

57 Ibid., pp. 467, 505.

58 Ibid., pp. 536–49.

59 *L'Histoire de Juliette, Œuvres*, vol. VIII, p. 399.

60 Cf. Horkheimer and Adorno, *Dialektik der Aufklärung*, pp. 86–7.

61 Cf. Sade, *La philosophie dans le boudoir*, p. 521.

62 d'Alembert, *Discours préliminaire*, pp. 95–6: 'le joug de la scolastique, de l'opinion, de l'autorité, et un mot des préjugés et de la barbarie'. Even the more moderate German Enlightenment coupled prejudice with barbarism, cf., *e.g.*, Lessing, 'Das Neueste aus dem Reiche des Witzes', p. 84.

63 Voltaire, 'Préjugés', p. 456: 'Il y a des préjugés universels, nécessaires, et qui sont la vertu même. Par tous pays on apprend aux enfants à reconnaître un Dieu rémunérateur et vengeur;

à respecter, à aimer leur père et leur mère; à regarder le larcin comme un crime, le mensonge intéressé comme un vice, avant qu'ils puissent deviner ce que c'est qu'un vice et une vertu'.

64 Aristotle, *Topica* I, 11, 105a3–7: Οὐ δεῖ δὲ πᾶν πρόβλημα οὐδὲ πᾶσαν θέσιν ἐπισκοπεῖν, ἀλλ' ἥν ἀπορήσειεν ἄν τις τῶν λόγου δεομένων καὶ μὴ κολάσεως [...] · οἱ μὲν γὰρ ἀποροῦντες 'πότερον δεῖ τοὺς θεοὺς τιμᾶν καὶ τοὺς γονεῖς ἀγαπᾶν ἤ οὔ' κολάσεως δέονται.

65 For one, Tatianus, *Oratio ad Graecos*.

66 Cf. Schelling, *Philosophische Untersuchungen über das Wesen der menschlichen Freiheit*, pp. 284–5.

67 *Morgenröthe*, § 267, p. 211: 'Ein edler Charakter unterscheidet sich von einem gemeinen dadurch, dass er eine Anzahl Gewohnheiten und Gesichtspuncte *nicht zur Hand hat*'.

68 du Marsais, *Essai sur les Préjugés*, vol. I, p. 23. La Mettrie, *L'homme machine*, p. 17: 'les ont conduits à mille préjugés, et pour tout dire en un mot, au fanatisme'.

69 *Morgenröthe*, § 31, p. 41.

70 *Cursus der Philosophie*, pp. 216–17: 'Der Mangel an Einsicht und die erworbenen Missvorstellungen werden hier mit den ursprünglich falschen Richtungen der Naturantriebe oder Culturverzerrungen die Haupthindernisse einer Verständigung im Wollen bilden. Handelt der Eine nach Wahrheit und Wissenschaft, der Andere aber nach irgend einem Aberglauben oder Vorurtheil, so ist Uebereinstimmung nur zufällig, und es müssen der Regel nach gegenseitige Störungen eintreten. Die Entscheidung solcher moralischer Conflicte auf dem Wege echter Verständigung, nämlich durch schliessliche Aufklärung des irrenden Theils, wird selbst dann nur selten gelingen, wenn kein ursprüngliches Uebelwollen im Spiele ist. Für die menschlichen Gesammtgruppen ist zu einer solchen, durch die Erkenntniss zu vermittelnden Ausgleichung, noch eher als dem Einzelnen gegenüber einige Aussicht vorhanden; indessen wird bei einem gewissen Grad von Unfähigkeit, Rohheit oder böser Charaktertendenz in allen Fällen der Zusammenstoss erfolgen müssen. Die Verletzung kann schon in dem unberechtigten Widerstande des unwissenden oder sonst fehlgreifenden Theils gegen das an sich zulässige Verhalten des andern Theils liegen, der alsdenn ein Recht haben wird, sich auch gegen den Willen des andern freie Bahn zu schaffen. Es sind nicht blos Kinder und Wahnsinnige, denen gegenüber die Gewalt das letzte Mittel ist. Die Artung ganzer Naturgruppen und Culturclassen von Menschen kann die Unterwerfung ihres durch seine Verkehrtheit feindlichen Wollens im Sinne der Zurückführung desselben auf die gemeinschaftlichen Bindemittel zur unausweichlichen Notwendigkeit machen. Der fremde Wille wird auch hier noch als gleichberechtigt erachtet; aber durch die Verkehrtheit seiner verletzenden und feindlichen Bethätigung hat er eine Ausgleichung herausgefordert, und wenn er Gewalt erleidet, so erntet er nur die Rückwirkungen seiner eignen Ungerechtigkeit'.

71 *Of the Conduct of the Understanding*, § 10, p. 228.

72 Cf. ibid., § 42, p. 279, where prejudice is represented as a form of partiality.

73 du Marsais, *Essai sur les Préjugés*, vol. II, p. 105.

74 *History of Civilization in England*, p. 10. As Gibbon noted, the same result, toleration, can actually be associated with highly divergent, even with logically incompatible, forms of indifference: 'The various modes of worship which prevailed in the Roman world were all considered by the people as equally true; by the philosopher as equally false; and by the magistrate as equally useful. And thus toleration produced not only mutual indulgence, but even religious concord' (*The History of the Decline and Fall of the Roman Empire*, p. 28).

75 For this reason, money, and in particular much money, has, as Kant points out, become the touchstone for serious conviction: 'Der gewöhnliche Probierstein: ob etwas bloße Überredung, oder wenigstens subjektive Überzeugung, d.i. festes Glauben sei, was jemand behauptet, ist das *Wetten*. Öfters spricht jemand seine Sätze mit so zuversichtlichem und unlenkbarem Trotze aus, daß er alle Besorgnis des Irrtums gänzlich abgelegt zu haben scheint. Eine Wette macht ihn stutzig. Bisweilen zeigt sich, daß er zwar Überredung genug, die auf einen Dukaten an Wert geschätzt werden kann, aber nicht auf zehn, besitze. Denn den ersten wagt er noch wohl, aber bei zehnen wird er allererst inne, was er vorher nicht bemerkte, daß es nämlich doch wohl möglich sei, er habe sich geirrt' (*Kritik der reinen Vernunft* A 824–5 = B 852–3, pp. 690–91).

76 Voltaire, 'Préjugés', S. 456; cf. § 91.

77 '*Der Mangel einer großen neugestaltenden Idee bedeutet zu allen Zeiten eine Beschränkung der Kampfkraft. Die Überzeugung vom Recht der Anwendung selbst brutalster Waffen ist stets gebunden an das Vorhandensein eines fanatischen Glaubens an die Notwendigkeit des Sieges einer umwälzenden neuen Ordnung dieser Erde. Eine Bewegung, die nicht für solche höchste Ziele und Ideale ficht, wird daher nie zur letzten Waffe greifen*' (pp. 596–7).

78 Cf., *e.g.*, Locke, *Essay*, IV, xvii, 24, vol. III, pp. 136–7; *Of the Conduct of the Understanding*, § 6, p. 217. The rhetoric of reasons is fully unfolded in Kant where they appear at the end of a therapeutic procedure that starts with the 'purification' from prejudice (implying that it is a kind of dirt) and healing from the 'blindness' it has produced: 'Ich habe meine Seele von Vorurteilen gereinigt, ich habe eine jede blinde Ergebenheit vertilgt, welche sich jemals einschlich, um manchem eingebildeten Wissen in mir Eingang zu verschaffen. Jetzo ist mir nichts angelegen, nichts ehrwürdig, als was durch den Weg der Aufrichtigkeit in einem ruhigen und vor alle Gründe zugänglichem Gemüte Platz nimmt' (*Träume eines Geistersehers*, I, 4, p. 960).

79 'In unserer reflexionsreichen und räsonierenden Zeit muß es einer noch nicht weit gebracht haben, der nicht für alles, auch für das Schlechteste und Verkehrteste, einen guten Grund anzugeben weiß. Alles, was in der Welt verdorben worden ist, das ist aus guten Gründen verdorben worden. Wenn auf Gründe provoziert wird, so ist man zunächst geneigt, davor zurückzutreten; hat man dann aber die Erfahrung gemacht, wie es sich damit verhält, so wird man harthörig dagegen und läßt sich dadurch nicht weiter imponieren' (*Enzyklopädie*, § 121 Zus., p. 252; cf. § 122 Anm., p. 253). Consistently, there is a positive usage of 'prejudice' in Hegel. Cf., *e.g.*, *Vorlesungen über die Geschichte der Philosophie*, p. 23: 'Es ist ein altes Vorurteil, daß das, wodurch sich der Mensch von dem Tiere unterscheidet, das Denken ist; wir wollen dabei bleiben'.

80 Cf. Aristotle, *Metaphysica* III, 4, 1006a8–9: ὅλως μὲν γὰρ ἁπάντων ἀδύνατον ἀπόδειξιν εἶναι (εἰς ἄπειρον γὰρ ἂν βαδίζοι, ὥστε μηδ' οὕτως εἶναι ἀπόδειξιν).

81 *Analytica posteriora* II, 19, 100b13–15: ἀποδείξεως ἀρχὴ οὐκ ἀπόδειξις, ὥστ' οὐδ' ἐπιστήμης ἐπιστήμη. Εἰ οὖν μηδὲν ἄλλο παρ' ἐπιστήμην γένος ἔχομεν ἀληθές, νοῦς ἂν εἴη ἐπιστήμης ἀρχή. Cf. II, 3, 90b19–27.

82 Cf. Hegel, *Phänomenologie des Geistes*, pp. 404, 413.

83 *Kritik der reinen Vernunft* A 642–68 = B 670–96, pp. 563–82: 'regulativen Gebrauch der Ideen'.

Bibliography

Addison, Joseph, and Richard Steele, *The Spectator*, vol. III [1712], ed. Gregory Smith (London: Dent, 1958)

d'Alembert, Jean Le Rond, *Discours préliminaire de l'Encyclopédie* [1751], ed. Jean-Louis Ferrier (Paris: Gonthier, 1965)

Amiel, Henri-Frédéric, *Journal intime*, Edition intégrale, vol. IV: December 1860– May 1863, ed. Philippe M. Monnier and Anne Cottier-Duperrex (Lausanne: Editions l'Age d'Homme, 1981)

Anonymus [*i.e.*, Anthony Collins], *A Discourse of Free-Thinking, Occasion'd by The Rise and Growth of a Sect call'd Free-Thinkers* (London: anonymous publisher, 1713)

Anonymus [*i.e.*, Claude-Adrien Helvétius], *De l'Esprit* (Paris: Durand, 1758)

Anonymus [*i.e.*, Friedrich II., 'der Große'], *Examen de l'essai sur les préjugés*, publ. under the direction of abbé N. Bastiani (London [*i.e.*, Berlin]: Nourse [*i.e.*, Voss], 1770)

Aquinas, Thomas, *Summa Theologica*, transl. by Fathers of the English Dominican Province, vol. X: II, qq. XLVII – LXXIX (London: Burns Oates & Washbourne, 1929)

Aristotle, *Analytica posteriora*, in *Analytica priora et posteriora*, ed. William David Ross and L. Minio-Paluello (Oxford: Clarendon Press, 1982), pp. 114–83

Aristotle , *Topica*, in *Topica et Sophistici elenchi*, ed. William David Ross (Oxford: Clarendon Press, 1984), pp. 1–189

Aristotle, *Metaphysica*, ed. Werner Jaeger (Oxford: Clarendon Press, 1980)

Arnauld, Antoine, and Pierre Nicole, *La Logique ou L'Art de penser, contenant, outre les règles communes, plusieurs observations nouvelles, propres à former le jugement* [1662], ed. Louis Marin (Paris: Flammarion, 1970)

Augustinus, Aurelius, *De civitate Dei contra paganos* [AD 413–426], I, ed. George E. McCracken, vol. I (Cambridge, Mass.: Harvard University Press – London: Heinemann, 1966)

Bacon, Francis, *The Works*, ed. James Spedding, Robert Leslie Ellis and Douglas Denon Heath, vol. I: *Philosophical Works* I, New edition (London: Longmans & Co. *etc.*, 1889)
    'Præfatio' to *Instauratio Magna* [1620], pp. 125–33
    Novum Organum, sive Indicia Vera de Interpretatione Naturæ [1620], pp. 149–365

Barbauld, Anna Lætitia, 'On prejudice', *The Works*, ed. Lucy Aikin, vol. II (London: Longman, Hurst, Rees *etc.*, 1825), pp. 321–37

Bayle, Pierre, Art. 'Jonas' [1696], *Dictionaire historique et critique*, 5th ed., ed. M. des Maizeaux, vol. III: G–L (Amsterdam: Compagnie des Libraires, 1734), pp. 464–8

Bellon de Saint-Quentin, J., *Superstitions anciennes et modernes, préjugés vulgaires, qui ont induit les peuples à des usages et à des pratiques contraires à la religion*, 4 vols. (Amsterdam: Bernard, 1733–1736)

Best, W.M., *A Treatise of Presumptions of Law and Fact, with the Theory and Rules of Presumptive or Circumstantial Proof in Criminal Cases* (Philadelphia: Johnson, 1845)

Bittner, Rüdiger, 'What is Enlightenment?' [1987], in *What is Enlightenment? Eighteenth-century answers and twentieth-century questions*, ed. James Schmidt (Berkeley – Los Angeles: University of California Press, 1996), pp. 345–58

Blackstone, William, *Commentaries on the Laws of England*, 4th ed., vol. IV: *Of Public Wrongs* (Oxford: Clarendon Press, 1770)

Bodin, Jean, *De la démonomanie des sorciers* (Paris: Du Puys, 1580)

Bonald, Louis Gabriel Ambroise de, *Œuvres complètes*, ed. Jacques Paul Migne, vol. III (Paris: Ateliers Catholiques, 1864)
'Sur les préjugés', clmn. 803–10
'Pensées sur la morale', clmn. 1372–91

Boswell, James, *Life of Johnson* [1791], ed. George Birkbeck Hill, rev. Lawrence Fitzroy Powell, vol. II (Oxford: Clarendon Press, 1934)

Bruyère, Jean de La, *Les Caractères, ou les Mœurs de ce Siècle* [1688], *Œuvres*, ed. Daniel Delafarge, vol. III (Paris: L'Édition d'Art H. Piazza, 1928)

Buckle, Henry Thomas, *History of Civilization in England*, vol. II [1861] (London: Grant Richards, 1903)

Burke, Edmund, *The Works*, New edition (London: Rivington, 1826)
vol. I: *A Philosophical Enquiry into the Origin of our Ideas of the Sublime and Beautiful* [1756/57], pp. 81–322
vol. III: 'Speech on Moving his Resolutions for Conciliation with the Colonies' [1775], pp. 23–132
vol. IV: 'A Representation to his Majesty, moved in the House of Commons' [1784], pp. 133–81
vol. V: *Reflections on the Revolution in France, and on the Proceedings of certain Societies in London relative to that Event* [1790], pp. 27–438
vol. IX: 'Letter to William Smith, 29 January 1795', pp. 399–411
vol. X: 'On the Reform of the Representation in the House of Commons' [1782], pp. 92–108

Cervantes Saavedra, Miguel de, *El ingenioso hidalgo Don Quijote de la Mancha* [1605–1615], ed. Francisco Rodríguez Marín, 8 vols. (Madrid: La Lectura, 1911–1913)

Chesterfield, Philip Dormer Stanhope, Earl of, 'Letter to his son, 7 February 1749', *The Letters*, ed. Bonamy Dobrée, vol. IV: 1748–1751 (London: Eyre & Spottiswoode, 1932), pp. 1304–9

Chesterfield, Philip Dormer Stanhope, Earl of, 'On Prejudices' [1755], *Miscellaneous Works*, ed. M. Maty, 2nd ed., vol. II (London: Dilly, 1779), pp. 257–61

Chladenius, Johann Martin, *Einleitung zur richtigen Auslegung vernünfftiger Reden und Schriften* (Leipzig: Lanckischen, 1742)

Coleridge, Samuel Taylor, *Table Talk* [1811–1834], recorded by John Taylor Coleridge, *Collected Works*, Vol. XIV/1, ed. Carl Woodring (Princeton: Princeton University Press, 1990)

Collingwood, Robin George, 'Can historians be impartial?' [1936], *The principles of history and other writings in philosophy of history*, ed. W.H. Dray and W.J. van der Dussen (Oxford: Oxford University Press, 1999), pp. 209–18

Collins, Anthony → Anonymus

Condorcet, Marie Jean Antoine Nicolas de Caritat, Marquis de, *Esquisse d'un tableau historique du progrès de l'esprit humain* [1793/94], ed. Monique Hincker and François Hincker (Paris: Editions Sociales, 1966)

Corbin, Alain, *Le Miasme et la Jonquille: L'odorat et l'imaginaire social XVIIIe – XIXe siècles* (Paris: Aubier Montaigne, 1982)

Descartes, René, *Œuvres*, ed. Charles Adam and Paul Tannery (Paris: Vrin, 1964)
vol. VII: *Meditationes de prima philosophia* [1641]
vol. VIII/1: *Principia Philosophiae* [1644]
vol. IX/1: 'Lettre à Monsieur C.L.R. [Clerselier]' [1646], pp. 202–17

Descartes, René, *Discours de la Méthode* [1637], ed. and comm. Étienne Gilson, 4th ed. (Paris: Vrin, 1967)

Diderot, Denis, Art. 'éclectisme' [1751], *Œuvres complètes*, Édition critique et annotée, ed. John Lough and Jacques Proust, vol. VII: *Encyclopédie* III (Lettres D – L) (Paris: Hermann, 1976), pp. 36–113

Diderot, Denis, 'Lettre sur l'Examen de l'essai sur les préjugés' ('Pages contre un tyran') [1771], *Œuvres politiques*, ed. Paul Vernière (Paris: Garnier, 1963), pp. 127–48

Duclos, Charles Pinot, *Considérations sur les mœurs de ce siècle* [1750], ed. F.C. Green (Cambridge: Cambridge University Press, 1939)

Dühring, Eugen, *Cursus der Philosophie als streng wissenschaftlicher Weltanschauung und Lebensgestaltung* (Leipzig: Koschny (Heimann), 1875)

Fichte, Johann Gottlieb, *Grundlage der gesammten Wissenschaftslehre* [1794/1802], *Werke*, ed. Immanuel Hermann Fichte, vol. I (Berlin: de Gruyter, 1971), pp. 83 – 328

Flaubert, Gustave, *Dictionnaire des idées reçues* [1850–1880]*, Édition diplomatique des trois manuscrits de Rouen par Lea Caminiti* (Napoli: Liguori – Paris: Nizet, 1966)

Fontenelle, Bernard Le Bovier de, *Nouveaux Dialogues des Mortes* [1683], édition critique, ed. Jean Dagen (Paris: Didier, 1971)

Fontenelle, Bernard Le Bovier de, 'Histoire des oracles' [1696], *Œuvres complètes*, ed. G.-B. Depping, vol. II (Genève: Slatkine, 1968), pp. 85–167

Friedrich II., 'der Große' → Anonymus

Gadamer, Hans-Georg, *Wahrheit und Methode: Grundzüge einer philosophischen Hermeneutik* [1960], 3rd ed. (Tübingen: Mohr (Siebeck), 1972)

Gadamer, Hans-Georg, 'Semantik und Hermeneutik' [1968], *Hermeneutik II: Wahrheit und Methode* (Tübingen: Mohr (Siebeck), 1986), pp. 174–83

Galilei, Galileo, *Dialogue Concerning the Two Chief World Systems – Ptolemaic & Copernican* [*Dialogo sopra i due sistemi del mondo* (1632), engl.], transl. Stillman Drake, pref. Albert Einstein (Berkeley – Los Angeles: University of California Press, 1962)

Gibbon, Edward, *The Decline and Fall of the Roman Empire* [1776–1788], ed. J.B. Bury, vol. I, 6th ed. (London: Methuen, 1912)

Gibbon, Edward, *Memoirs of My Life* [1788–1793], ed. Georges A. Bonnard (London: Nelson, 1966)

Glanvill, Joseph, *The Vanity of Dogmatizing: or Confidence in Opinions manifested in a Discourse of the Shortness and Uncertainty of our Knowledge, and its Causes* (London: Eversden, 1661)

Goethe, Johann Wolfgang von, *Werke, Hamburger Ausgabe* (Hamburg: Wegner)
vol. I (ed. Erich Trunz, 8th ed., 1966): 'Gern wär' ich Überlieferung los' [1827/32], p. 310
ibid., 'Den Originalen' [1827/32], p. 318
vol. XII (ed. Hans Joachim Schrimpf, 6th ed., 1967): *Maximen und Reflexionen* [1809–1832], pp. 364–547

Hamann, Johann Georg, 'Brief an Christian Jacob Kraus' [1784], in *Was ist Aufklärung? Thesen und Definitionen*, ed. Ehrhard Bahr (Stuttgart: Reclam, 1974), pp. 17–22

Hanke, Lewis, *The First Social Experiments in America: A Study in the Development of Spanish Indian Policy in the Sixteenth Century* (Cambridge, Mass.: Harvard University Press, 1935)

Hazlitt, William, *The Complete Works*, ed. P.P. Howe, vol. XX (London – Toronto: Dent & Sons, 1934)
'Prejudice' [1830], pp. 316–21
'Paragraphs on prejudice', pp. 324–30

Hegel, Georg Wilhelm Friedrich, *Werke in zwanzig Bänden*, ed. Eva Moldenhauer and Karl Markus Michel (Frankfurt/M.: Suhrkamp, 1986)
vol. III: *Phänomenologie des Geistes* [1807]
vol. VIII: *Enzyklopädie der philosophischen Wissenschaften im Grundrisse, Erster Teil: Die Wissenschaft der Logik* [1830]
vol. XVIII: *Vorlesungen über die Geschichte der Philosophie I* [1817–1831]

Heidegger, Martin, *Sein und Zeit* [1927], 16th ed. (Tübingen: Niemeyer, 1986)

Heine, Heinrich, 'Über die französische Bühne' [1837], *Werke, Historisch-kritische Gesamtausgabe*, vol. XII/1, ed. Jean-René Derré and Christiane Giesen (Hamburg: Hoffmann & Campe, 1980), pp. 227–90

Helvétius, Claude-Adrien → Anonymus

Herder, Johann Gottfried, *Abhandlung über den Ursprung der Sprache* [1772], *Sämtliche Werke*, ed. Bernhard Suphan, vol. V (Berlin: Weidmann, 1891), pp. 1– 56

Hilberg, Raul, *The Destruction of the European Jews*, 2nd ed. (Chicago: Quadrangle Books, 1967)

Hitler, Adolf, *Mein Kampf* [1925/26] (München: Eher, 1934)

Hobbes, Thomas, *The English Works*, ed. William Molesworth (London: Bohn)
vol. III (1839): *Leviathan, or the matter, form, and power of a commonwealth ecclesiastical and civil* [1651]
vol. VI (1840): *A Dialogue between a Philosopher and a Student of the Common Laws of England* [1681], pp. 1–160

Holbach, Paul-Henry Thiry d', *Lettres à Eugénie ou préservatif contre les préjugés* (London: N.N., 1768)

Holbach, Paul-Henry Thiry d', *Système de la Nature, ou des lois du monde physique et du monde moral* [1770], nouvelle édition, ed. Yvon Belaval (Hildesheim: Olms, 1966)

Horkheimer, Max, 'Über das Vorurteil' [1961], in Max Horkheimer and Theodor W. Adorno, *Sociologica II. Reden und Vorträge*, 3rd ed. (Frankfurt/M.: Europäische Verlagsanstalt, 1973), pp. 87–93

Horkheimer, Max and Theodor W. Adorno, *Dialektik der Aufklärung* [1944/47] (Frankfurt/M.: Fischer, 1984)

Humboldt, Wilhelm von, 'Über den Entwurf zu einer neuen Konstitution für die Juden' [1809], *Gesammelte Schriften*, ed. Königlich Preußische Akademie der Wissenschaften, vol. X, ed. Bruno Gebhardt (Berlin: Behr, 1903), pp. 97–115

Hume, David, *The Philosophical Works in four volumes*, ed. Thomas Hill Green and Thomas Hodge Grose, Reprint (Aalen: Scientia, 1964)
vol. III: 'Of the Standard of Taste' [1757], pp. 266–84
vol. IV: 'Of Moral Prejudices' [1742], pp. 371–5

Hume, David, *A Treatise of Human Nature* [1739/40], ed. Lewis Amherst Selby-Bigge, 2nd ed., rev. Peter Harold Nidditch (Oxford: Clarendon Press, 1985)

Hume, David, *The History of England* [1754–62] (London: Virtue, n.d.)

Hutcheson, Francis, *An Inquiry concerning Beauty, Order, Harmony, Design* [1725], ed. Peter Kivy (The Hague: Nijhoff, 1973)

Hutcheson, Francis, *An Essay on the Nature and Conduct of the Passions and Affections, with Illustrations on the Moral Sense* (London: Darby & Browne, 1728)

James, Henry, 'Letter to Thomas Sergeant Perry, 1 November 1863', *Letters*, ed. Leon Edel, vol. I: 1843–1875 (London: Macmillan, 1974), pp. 43–8

Jean Paul, *Sämtliche Werke*, ed. Norbert Miller, Pt. II, vol. 1: *Jugendwerke I* (München: Hanser, 1974)
'Unterschied zwischen dem Narren und dem Dummen' [1781], pp. 260–6
'Von der Dumheit' [1781], pp. 266–75

Jeaucourt, Louis Chevalier de, Art. 'préjugé', *Encyclopédie, ou dictionnaire raisonné des sciences, des arts et des métiers, par une société de gens de lettres*, ed. Denis Diderot and Jean Baptiste le Rond d'Alembert, vol. XXVII (Lausanne – Bern: Sociétés Typographiques, 1780), pp. 237–9

Justinian I, Emperor, *Digesta* [AD 533], transl. Alan Watson *etc.* (Philadelphia: University of Pennsylvania Press, 1998), vol. I

Kant, Immanuel, *Werke in zehn Bänden*, ed. Wilhelm Weischedel (Darmstadt: Wissenschaftliche Buchgesellschaft, 1968)

vol. I (3rd ed.): *Gedanken von der wahren Schätzung der lebendigen Kräfte, und Beurteilung der Beweise, derer sich Herr von Leibniz und andere Mechaniker in dieser Streitsache bedienet haben, nebst einigen vorhergehenden Betrachtungen, welche die Kraft der Körper überhaupt betreffen* [1746], pp. 7–218

vol. II (3rd ed.): *Träume eines Geistersehers, erläutert durch Träume der Metaphysik* [1766], pp. 919–89

vol. III and IV (continuous pagination) (3rd ed.): *Kritik der reinen Vernunft* [1781/ 1787]

vol. V (3rd ed.): 'Was heisst: Sich im Denken orientieren?', pp. 265–83

ibid., *Logik: Ein Handbuch zu Vorlesungen* [1800], ed. Gottlob Benjamin Jäsche, pp. 417–582

vol. VIII (3rd ed.): *Kritik der Urteilskraft* [1790]

vol. IX (2nd ed.): 'Beantwortung der Frage: Was ist Aufklärung?' [1783], pp. 51–61

Kant, Immanuel, *Gesammelte Schriften* (de Gruyter) [Academy edition]

vol. XVI (1924): *Reflexionen zur Logik*, ed. Königlich Preußische Akademie der Wissenschaften (Berlin – Leipzig)

vol. XVIII (1928): *Reflexionen zur Metaphysik*, ed. Preußische Akademie der Wissenschaften (Berlin – Leipzig)

vol. XXIV/1 (1966): *Einleitung in die Vernunft-Lehre* [*Logik Blomberg*], ed. Deutsche Akademie der Wissenschaften (Berlin)

Kater, Michael H., *Das 'Ahnenerbe' der SS 1935–1945: Ein Beitrag zur Kulturpolitik des Dritten Reiches*, 2nd ed. (München: Oldenbourg, 1997)

Kiesewetter, Johann Gottfried Carl Christian, 'Ueber Vorurtheil', *Deutsche Monatsschrift* III (1790), pp. 349–56

Kleist, Heinrich von, 'Brief an Ulrike von Kleist, 21 November 1811', *Briefe Heinrich von Kleists*, ed. Friedrich Michael (Leipzig: Insel, 1925), p. 272

Kraus, Karl, *Sprüche und Widersprüche* [1924] (Frankfurt/M.: Suhrkamp, 1966)

La Mettrie, Julien Offray de, *L'homme machine* [1748], ed. Gertrude Carman Bussey (La Salle, Ill.: Open Court, 1912)

Leibniz, Gottfried Wilhelm, *Die philosophischen Schriften*, ed. C.J. Gerhardt, 7 vols., Reprint (Hildesheim: Olms, 1960–1961)

Lessing, Gotthold Ephraim, *Werke* (München: Hanser)

vol. I (1970): *Die Juden* [1749], ed. Sibylle von Steinsdorff, pp. 375–414

ibid., *Der Misogyn* [1748], ed. Sibylle von Steinsdorff, pp. 423–72

vol. III (1972): 'Das Neueste aus dem Reiche des Witzes, als eine Beilage zu den Berlinischen Staats- und Gelehrten Zeitungen' [1751], ed. Karl S. Guthke, pp. 83–142

Libanios, Τίμων ἐρῶν ' Ἀλκιβιάδου ἑαυτὸν προσαγγέλει [c. AD 360], *Opera*, vol. V, ed. R. Förster (Leipzig: Teubner, 1909)

Lichtenberg, Georg Christoph, *Schriften und Briefe* [1764–1799], ed. Wolfgang Promies, vol. I (München: Hanser, 1968)

Lifton, Robert Jay, *The Nazi Doctors: Medical Killing and the Psychology of Genocide* (London: Macmillan, 1986)

Locke, John, *The Works in ten volumes*, New edition (London: Tegg *etc.*, 1823)

    vols. I–III: *An Essay concerning Human Understanding* [1690]

    vol. III: *Of the Conduct of the Understanding* [1697], pp. 203–89

    vol. VI: 'A Third Letter for Toleration' [1692], pp. 139–546

    vol. IX: *Some Thoughts concerning Education* [1690], pp. 1–205

Maistre, Joseph de, *Œuvres complètes*, vol. 1, ed. Rodolphe de Maistre, 3rd ed. (Lyon – Paris: Vitte, 1924)

    Etude sur la souveraineté [1794/95], pp. 309–553

    Essai sur le principe générateur des constitutions politiques et des autres institutions humaines [1809], pp. 221–307

D.M. [*i.e.*, César Chesneau du Marsais], *Essai sur les Préjugés, ou, De l'influence des opinions sur les mœurs et sur le bonheur des Hommes* [1770] (Paris: Desray, 1792)

Marx, Karl, and Friedrich Engels, *Manifest der Kommunistischen Partei* [1848], *Werke*, ed. Institut für Marxismus-Leninismus beim ZK der SED, vol. IV (Berlin: Dietz, 1959), pp. 459–93

Maupertuis, Pierre Louis Moreau de, *Briefe des Herrn von Maupertuis* [1752] (Hamburg: Bene, 1753)

Meier, Georg Friedrich, *Auszug aus der Vernunftlehre* [1752], in Immanuel Kant, *Gesammelte Schriften*, ed. Königlich Preußische Akademie der Wissenschaften, vol. XVI (Berlin – Leipzig: de Gruyter, 1924)

Meiszner, Rudolf, Art. 'Vorurteil', in *Deutsches Wörterbuch von Jacob und Wilhelm Grimm*, ed. Deutsche Akademie der Wissenschaften zu Berlin, vol. XII/2 (Leipzig: Hirzel, 1951), col. 1856–63

Melville, Herman, *Moby-Dick or The Whale* [1851], *The Writings of Herman Melville: The Northwestern-Newberry Edition*, vol. VI, ed. Harrison Hayford, Hershel Parker and G. Thomas Tanselle (Evanston – Chicago: Northwestern University Press and Newberry Library, 1988)

Montaigne, Michel de, *Les essais: Édition conforme au texte de l'exemplaire de Bordeaux*, 2 vols. (continuous pagination), ed. Pierre Villey, 3rd ed. (Paris: Presses Universitaires de France, 1978)

    vol. I: 'De la coustume et de ne changer aisément une loy receüe' [1572/88], pp. 108 – 123

    ibid., 'De la præsumption' [1578–80], pp. 631–62

    vol. II: 'De l'art de conferer' [1586/87], pp. 921–43

    ibid., 'De la vanité' [1586], pp. 944–1001

    ibid., 'Des boyteux' [1585], pp. 1025–35

Montesquieu, Charles de Secondat, Baron de La Brède et de, *Œuvres complètes*, ed. Édouard Laboulaye (Paris: Garnier)

    vol. I (1875): *Lettres persanes* [1721]

    vol. III (1876): *De l'esprit des lois*, Nouvelle édition [1749/1757], I

Mozart, Wolfgang Amadeus, *Neue Ausgabe sämtlicher Werke*, II/5: *Opern und Singspiele*

    vol. 18: *Così fan tutte ossia La Scuola degli Amanti* [1789/90], ed. Faye Ferguson and Wolfgang Rehm (Kassel – Basel – London – New York: Bärenreiter, 1991)

    vol. 19: *Die Zauberflöte* [1791], ed. Gernot Gruber and Alfred Orel (Kassel – Basel – Paris – London: Bärenreiter, 1970)

Nicolai, Friedrich, *Das Leben und die Meinungen des Herrn Magister Sebaldus Nothanker* [1773–76], ed. Fritz Brüggemann (Darmstadt: Wissenschaftliche Buchgesellschaft, 1967)

Nietzsche, Friedrich, *Sämtliche Werke, Kritische Studienausgabe in 15 Bänden*, ed. Giorgio Colli and Mazzino Montinari (München: Deutscher Taschenbuch Verlag – Berlin: de Gruyter, 1980)

    vol. 1: 'Vom Nutzen und Nachtheil der Historie für das Leben', *Unzeitgemäße Betrachtungen, Zweites Stück* [1873], pp. 243–334

    vol. 2: *Menschliches, Allzumenschliches: Ein Buch für freie Geister* [1878–1880]

    vol. 3: *Morgenröthe: Gedanken über die moralischen Vorurtheile* [1881], pp. 9–331

    ibid., *Die fröhliche Wissenschaft* [1882], pp. 343–651

    vol. 5: *Jenseits von Gut und Böse: Vorspiel einer Philosophie der Zukunft* [1886], pp. 9–243

    vol. 6: *Ecce homo: Wie man wird, was man ist* [1888], pp. 255–374

Olden, Rudolf, *Hitler* (Amsterdam: Querido, 1936)

The Oxford English Dictionary, vol. V (Oxford: Clarendon Press, 1961)

Pascal, Blaise, *Pensées sur la religion et sur quelques autres sujets* [1654–1662], ed. Louis Lafuma, vol. I: *Textes* (Paris: Éditions du Luxembourg, 1952)

Peirce, Charles Sanders, 'The Order of Nature' (6.395–6.427.) [1878], *Collected Papers*, ed. Charles Hartshorne and Paul Weiss, vol. VI: *Scientific Metaphysics* (Cambridge, Mass.: Harvard University Press, 1960), pp. 283–301

Périer, Marguerite, 'Mémoire sur la vie de Monsieur Pascal' [1713–1733], in Blaise Pascal, *Pensées sur la religion et sur quelques autres sujets*, ed. Louis Lafuma, vol. III: *Documents sur la vie de Pascal* (Paris: Éditions du Luxembourg, 1952), pp. 59–67

Plato, *Sämtliche Werke*, ed. Karlheinz Hülser, Greek text according to the complete edition of the Association Guillaume Budé (Frankfurt/M.: Insel, 1991) (cited according to the pagination of the edition by Henricus Stephanus, Paris 1578)

    vol. I: *Apology*, pp. 197–261

    vol. III: *Meno*, pp. 9–101

    vol. IV: *Phaedo*, pp. 185–347

Pope, Alexander, *An Essay on Man, Being the First Book of Ethic Epistles to Henry St. John, Lord Bolingbroke* (London: Gilliver, 1734)

Poullain de la Barre, François, *De L'Égalité des Deux Sexes Discours Physique et Moral (Où l'on voit l'importance de se défaire des Préjugez.)* (Paris: Du Puis, 1673)

Quincey, Thomas de, 'Philosophy of Herodotus' [1842], *Collected Writings*, ed. David Masson, vol. VI (London: Black, 1897), pp. 96–138

Reid, Thomas, *Essays on the Intellectual Powers of Man* [1785], *New Edition* (London: Griffin, 1865)

Reynolds, Joshua, *The Complete Works* (London: McLean, 1824)
vol. I: 'Seventh Discourse on Art' [1776], pp. 145–86
vol. III: 'Notes on "The Art of Painting"' [1783], pp. 89–164

Riem, Andreas, 'Ueber Aufklärung, ob sie dem Staate – der Religion – oder überhaupt gefährlich sey und seyn könne? Ein Wort zur Beherzigung für Regenten, Staatsmänner und Priester. Ein Fragment' [1788], in *Bibliothek der Deutschen Aufklärer des achtzehnten Jahrhunderts*, ed. Martin von Geismar, vol. II (Leipzig: Wigand, 1847), pp. 313–44

Rousseau, Jean-Jacques, *Œuvres complètes* (Paris: Gallimard)
vol. I (1959): *Les confessions* [1770], ed. Bernard Gagnebin and Marcel Raymond, pp. 1–656
ibid., *Rousseau juge de Jean Jaques* [1772–1776], ed. Robert Osmont, pp. 657–992
vol. IV (1969): *Émile ou De l'éducation* [1762], ed. Bernard Gagnebin and Marcel Raymond, pp. 239–877

Russell, Bertrand, 'The Superior Virtue of the Oppressed', *Unpopular Essays* (London: Allen & Unwin, 1950), pp. 80–7

Sade, Donatien-Alphonse-François, Marquis de, *Œuvres complètes*, *Édition définitive*, ed. Gilbert Lely (Paris: Cercle du livre précieux, 1966)
vol. III: *La philosophie dans le boudoir ou Les instituteurs immoraux, Dialogues destinés à l'éducation des jeunes demoiselles* [1795], pp. 347–577
vols. VIII–IX: *L'Histoire de Juliette, ou les prospérités du vice* [1797]

Sailer, Johann Michael, *Vernunftlehre für Menschen, wie sie sind, das ist: Anleitung zur Erkenntnis und Liebe der Wahrheit, Sämmtliche Werke*, ed. Joseph Widmer, *Philosophische Abtheilung*, vol. II, 3rd ed. (Sulzbach: Seidel, 1830)

Schelling, Friedrich Wilhelm Joseph von, *Philosophische Untersuchungen über das Wesen der menschlichen Freiheit und die damit zusammenhängenden Gegenstände* [1809], *Werke*, ed. Manfred Schröter, vol. IV (München: Beck, 1927), pp. 223–308

Schlegel, Friedrich, *Philosophische Lehrjahre* I [1796–1806], *Kritische Friedrich-Schlegel-Ausgabe*, vol. XVIII, ed. Ernst Behler (München – Paderborn – Wien: Schöningh, 1963)

Sextus Empiricus, *Pyrrhoneion hypotyposeon* [c. AD 180–200], *Outlines of Pyrrhonism, The works*, ed. & transl. R.G. Bury, vol. I (Cambridge, Mass.: Harvard University Press – London: Heinemann, 1967)

Shaftesbury, Anthony Ashley Cooper, Third Earl of, *Characteristics of Men, Manners, Opinions, Times* [1711], ed. John MacKinnon Robertson, vol. II (Indianapolis – New York: Bobbs-Merrill, 1964)

Shirer, William L., *The Rise and Fall of the Third Reich: A History of Nazi Germany* (New York: Simon & Schuster, 1960)

Simmel, Georg, *Gesamtausgabe* (Frankfurt/M.: Suhrkamp)

    vol. II (1989): *Über sociale Differenzierung: Sociologische und psychologische Untersuchungen* [1890], ed. Heinz-Jürgen Dahme, pp. 109–295

    vol. XI (1992): *Soziologie: Untersuchungen über die Formen der Vergesellschaftung* [1908], ed. Otthein Rammstedt

Sophocles, *Antigone, Sophocles in 2 Volumes*, ed. & transl. F. Storr, vol. I (Cambridge, Mass.: Harvard University Press – London: Heinemann, 1962), pp. 309–419

Spenser, Edmund, *A view of the present state of Ireland* [1596], ed. William Lindsay Renwick (Oxford: Clarendon Press, 1970)

Spinoza, Benedictus, *Tractatus de intellectus emendatione* [1677], *Opera*, ed. Carl Gebhardt, vol. II (Heidelberg: Winter, 1925), pp. 1–40

Sprat, Thomas, *The History of the Royal-Society of London, For the Improving of Natural Knowledge* (London: Martyn, 1667)

Stephen, James Fitzjames, *A Digest of the Law of Evidence* [1876], 12th ed., rev. Harry Lushington Stephen and Lewis Frederick Sturge (London: Macmillan, 1948)

Swift, Jonathan, *The Prose Works*, ed. Herbert Davis (Oxford: Blackwell)

    vol. I (1939): 'A Full and True Account of the Battel Fought last Friday, between the Antient and the Modern Books in St. James's Library' ('The Battle of the Books') [1710], addendum to 'A Tale of a Tub', pp. 138–65

    ibid., 'Thoughts on Various Subjects' [1696–1707], pp. 241–5

    vol. XII (1955): 'A Modest Proposal for Preventing the Children of poor People in Ireland, from being a Burden to their Parents or Country; and for making them beneficial to the Publick' [1729], pp. 109–18

Tatianus, *Oratio ad Graecos* [AD 152–155], in *Die ältesten Apologeten: Texte mit kurzen Einleitungen*, ed. Edgar J. Goodspeed (Göttingen: Vandenhoeck & Ruprecht, 1914), pp. 266–305

Tertullianus, Quintus Septimius Florens, *De carne Christi* [c. AD 205], *Corpus Scriptorum Ecclesiaticorum Latinorum*, vol. LXX, ed. A. Kroymann (Wien: Tempsky, 1942)

Thomasius, Christian, 'De Praejudiciis oder von den Vorurteilen' [1691/1696], in Fritz Brüggemann (ed.), *Aus der Frühzeit der Deutschen Aufklärung: Christian Thomasius und Christian Weise* (Darmstadt: Wissenschaftliche Buchgesellschaft, 1966), pp. 30–60

Toland, John, 'The Origin and Force of Prejudices', *Letters to Serena* (London: Lintot, 1704), pp. 1–18

Toland, John, *Adolf Hitler* (Garden City, New York: Doubleday & Co., 1976)

Vergilius Maro, Publius, *Aeneis* [29–19 BC], *The Aeneid, Virgil in 2 Volumes*, ed. & transl. H. Rushton Fairclough (New York: Putnam's – London: Heinemann, 1916)

Voltaire, *Œuvres complètes, Nouvelle édition* (Paris: Garnier)

    vol. IX (1877): 'Poëme sur la loi naturelle' [1752], pp. 439–64

    vol. XII (1878): *Essai sur les mœurs et l'esprit des nations et sur les principaux faits de l'histoire, depuis Charlemagne jusqu'a Louis XIII* II [1756]

Voltaire, *Les Œuvres complètes* (Oxford: Voltaire Foundation)

    vol. XXXVI (1994): 'Préjugés', *Dictionnaire philosophique* [1764], ed. Christiane Mervaud, pp. 456–460

    vol. CI (1971): 'Lettre à Théodore Tronchin' [1756], *Correspondence and related documents* 1756–1757, ed. Theodore Besterman, pp. 158–9

Whately, Richard, *Elements of Rhetoric, Comprising an Analysis of the Laws of Moral Evidence and of Persuasion* [1828], ed. Douglas Ehninger (Carbondale: Southern Illinois University Press, 1963)

Wieland, Christoph Martin, 'Gedanken von der Freiheit über Gegenstände des Glaubens zu philosophieren' [1788], *Werke*, vol. III, ed. Fritz Martini and Reinhard Döhl (München: Hanser, 1967), pp. 493–549

Wieland, Christoph Martin, 'Etwas über die Vorurtheile überhaupt' [1798], in Bernd Weyergraf, *Der skeptische Bürger: Wielands Schriften zur Französischen Revolution* (Stuttgart: Metzler, 1972), pp. 146–51

Young, Edward, *Conjectures on Original Composition* [1759], in *English Critical Essays: Sixteenth, Seventeenth and Eighteenth Centuries*, ed. Edmund D. Jones (London – New York – Toronto: Oxford University Press, 1975), pp. 270–311

Zola, Émile, 'J'accuse: Lettre à M. Félix Faure, président de la République' [1898], *Œuvres complètes*, ed. Henri Mitterand, vol. XIV (Paris: Cercle du livre précieux, 1970), pp. 921–31

Zollikofer, Daniel Cornelius, 'Neunter Discours', in Johann Jakob Bodmer and Johann Jakob Breitinger, *Die Discourse der Mahlern*, Zweyter Theil (Zürich: Lindinner, 1722), pp. 65–71

Index of Names

Numbers refer to paragraphs, *P* signifies the preface.

Index of Subjects

Numbers refer to paragraphs, *P* signifies the preface.